WRITE GREAT FICTION

Dialogue

WRITE GREAT FICTION

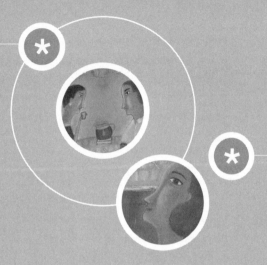

Dialogue

[TECHNIQUES AND EXERCISES FOR CRAFTING EFFECTIVE DIALOGUE]

BY GLORIA KEMPTON

WRITER'S DIGEST BOOKS

Writer's Digest Books
Cincinnati, Ohio
www.writersdigest.com

[COPYRIGHT]

Visit our Web site at www.writersdigest.com for information on more resources for writers.

To receive a free weekly e-mail newsletter delivering tips and updates about writing and about Writer's Digest products, register directly at our Web site at http://newsletters.fwpublications.com.

16 15 14 13 12   12 11 10 9

Library of Congress Cataloging-in-Publication Data
Kempton, Gloria
   Write great fiction : dialogue : techniques and exercises for crafting effective dialogue/
   by Gloria Kempton.
      p. cm.
   Includes index.
   ISBN-13: 978-1-58297-289-3 (pbk : alk. paper)
   ISBN-10: 1-58297-289-3 (pbk : alk. paper)
   1. Fiction--Technique. 2. Dialogue. I. Title

PN3383.D53K46 2004
808.3--dc22   2004053005

Edited by Kelly Nickell and Michelle Ruberg
Designed by Stanard Design Partners
Interior and Cover Illustrations by Getty Images
Cover by Nick Gliebe/Design Matters
Production coordinated by Robin Richie and Logan Cummins

[ABOUT THE AUTHOR]

Gloria Kempton is an author, writing coach and former magazine and book editor. She is the author of several nonfiction books, including *Love One Another, Forgive One Another,* and *The Passionate Edge,* and two young adult novels, *Jocelyn* and *Andrea.* She's also a contributing editor to *Writer's Digest* magazine and an instructor with the Writer's Digest School's www.WritersOnlineWorkshops.com. In the past, she has worked as a free-lance book editor for a large number of major publishers. Kempton also speaks at and conducts workshops at writers conferences across the country each year; these include the National Writer's Association Conference, the Pacific Northwest Writer's Conference, and the Maui Writer's Conference. She teaches writing at Bellevue Community College in Bellevue, WA, and leads writing workshops in the Seattle area and at her beach house on the Oregon coast. You can contact her through her Web site: www.writers recharge.com.

[DEDICATION]

I dedicate this book to all of you who have talked to me throughout my life and who will now find yourselves in the following pages.

[ACKNOWLEDGMENTS]

I'd like to thank Kelly Nickell, my editor at Writer's Digest Books, for pushing me and challenging me and not letting me get by with writing a shallow book on the subject of fictional dialogue. Because of her help, I believe I've covered the subject with some originality and fresh insights that haven't been used in other books on the same subject. Thanks, Kelly, for your pokes and prods at each step of the writing process to move more deeply into my topic.

table of contents

introduction

Dialogue is conversation—nothing more, nothing less. How hard do we really think about the conversations in which we engage on a daily basis? How difficult do we make them? How much stress do we create for ourselves trying to make sure we pronounce every word correctly, say exactly what we mean, use the tone that reveals or hides our true feelings, arrange our body so it lines up with what we're saying, make sure we're giving the other person a chance to talk so we're not giving speeches... I'm exhausted just thinking about it. Of course we don't stress out this way when we're just standing on the sidewalk talking to a neighbor. But we do it when we're creating dialogue for our characters, which is what makes writing dialogue so very difficult.

But it's not difficult. We *make* it difficult.

That's my premise for this book. My goal is to break down the process of writing dialogue so it becomes more natural for writers, as natural as breathing and talking—two things we've been doing ever since we were born. Yes, we were talking as soon as we were breathing; we just didn't have the words. Just like we don't now breathe the way we naturally should (many of us walk around holding our breath), we also usually don't talk the way we'd like to be heard, so when we sit down to re-create dialogue we start thinking too hard about it and become paralyzed.

Somewhere along the line, someone tried to teach us how we *should* talk and then we learned how. We were praised for talking correctly and criticized for talking incorrectly.

"Mom, you don't have to yell, I can hear you."
"Don't use that tone with me, young man."

"Can I have more potatoes?"
"No, Susie, it's *may* I have more potatoes?"

"He's a dork, Mom."

"Don't call people names—it's not nice."

So here we are. We think we know how to talk correctly, so we don't worry about it so much in everyday conversation. But when we actually sit down to re-create dialogue on the page, suddenly we feel a lot of self-doubt and are faced with our own inadequacies. Maybe the real question we're asking at an unconscious level is not, "Can I write dialogue?" but "Am I talking correctly?" I don't know for sure, but I do know that we can make this process easier by doing something a little "zenny": When we're about to write a piece of dialogue, any dialogue, we must remember to forget.

Forget what?

That we're writing dialogue. We must slip inside of our characters and become them. From inside of our characters, we begin speaking. In the book *Finding Your Writer's Voice: A Guide to Creative Fiction,* authors Thaisa Frank and Dorothy Wall tell us this: "Great impersonators throw aside their own way of talking and take on the voice of another. As you work with character, letting yourself become possessed by this person, you want to abandon the automatic voice in your head that offers dialogue as *you* would speak it, and become the voice of this other person." Okay, it sounds like channeling. We've gone from Zen to New Age. Call it what you want—it works.

I've been writing dialogue for many years. I struggle with description, setting, and plot, but I seldom struggle with dialogue. I didn't know writers struggled with dialogue until I started coaching writers and heard them express their fears of not doing it "right."

I'm here to tell you there is no "right" way—I don't care what you've heard from other writing instructors and read in other writing books. There is only *your* way. Yours is the "right" way. And your job as writer is to learn to access the voice inside of yourself that you need for a particular piece of dialogue, no matter who's speaking it. Sure, you can do research, read books like this one, watch movies, and listen to how folks on the street talk. But ultimately, our characters come from somewhere inside of us, and if we want to be true to ourselves and our characters, whether fictional or real, we have to start giving them a voice.

As I prepared to write this book, I began to explore why dialogue has always come easily for me. I realized that it's because at a very early age, when I began to read fiction, I became the characters I was reading about. I slipped into their heads, only to emerge when I'd finished the story. When I started to write my own stories at the tender age of nine, I had formed a useful writing habit: I became my characters. I easily slipped into my characters, speaking from inside their heads.I was all of them —the sane to the insane, the kind to the brutal, the boring to the quirky.

You may wonder, "But how do I do that? How do I slip inside of my characters? How does that work, practically speaking? I'll be answering these questions in the following pages. You see, once we understand that our characters are not outside of us but within us, it takes the mystery out of *how* to write dialogue for any character. If we pull our characters up from inside of us instead of approach them from the outside, writing dialogue becomes an organic process.

Writing dialogue is simply giving a voice to the characters that live inside of us. I don't mean to make this sound spooky—you don't have to go into a dark room and turn around three times while repeating, "I love green eggs and ham."

All you have to do is want to write *authentic* dialogue. And when you let yourself do that, you'll discover the satisfaction in writing the kind of dialogue that delivers your character's true voice to the reader.

I have news for you. Not only is there no "right" way to write dialogue, and not only does writing dialogue not have to be as difficult as we like to make it, but writing dialogue can actually be fun.

My twofold mission in this book is: (1) to equip you with specific literary tools that will help you remember to forget that you're writing dialogue, which in turn will cause you to relax so your character's dialogue will emerge from who that character is, rather than from your personal agenda for the story, and (2) to remind you over and over again that the art of writing dialogue can be a lot of fun and is learned by exercising your freedom to color outside of the lines.

You'll find that this book will become your best friend on the journey to remember to forget you're writing dialogue and in your intention to no longer struggle but have fun learning to access the many voices inside of you.

chapter 1

[RELEASING THE VOICE WITHIN — THE PURPOSE OF DIALOGUE]

You're at the bookstore browsing through the fiction section. You're perusing titles, grabbing books off the shelf and skimming the back cover copy, then finally leafing through the novels one by one. Whether it's conscious or unconscious, guess what you're looking for.

Space. The eye is naturally drawn to space. Plenty of white space on each page. In a nonfiction book, that may mean text broken up with a subhead or sidebar here and there. In a novel that means dialogue.

Do you remember those novels teachers made us read in high school? *Great Expectations. Madame Bovary. Lord of the Flies.* Page after page of blocks of text. Long passages of boring narrative.

Dialogue not only creates space on the page, which is visually appealing, but it's also what brings characters to life in a story, which is emotionally appealing. We're much more interested in a story's setting when it comes through a scene of dialogue. Dialogue reveals the characters' motives and opposing agendas. Our characters' tense words let readers know where our characters are internally and create suspense for what's ahead in the story. The onset of a dialogue scene immediately propels the story into high gear. Through dialogue, we can give readers a very real sense of a story's setting. If done well, dialogue can even communicate the story's theme. Effective dialogue delivers all of these things to eager readers. This is the kind of dialogue we, as writers, want to create.

How?

In later chapters, we'll explore how to create the kind of dialogue that succeeds at all of the above, but for right now, it's enough to try to understand what we owe our readers when we engage them in a scene of dialogue.

We need to understand what it looks like to create dialogue that delivers before we can learn how to actually make it happen.

Effective dialogue, the kind of dialogue that connects with readers and makes them care about our characters and their struggles, can accomplish many purposes simultaneously. Let's take a look at them one by one.

CHARACTERIZES/REVEALS MOTIVES

We introduce our characters to our readers through dialogue. Dialogue combined with facial expressions and body language indicates to readers who our characters are. In real life, this is how we get to know one another. We start interacting. Sometimes this goes well, sometimes it doesn't. Through dialogue, we decide if we like someone or not. This is also how our readers decide if they like our characters. As they listen to them and watch them interact with each other, they decide if these are good guys or bad guys or a combination. It's in our power to evoke positive or negative feelings in our readers for our characters through the dialogue we create for them.

When a character speaks in a controlled tone, every word clipped and enunciated clearly, it could be that he's right on the edge, momentarily suppressing a ton of internal rage. On the other hand, if a character's voice is warm and inviting, this could reveal an internal sense of security and well-being. A character who rattles off words faster than the speed of light could be running away from himself, and a character who talks painfully slow may be unsure of himself, experiencing depression, or lacking in social skills.

Every one of your characters is driven by something—they all have agendas, motives, and reasons for what they want in your story. In some sense, motive is the most important element in a story because it drives the character from the inside to go after what he wants. It's the impetus behind and the reason for his goal. Without motive, there's no story. That's how important it is. Let's say you're writing a children's story. The protagonist's goal could be to win the spelling bee. The motive? To earn her father's approval. This could also be an adult story. The goal would be different, but the motive could be the same.

The most effective way to reveal your characters' motives is through their own mouths. Again, in real life, we do this all the time. I remember a friend once telling me that another person had insinuated she had done something rude. "I don't want everyone to think I'm not nice," she told me.

Right away I knew that it wasn't that my friend actually cared if she was nice or not; what she cared about was how others perceived her. What she cared about was her image. I'm not making a value judgment here. I don't have to. She opened her own mouth and revealed her motive herself—wanting others to think well of her. We do it all the time. Whenever your characters open their mouths, they start telling the truth about what's motivating them. This is what you want to do. This is good. You want your dialogue to deliver your characters' motives to your reader. Again, this is how your reader is signaled as to how to feel about your characters. Motives, even more than behavior, reveal whom our characters are deep down inside because behavior is external and motives are internal. Effective dialogue brings up who our characters are at their core. It's powerful stuff.

The following scene of dialogue shows the motives of the antagonist, Sean Dillon, in Jack Higgins' novel *Eye of the Storm*. Dillon is a terrorist, has been one for twenty years, and "he hasn't seen the inside of a cell once," according to KGB agent Josef Makeev. After going undercover and trying unsuccessfully to catch Dillon, Makeev discusses the terrorist, who was also once an actor, with another KGB agent, Michael Aroun.

> "As I said, he's never been arrested, not once, and unlike many of his IRA friends, he never courted media publicity. I doubt if there's a photo of him anywhere except for the odd boyhood snap."
>
> "What about when he was an actor?"
>
> "Perhaps, but that was twenty years ago, Michael."
>
> "And you think he might undertake this business if I offer him enough money?"
>
> "No, money alone has never been enough for this man. It always has to be the job itself where Dillon is concerned. How can I put it? How interesting it is. This is a man to whom acting was everything. What we are offering him is a new part. The Theatre of the Street perhaps, but still acting." He smiled as the Mercedes joined the traffic moving around the Arc de Triomphe. "Let's wait and see. Wait until we hear from Rashid."

A character won't always admit his own motives in conversation with others, usually because he doesn't even know himself why he does what he does. This is often especially true of the antagonist. So having other characters talk about the antagonist's motives is an effective way to show the antagonist's motivation.

SETS THE MOOD IN THE STORY

Every story, no matter what kind, evokes emotion in the reader. Or it should, if you want to hold your reader's attention. The story's emotional pull ultimately creates the story's mood. The mood, the emotion, is what keeps pulling at the reader, compelling her to keep turning the pages. The mood can be setting. It can be the characters and their motives. It can be how quickly or slowly the plot moves.

Dialogue is a tool you can use to create your story's mood. In a mystery or horror story, the dialogue should evoke fear in the reader. In a romance, we're looking for that warm, fuzzy dialogue that budding love brings. In a mainstream or literary story, it may be one of any number of atmospheres we want to create and emotions we want to evoke as we go about creating a scene of dialogue. When characters are interacting, they're exchanging feelings. As the writer, you're in charge of creating the story's mood. Certainly, sometimes the mood just kind of evolves as our characters start talking, but you can also direct the dialogue so you're controlling the mood.

In Anna Quindlen's first-person novel *One True Thing,* the relationship between the protagonist, Ellen Gulden, and her father, the antagonist, George Gulden, is a hostile one. He has convinced Ellen to come and be her mother's caretaker as she wastes away from cancer. Ellen grudgingly agrees, and her attitude toward this task quickly becomes the story's mood. In the following scene of dialogue, we begin to see just what her attitude is.

> "Ellen, there is no reason for the two of us to be at cross-purposes. Your mother needs help. You love her. So do I."
>
> "Show it," I said.
>
> "Pardon me!"
>
> "Show it. Show up. Do you grieve? Do you care? Do you ever cry? And how did you let her get to this point in the first place? When she first felt sick, why didn't you force her to go to the doctor?"
>
> "Your mother is a grown woman," he said.
>
> "Sure she is. But wasn't it really that you didn't want your little world disrupted, that you needed her around to keep everything running smoothly? Just like now you need me around because she can't. You bring me here and drop me down in the middle of this mess and expect me to turn into one kind of person when I'm a completely different kind and to be a nurse and a friend and a confidante and a housewife all rolled up in one."
>
> "Don't forget being a daughter. You could always be a daughter."

"Oh, Papa, don't try to make me feel guilty."

As the story progresses, we watch the plot events transform Ellen, and by the end of the story she's a different person. But this is the mood that permeates the story, and the author often uses dialogue to bring it out.

INTENSIFIES THE STORY CONFLICT

We can use dialogue to keep raising the stakes for our protagonist, to keep him in hot water, to keep propelling the story forward. Your character has a goal. He wants something—desperately. In the movie *ET*, we remember one line vividly: "ET phone home." This one line of dialogue—three words—contains the essence of what ET is all about. This little creature just wanted to go back home. Desperately.

Now, it's up to you to keep throwing obstacles at your protagonist to keep him from easily getting what she wants. These obstacles come from within and without the character. The other characters come against your protagonist. The protagonist sabotages herself. This is called story conflict, and you can reveal it and keep intensifying it through dialogue. You want to use dialogue to keep reminding the reader just how desperate your character is to achieve her goal.

Every scene of dialogue, in some way, needs to move the story conflict forward. We need to be in a different place at the end of a scene of dialogue than we were at the beginning. The situation should grow continually worse every time our characters open their mouths to talk to one another. Our protagonist is becoming more desperate. Our antagonist seems surer of victory; we know because of the confidence we give to his tone of voice. Our supporting characters keep reminding our protagonist of his goal, of where he's headed on the Hero's Journey. This is dialogue that does not stand still but moves the story forward with each scene.

In Jude Deveraux's romantic suspense novel *High Tide*, the protagonist, Fiona, is being set up for murder. A businesswoman, she is visiting her wealthy client, Roy Hudson, on his boat, when he starts hitting on her. She fights him off, eventually falling into an exhausted sleep on the boat and waking up in the middle of the night with his body on top of hers—his very *dead* body. The hero, Ace Montgomery, and Ellen are talking about the murder in the following scene of dialogue.

She took a deep breath. "I want to know what's going on," she said as calmly as she could. "I am wanted for murder. The newspaper—"

"No, we are wanted for murder." He'd put the frozen packages back into the freezer and was now looking in the cupboards. "You know how to make pancakes?"

At that Fiona put her arms straight down to her sides, her hands in fists, opened her mouth, and let out a scream.

Ace had his hand over her mouth before she'd let an ounce of air escape her lungs. "What the hell do you think you're doing?" he demanded. "If someone heard you, they might investigate." Slowly, he removed his hand and nodded toward the countertop in the kitchen. "Now sit down while I make breakfast."

She didn't move. "So help me, if you don't tell me what's going on, I'll scream my head off."

"You really do have trouble with anger, don't you? Have you thought of seeing a counselor?"

At that Fiona opened her mouth again, but this time he didn't move. Instead, he just looked at her speculatively.

Closing her mouth, Fiona narrowed her eyes at him. "So why aren't we at the police station, Mr. Do-Gooder? Just hours ago you were telling me that I couldn't be a fugitive from justice, that I had to turn myself over to the police. But now that you're also accused, we're hiding."

"You want blueberries in your pancakes?"

"I want some answers!" she shouted at him.

Since this is a *romantic* suspense, Deveraux has to do double duty in intensifying the conflict in each scene; she has both the plot—the murder—and the relationship between the hero and the heroine to develop. This scene works well on both levels as Fiona is screaming at Ace to give her some answers about the murder—she's scared to death at being a suspect—while furious at him for not being more direct with her. As you probably know, when writing romance, the hero and heroine often start out intensely disliking each other. A scene of dialogue showing this is a lot more fun than the protagonist simply telling us from inside her head.

CREATES TENSION AND SUSPENSE

As a writing coach, I have worked with hundreds of fiction and nonfiction writers over the years, and the weakness I see most often in scenes of dialogue is the lack of tension and suspense. Nothing is at stake. The characters are just chatting about something or other. Making small talk. Having a tea party. Ho-hum.

Dialogue's purpose, and there is no exception to this, is to create tension in the present and build suspense for what's to come. As a fiction writer, you want to remember this. No matter what kind of scene you're writing, no matter the genre, tension and suspense must be included, most often at the core of the scene. Successful authors know this. Robin Cook, the author of a number of successful medical mysteries, is such an author. His stories are full of tense dialogue scene after tense dialogue scene. The following excerpt is one from his novel *Fatal Cure*. It illustrates the kind of tension and suspense in a dialogue scene that grabs the reader by the gut so she couldn't stop reading even if the house was on fire.

The protagonist, Angela, is on a personal mission to find a killer. The reason this is personal for her is because her husband, David, has just discovered a body buried in the basement of the house they recently moved into. Prior to this scene, she confronted the Chief of Police about what she sees as incompetence and indifference in the police's search to find a suspect.

> "Don't you dare paint me as an hysterical female," Angela said as she got into the car.
>
> "Baiting the local chief of police like that certainly isn't rational," David said. "Remember, this is a small town. We shouldn't be making enemies."
>
> "A person was brutally murdered, the body dumped in our basement, and the police don't seem too interested in finding out who did it. You're willing to let it rest at that?"
>
> "As deplorable as Hodges' death was," David said, "it doesn't involve us. It's a problem that should be left up to the authorities."
>
> "What?" Angela cried. "The man was beaten to death in our house, in our kitchen. We're involved whether you want to admit it or not, and I want to find out who did it. I don't like the idea of the murderer walking around this town, and I'm going to do something about it. The first thing is we should learn more about Dennis Hodges."

Cook creates tension in this scene by pitting Angela and David against each in their different approaches to how this case should be handled. The suspense comes from Angela's determination to *do* something about the murderer walking around her town. She has spoken her commitment out loud and we know she means what she says. She's going to do something and we'll keep reading to find out what she does.

Effective dialogue always, always delivers tension.

Just for Fun

Take a notebook and go to the mall or a park or a café and eavesdrop on a conversation. Chances are, it will pretty mundane, as is. Now write a scene of dialogue, giving the conversation you just heard a purpose.

SPEEDS UP YOUR SCENES

As storytellers, we have a number of writing tools at our disposal—narration, action, description, and dialogue, to name a few. When you're considering how to pace a story, description and narration will move it slowly, steadily, and easily along. Action and dialogue will speed it up—dialogue even more than action. When characters start talking, the story starts moving. Usually. There are always the dull chatting scenes I mentioned above. But we're talking here about effective dialogue—dialogue that delivers.

Dialogue is a way to control the pace of our stories. Getting back to Angela and David—in this scene, David is talking to his daughter about the body he discovered in the basement. The first paragraph is a narrative one and moves more slowly than the scene of dialogue that follows.

> When it was almost seven Angela asked David if he would take Caroline and Arni home. David was happy to do it, and Nikki came along. After the two children had been dropped off, David was glad for the moments alone with his daughter. First, they talked about school and her new teacher. Then he asked her if she thought much about the body discovered in the basement.
>
> "Some," Nikki said.
>
> "How does it make you feel?" David asked.
>
> "Like I don't want to ever go in the basement again."
>
> "I can understand that," David said. "Last night when I was getting firewood I felt a little scared."
>
> "You did?"

"Yup," David said. "But I have a little plan that might be fun and it might help. Are you interested?"

"Yeah!" Nikki said with enthusiasm. "What?"

"You can't tell anybody," David said.

"Okay," Nikki promised.

David outlined his plan as they continued home. "What do you say?" he asked once he had finished.

"I think it's cool," Nikki said.

"Remember, it's a secret," David said.

"Cross my heart."

In the narrative paragraph that follows this scene, David goes into the house and makes a phone call, and we learn that he's experienced some distress about two of his patients who had previously died. Here things slow down as the author begins feeding us necessary information in narrative. The narrative slows the story back down after the scene of dialogue. What makes dialogue move more quickly than narrative? It's the quick back-and-forth of the character's words to one another, like a tennis ball being batted back and forth across the court.

It's obvious which part of the above excerpt moves more quickly. Of course, there are times when you want a scene to move more slowly, so I'm not saying that it's always best to use dialogue. But when you need to speed up a scene, this is its purpose. This is what it will do for you.

ADDS BITS OF SETTING/BACKGROUND

Do you ever find it difficult to get the setting and background into your story in an interesting way? Here dialogue comes to the rescue once again.

As writers, we have a tendency to want to use narrative to set up every scene for the reader before the action starts, which is unnecessary. Once the action in a scene is rolling along, you can use dialogue to throw in what you need us to know at that moment about the setting and story background. In Joyce Carol Oates' novel *We Were the Mulvaneys*, Patrick, the viewpoint character in this scene, and his sister, Marianne, haven't seen each other for a few years. He has just asked her how she did in college and she's told him she had to take a couple of incompletes. Listen to how Marianne describes the town she now lives in, Kilburn, and later how the author slips in a few details of the current setting, Patrick's room.

"Well—" Marianne squirmed, pulling at her spiky hair. "Things sort of came up. Suddenly."

"What kind of things?"

"An emergency at the Co-op, just after Thanksgiving. Aviva who was assistant store manager got sick—"

"Store? What store?"

"Oh Patrick, I must have told you—didn't I? In Kilburn, in town, we have a Green Isle outlet. We sell preserves, fresh preserves, fresh produce in the summer, baked goods—my zucchini-walnut bread is one of the favorites. I—"

"And you work in the store? How many hours a week?"

Marianne dipped her head, avoiding Patrick's interrogative gaze. "We don't think in terms of hours—exactly," she said. She was sitting on Patrick's sofa (not an item from home, part of the dull spare slightly shabby furnishings of the apartment) while Patrick sat facing her, in a rather overbearing position, on his desk chair, his right ankle balanced on his left knee in a posture both relaxed and aggressive.

Thinking Pinch-style I have a right to ask, who else will ask if I don't?

"What terms do you think in, then?"

"The Green Isle Co-op isn't—a formally run organization, like a business. It's more like a—well, a family. People helping each other out. From each what he or she can give; to each, as he or she requires."

Here we get a sense of *who* the town is as a character as well as some physical details. Setting and background can actually be made interesting when incorporated into a dialogue scene. The reader experiences the setting through the viewpoint character's observations, and depending on the character, this could prove very interesting indeed. As long as there's *tension*, of course.

COMMUNICATES THE THEME

In his memoir *On Writing,* Stephen King writes: "When you write a book, you spend day after day scanning and identifying the trees. When you're done, you have to step back and look at the forest…it seems to me that every book—at least every one worth reading—is about *something*."

This *something* is better known as theme. What's your story *about*? What do you want your story to say to your reader? In its simplest form, theme is your story's conflict and resolution.

Theme is something we need to weave through our stories in bits and pieces, letting it pop up here and there to reveal what the story is all *about*. Dialogue is definitely a fiction element that pops everything up and out. When characters are talking, whispering, shouting, hissing, grumbling, sneering, or moaning, the reader is listening. If you can sneak your theme into the dialogue, your reader will hear it in a way that it can't be heard in narrative.

Back to *One True Thing* for a moment. The author, Anna Quindlen, is an expert at writing about something in this novel and weaves the theme all through the narrative in the story. Toward the end of the novel, when Ellen is on the stand for her mother's murder, the author uses dialogue to bring it out once more. The prosecutor has just asked her if she loved her mother. This is her answer:

> "The easy answer is yes. But it's too easy just to say that when you're talking about your mother. It's so much more than love—it's, it's everything, isn't it?" as though somehow they would all nod. "When someone asks you where you come from, the answer is your mother." My hands were crossed on my chest now, and the woman in the blue suit turned her rings. "When your mother's gone, you've lost your past. It's so much more than love. Even when there's no love, it's so much more than anything else in your life. I did love my mother, but I didn't know how much until she was gone."

This isn't the entire theme, but certainly one important part of it, and when Ellen speaks these words, the reader knows exactly what she's talking about because the themes in our lives are universal. Dialogue is not only a faster and more effective way to communicate the theme than to use long paragraphs of dry exposition, but it's also more emotional, up-front, and personal with the reader. You have to be careful, of course, that the characters aren't simply preaching and moralizing to each other just to make sure the reader gets *your* message. If you have a philosophy or idea you want to get across in your book—and you should—then it's perfectly natural to have your characters discussing this idea. If the theme is woven in in other ways throughout other scenes, your characters' dialogue about it in any one scene will feel natural. Use dialogue to convey your story's theme to your reader.

We will cover all of the above in more detail in future chapters. There's a lot to learn about how to get your dialogue to deliver in a way that engages your reader at an emotional level.

But before we get into the nuts and bolts of writing dialogue, there are a few fears we should dispel so you feel free to bring your characters onstage and let them loose to be their authentic selves. We'll deal with these fears in the next chapter.

EXERCISES

The following exercises are designed to give you the opportunity to practice the purposes of dialogue and release the voice inside of yourself through fictional characters.

EXERCISE 1

Characterizes/reveals motives. Consider the background of both your protagonist and antagonist. Write a scene where both of them show up and have to talk to each other, whether they want to or not. In this scene, find a way to insert a bit of motivation into the dialogue so we have sympathy for both characters.

EXERCISE 2

Sets the mood in the story. Place two characters in a setting that will enhance the story's mood. A dark, creepy alley in a horror story, a bright island beach in a romance, or you might want to reverse these for something different—a dark alley in a romance or an island beach in a horror story. Write a scene of dialogue focusing on the mood/emotion you want to convey in the overall story.

EXERCISE 3

Intensifies the story conflict. Two characters are arguing about the moral issues concerning abortion, or the death penalty, or assisted suicide, or another hot topic of your choosing. Write a scene of dialogue that intensifies the conflict between these two characters. Show the conflict escalating as they continue to argue.

EXERCISE 4

Creates tension and suspense. Two characters are in a fender bender. One, the antagonist, has yet to get a learner's permit and was taking the family car out for a joyride without insurance. Write a scene of dialogue that's full of tension and suspense for what's ahead for both characters.

EXERCISE 5

Speeds up your scenes. Find a bit of ponderous narrative in one of your own story scenes and transition into dialogue, using it to speed up the scene. Resist using much narrative or action; try to create most of the scene using just dialogue so you can discover how dialogue quickly speeds up the pace in a scene. If you're not far enough into a story of your own, complete this exercise with a novel on your bookshelf.

EXERCISE 6

Adds bits of setting/background. Find a line of dialogue, either in something you've written or in a novel you've read, that reveals the story's setting. If it's out of another author's novel, study how the writer managed to insert bits of the setting into the dialogue to make it seem like a natural part of the discussion between the characters.

EXERCISE 7

Communicates the theme. Pull at least three novels off your bookshelf and see if you can find a line or two of dialogue that communicates the story's theme. If you can't find anything, create a line of dialogue that clearly conveys what you believe the story to be *about*.

chapter 2

[MUTE CHARACTERS
AND STORIES—
ABOLISHING YOUR FEARS]

"Are you planning to use any dialogue in your novel?" As a writing coach, this is the first time I'd ever had to ask a writer this question. New writers often use too much dialogue, but seldom none at all.

"Well, sure." Carol shifted uncomfortably as she studied her manuscript.

"We're into the third chapter and all of the characters are passing each other without speaking." I'd already noticed this in previous readings of the first couple of Carol's novel chapters, but we were working on other things and I hadn't gotten around to mentioning it.

"Yeah, well, I know I have to get it in there pretty soon." She flipped a few pages over. "I have a question about where the comma goes in this one sentence on page five."

I'm not a therapist, but I knew Carol was avoiding the subject of dialogue—again. She never wanted to talk about it. Turns out when I finally did make her talk about it that she was scared of dialogue. Afraid that when her characters started talking, they would sound stupid, not at all profound and mysterious as she imagined them to be in her mind. She didn't want to dispel their mysteriousness by letting them open their mouths and make fools out of themselves and especially out of her. This is the first time I got anyone to admit this, but I have a feeling it's a common problem with both nonfiction and fiction writers. I've noticed that nonfiction writers avoid dialogue most of the time because they don't feel like they have to use it. Fiction writers know at some point they have to use it, but they do so with great trepidation.

Writing dialogue happens to be something I've always enjoyed. Part of the reason for this, I suspect, is that I tend to create and write about characters much like myself. I haven't taken a lot of risks in my fiction—creating stories I couldn't live, creating characters I couldn't be. I can appreciate the fear around dialogue, especially if you have to work with characters with dialect or speech impediments or who live in another world you've never experienced, whether real as in another part of the planet or on another planet altogether as in science fiction or fantasy.

Since the premise of this book is to learn to release the voice within us and create dialogue that delivers our story to the reader, no matter what kind of character we're creating, we have to first begin to understand the hindrances, conscious and unconscious, that keep us from plunging right in and doing it. We have fears about dialogue that handicap us and keep us from relaxing while we're writing, misconceptions that create pressure to do it "right." And that's where the paralysis comes in that Carol experienced. The good news is that bringing these fears and misconceptions out into the open allows us to see them for what they are and determine to not be driven by them any longer. Good writing of any kind, whether we're writing dialogue, exposition, action, or description, can happen only when we're relaxed and not worrying about the mechanics. That's the purpose of this book—to help you relax by showing you how you can become more comfortable with your voice and to teach you the mechanics so you can practice and make them automatic.

Natalie Goldberg tells us in *Writing Down the Bones,* "Don't think. Don't get logical." She goes on to say that "…the aim is to burn through to first thoughts, to the place where energy is unobstructed by social politeness or the internal censor, to the place where you are writing about what your mind actually sees and feels, not what it thinks it should see or feel."

Our fears and misconceptions prevent us from burning through to first thoughts. When we're full of fear, we have no choice but to write out of what our fear brings up. The flow of energy Natalie is talking about is blocked, so we can't write about what our mind "actually sees and feels." The only way to defuse our fears is to bring them out into the open—so let's get started.

IDENTIFYING YOUR FEARS

Following is a list of our most common fears concerning dialogue.

- What if I let my character talk and he sounds stupid, not at all how I want my reader to perceive him?

- What if my characters start talking and they all sound the same?
- What if my characters don't sound like my reader expects them to?
- What if my dialogue sounds flat and boring and doesn't do anything to move the story forward?
- What if my dialogue sounds stilted and formal, and the reader can tell I'm trying to write dialogue rather than just letting my characters talk?
- What if I let my characters start talking and they run away with the scene?
- What if I don't put enough narrative in and the reader can't follow the dialogue? Worse yet, what if I put too much in and slow the dialogue way down?

You'll notice that all of the above fears start with "What if…" That's the nature of fear. It's always about something that might, that could happen, never what necessarily *will* happen.

Be honest. Have you ever experienced at least one of these fears when you're about to launch into a dialogue scene? The purpose of this book is to make you so comfortable with writing dialogue that there will be no place for fear. Once you're comfortable and relaxed, you'll find that fear will no longer be present.

I've always found that the best way to deal with fear of any kind is to face it straight on. So let's take the above fears and look at them one by one to defuse their power over us.

What if I let my character talk and he sounds stupid, not at all like I want my reader to perceive him? Okay, what if he does? There is more than one way you can look at this if it really happens, which it seldom does. Our characters don't often sound as stupid as we think they do. It's usually our perception of how they sound that's the problem. The real issue could be that we fear we sound stupid when we talk, so we project that fear onto our characters. But people just talk—sometimes saying stupid things and sometimes saying brilliant things. Do you know anyone who talks brilliantly 100 percent of the time? Or stupidly 100 percent of the time? Sometimes I amaze myself, I say such profound things. Other times I sound like the dumbest character on *Saturday Night Live*. What's my point?

That whether your characters sound stupid or not, which is purely subjective, they have to keep talking. Because that's what characters do. Characters in a novel talk.

You have to know your characters well. Let's say you've created a tough guy. You perceive him as tough and you want your reader to perceive him that way. You want your protagonist and your reader to be scared of this dude. Yet he comes onstage and sounds like Elmer Fudd: "Where is that wabbit anyway?" Sure, this is probably the worst it could get, but we're going for the worst scenario possible here. You have three options: (1) You fire him and create a new antagonist, someone who really is tough, (2) you let him provide the comic relief for the story, or (3) you stop drinking when you're writing because you write crap when you do.

Even worse, what if you suspect that your characters might sound stupid but you're not absolutely sure? First, try reading your dialogue out loud. If that doesn't work, try reading it to another person, preferably another writer. Another "cool" writer. Cool people always know when other people sound stupid. I'm only half kidding here. It's kind of a sixth sense.

All jokes aside, I understand that this is a serious problem, but it's not the end of the world. We can fix all of this stuff in the second draft. Keep writing.

What if my characters start talking and they all sound the same? This can be a real problem. Sometimes I wish I were an actor and had to worry about being only one character. When you have to be ten people at once, sometimes all in the same scene, well, it's schizophrenic, and you're in danger of your characters all sounding the same, unless you know each of your characters on an intimate level. After all, you're the one writing this story. It's your voice. You only have one voice.

At least that's what we think. Have you ever gotten mad at your kids? Made love? Worked in corporate America? Is your voice the same for all of these situations? I didn't think so. You can play different roles and your voice is just a little adjusted for all of them. Not your personality—your voice. This is what you have to understand in order to create all of these different characters and make sure they don't all sound the same.

When you sit down to write, you're in one character's head—hopefully, that of your viewpoint character. But you still have to jump around and play every role in the scene when you're actually writing. You have to do what works for you. I heard Barbara Kingsolver on the *Oprah Winfrey Show* talk about how she wrote *The Poisonwood Bible* five times, each time from a different character's point of view. Now, that's some serious writing, to make sure she knew each of her characters and how they viewed the situation in her story. I don't suggest you go to that extreme, but do whatever you have to do. If you just can't get into a character's head, then go hang out with someone like your character long enough so you can adapt your voice and make it authentically that character's. You might want to try writing the scene from one character's point of view and then another character's point of view so you're inside of each of the characters for that scene. Maybe you'll only need to do this a few times before you "get" the distinct voice of each character.

You can also stop writing for a moment, pull up a new page, and just start writing like a mad person in the character's point of view that you're having trouble with. Don't think about what you're writing. Write about anything. Explode. Write quietly. Hang back and then cut loose. Be that character for a few moments. Let him talk to you about how he feels about the state of the economy or his next-door neighbor, his bartending job, or his addiction to pornography. Then come back to your scene. I guarantee this character won't sound like anyone other than himself because you've actually *been* him for a moment in time. Hung out inside of him. Sometimes I wish writers would do this more often with their antagonists so their antagonists wouldn't always come across as one-dimensional.

Another thing that might help is to make sure that your characters have vastly different careers and lives. This isn't always possible, of course. For example, your viewpoint character might be a teacher who works at an elementary school. Some of the supporting characters may be fellow teachers. If this is the case, you might want to go back to your character sketches and make sure that you build into each of the other characters something different that would show up in their dialogue with each other. Maybe one could be from the South, even though the story takes place in Idaho. Maybe another could be a jazz musician in his spare time. Spending time developing your characters can ensure that they won't be carbon copies of each other.

What if my characters don't sound like my reader expects them to? Our reader immediately starts to create a picture in his mind of our characters the minute we introduce them, so we need to get our characters talking as soon as possible. If we wait too long, our reader will start to create a picture in his mind of our characters and then when the characters do start to talk, the reader is surprised because, well, that's not how she imagined this person would communicate at all. Have you ever really admired someone from afar and when you heard the person speak it was nothing like you expected?

I was "in love" with a Marine when I was in high school. He was very good-looking and would write the most romantic letters and send romantic gifts. When he would come home on leave (oh, this is painful to remember) he would show up on my porch and start talking—and, well, he had the worst lisp. I would always forget about that part, and when he spoke the fantasy would immediately crack open and I would be crushed. He was a really nice guy, but I couldn't get past that.

That's how your reader feels when you've described your character vividly in narrative and when he finally speaks it's just not at all what your reader expected. So, as I said above, get your character talking as soon as you can after you introduce him.

Also, be sure to paint a physical picture of him that connects to how he speaks. If he's in a suit and tie most of the time, he probably won't talk like a farmer. Likewise, if he wears bib overalls a lot, he probably won't be talking about the latest version of Microsoft Windows. I say *probably*, because you never know. But if you're going to break a stereotype, you need to somehow indicate that to the reader so when your character starts talking, your reader doesn't have to suspend disbelief. Along with his physical appearance, make sure the background you create for him connects as well. Your character is an entire package and when he speaks, your reader will only be surprised if one part of the package doesn't fit.

Fixing Your Own Story

As you're writing your current story, ask yourself:
- What am I afraid of?
- What's the worst thing that can happen if my characters sound stupid, all sound the same, or sound flat and boring/stilted and formal, or run away with the scene?
- If the worst thing happens, can I recover? How?

Now charge through your fear. As Susan Jeffers advises—feel it and write anyway.

What if my dialogue sounds flat and boring and doesn't do anything to move the story forward? This is an understandable fear. In real life, we sometimes say things and then walk away from the conversation knowing that we didn't connect with the other person the way we wish we had. This happens to all of us. But then there are other times that we speak brilliantly, surprising even ourselves. Does our real dialogue always move our lives or "stories" forward?

What happens is that we walk away knowing what we "should" have said. Don't you hate that?

If we want our characters' dialogue to be interesting and move the story forward, we have to know our stories very well. We have to know exactly where we want our characters to go and how we want them to get there. We have to know what our characters' intentions are in every single scene, and we have to cut away every single word of dialogue that doesn't in some way contribute to the plot we have planned for them. Taking characters on detours is what causes flat and boring plots. If you keep your characters and story on track, this is not something you'll have to worry about.

So chill. This is really a second-draft question. When our characters sound flat and boring in our first draft, we can take another look at the dialogue in our second draft and fix it. It's often not until our characters sound flat and boring that we even know what we want them to say and how we want them to sound. Sometimes that's all it takes. Even flat and boring isn't the end of the world. We see it, measure it against what we want our characters to come off like, and once we have something to measure it against, we know what to do. So, in that sense, flat and boring isn't so bad.

What if my dialogue sounds stilted and formal and the reader can tell I'm trying to write dialogue rather than just letting my characters talk? This is one of the worst fears because it's very real. I do happen to read a lot of dialogue that sounds stilted and formal and I know immediately that the writer is trying too hard. The writer is trying to write dialogue.

The dialogue has to emerge out of who the character is and his needs in the story, not out of the writer's need to tell a story. Do you understand the difference?

Stilted dialogue happens when we perceive what needs to be accomplished in our story and we set out to accomplish it. What happens is that we're writing the dialogue out of our need to tell the story rather than out of who our character is in the particular scene we're writing. We can definitely change this if we can just let go and quit trying to control the story.

If you're the kind of person who thinks through all of her words before she speaks them, this is probably your biggest dialogue challenge. I have a friend who recently started writing. She's a very calculated person. You can actually see the wheels in her mind turning in the middle of a conversation as she thinks through every sentence before she speaks. I wasn't surprised to read the dialogue in her first story and see the same thing.

Many of us are full of inhibitions when we sit down to write. Part of letting go of our inhibitions is letting go of our stories so our characters can act them out. Sometimes stilted dialogue only shows up when we reread what we've written. We recognize it when it happens, and that's what's important. If we can recognize it, we can fix it.

What if I let my characters start talking and they run away with the scene?
That would be just terrible, wouldn't it? To lose control of our characters, and therefore the story, just undoes us, doesn't it? Whoever told us we had to be in constant control of our stories, especially on the first draft? What if Fred's dialogue takes him toward Sally, that other woman, the one who was just a walk-on in your cast of characters? Now what? What's the worst that can happen? You might have to rewrite your outline or think through the story again to see if there's something that's supposed to happen that you're not letting happen. That would be terrible.

Dialogue tends to go that way. People start saying things they didn't expect to say, things get a little out of control, and sometimes people even end up fighting. Of course, in a story, that's not all bad. Actually, it's usually good because it means tension and conflict, which are definitely good for a story. So go ahead. Let your characters talk and quit interfering. If you were a character in a story, would you want someone looking over your shoulder every minute, making sure you were saying the "right" thing? You couldn't even be yourself. Let your characters be who they are. One way to get to know them is to bring them onstage and turn them loose in a scene of dialogue.

Sure, you may have an outline and you expect your characters to follow it. But it's kind of like when you have a goal for a conversation you plan to have with your partner, friend, or boss, and you find yourself saying things you hadn't planned to say at all. Sometimes this works out and sometimes it doesn't. But the fact is it happens, and you can't always control it. Often the words are out before you can reign them back in. Every once in a while you can catch yourself as it's happening, but most of the time you just keep talking, either making a fool of yourself or saying some really brilliant things that you hadn't anticipated at all. It all depends on the headspace you're in at the moment. That's true of your characters, as well. Their headspace is your headspace. Relax and let them be who and where they are. You can always reign them back in in another draft if that's what needs to happen.

What if I don't put in enough narrative and the reader can't follow the dialogue? Worse yet, what if I put in too much and slow the dialogue way down? Pacing can be such a bugaboo. When is it too much? When is it not enough? We'll talk more about this in chapter eight, but for right now, this is a very real fear.

You have to have a sense of rhythm to know when enough is enough and when too much is too much. Some scenes call for bare dialogue—dialogue with no added narrative or action. Other scenes need a lot of extra narrative so we understand the core of the dialogue. And still others need action so the dialogue doesn't drag. The perfect balance is sometimes hard to come by, but this fear doesn't have to paralyze you. The more you practice, the better you'll get at this. And if you go over a little bit—too much narrative or action, too much dialogue—you'll catch it in your rewrite because you'll be watching for it.

Dialogue functions like real-life conversations. We talk, we think, we act. We do all of this unconsciously. This is how you want to write dialogue, and if you're worried about what you're doing every minute, your dialogue will come across like that—jerky, stilted, and unnatural. Eventually, after you feel comfortable with dialogue, you won't even be asking this question because you'll intuitively know when to put in a bit of narrative here, a bit of action there, a line of dialogue here, and an identifying tag there all the way through a scene.

Remember Carol? I don't know if she ever got over her fear of writing dialogue. She stopped writing her novel. I think she got bored with it, which is understandable. A story without dialogue is boring indeed. And that should lead your list of fears: What if I become so afraid of writing dialogue that I don't write any?

Don't despair. You *will* become comfortable with dialogue because you're a storyteller, and all stories need dialogue to feel alive to the reader.

You will overcome your fear because you're committed to your story.

In the next chapter, we'll look at the different kinds of dialogue we need to create to make our characters sound authentic in the various fiction genres. In the meantime, keep reading. And for goodness sake, keep writing.

EXERCISES

Do you remember Susan Jeffers' book *Feel the Fear and Do It Anyway?* This is how you want to approach your fears about writing dialogue. You want to practice challenging them until confidence overrides the fear. Later in this book, we'll go through published excerpts and discuss specific tips that will assist you in this process. The more you challenge your fear by taking risks with your dialogue, the less often your fear will show up when you're writing. Let's take the above fears one by one and give you the opportunity to practice.

EXERCISE 1

What if I let my character talk and he sounds stupid, not at all like I want my reader to perceive him?

The wonderful thing about writing as opposed to speaking is that this is the world of second chances. We can rewrite and rewrite and rewrite as many times as we need to.

Consider one of the characters in a story you're writing. Or consider a character in a completely new story idea. You have a definite role for him in the story. Shine the spotlight on this one character. Know what he wants. Give him a goal in a scene. Be sure you know exactly how you want your reader to perceive him. Now go ahead and write a scene of dialogue, slipping into this character's persona so you can write him for who he really is. Don't think about how stupidly or brilliantly he's talking until after the scene is over.

Now go back and read what you wrote. Does he sound stupid? How stupid? If he sounds real stupid, you might have to "fire" him and create another character to take his place. If he sounds just a little stupid, you can probably revise the dialogue and edit out the stupid parts. If the stupidity persists, maybe he's a stupid character, and you need to go with that. Consider, too, that the problem may be with you. No, I don't mean that you're stupid. But maybe you can't look at your story objectively. Have someone else read your work and give you feedback. Those characters that you think sound stupid may sound just fine.

What if my characters start talking and they all sound the same?

Know your character. Ground yourself in all of their personas, protagonist and antagonist alike and all minor characters, no matter how unlikable. Write first-person character sketches, letting your characters tell you who they are. How do you get to know real people? By spending time with them. The more time you spend with them, the better you get to know them, and soon you can hardly remember when you didn't know them. If you absolutely can't slip inside of any one of your characters, fire him and get a new one to take his place.

Create one scene in your story that includes all of your characters. Now write that scene from each character's point of view, one at a time. Focus on dialogue as the main way of recording the event. If it's impossible to put all the characters in one scene (maybe they lived at different times), then have the odd character reflect back on or project forward to the same scene the others experienced. What you want to do is create the same event for everyone, but show how they all experience it differently. Let each of them tell you about the event in his or her own words. This may include slang, dialect, or certain words or phrases that the other characters would never think to use.

When you reread these scenes, do your characters all sound alike? Have you created your character charts? If not, do that right away. If so, pull out some of the external or internal traits and feed them into the dialogue of the characters that sound alike. This will accomplish what I mentioned earlier in the chapter—the other parts of your characters' lives are different, and they can bring some of that difference into their dialogue. If you have to do this more than once to achieve your goal—write a scene from everyone's viewpoint—then do it as many times as it takes to really get to know these people.

EXERCISE 3

What if my characters don't sound like my reader expects them to?

This problem is easily fixed if you get your characters talking right away, like I suggested earlier. But for practice consider the following:

You've portrayed a character as a Harvard-educated woman. A physicist with two kids, recently divorced, out to lunch with friends, she's complaining about her boss. Suddenly she says, "Well, give me a two-by-four and I'll show him that I'm no ninny" or some such uneducated line.

You're appalled. Where did that come from? Clearly, from somewhere inside of you that at one time had an abusive boss or husband or father or whatever. Okay, so it's not what this character would normally say. A lot of writing fiction is about working through our unresolved issues. Sometimes we need to follow and sometimes we need to reign that character in. Part of being a writer is knowing when to do what. Anyway, you're going to have to get this character off that subject, and work it out in another book, maybe non-fiction, or you're going to just let her go for it and clean it up later. Getting back to your Harvard-educated character—in this case, reign her back in. Rewrite just that one line so it sounds like an intelligent complaint about the boss. Maybe something like, "He seems to think that if we aren't all working twelve-hour days, as he does, that we're not committed to the company. I suppose I'll need to address this in our next staff meeting." You get the idea.

EXERCISE 4

What if my dialogue sounds flat and boring and doesn't do anything to move the story forward?

As for flat and boring, well, maybe your character needs to get a life. But, yes, it is absolutely necessary that every scene of dialogue move the story forward, and so yes, you need to do something about this. If you recognize that you write the kind of dialogue that doesn't keep the plot moving, then you're already ahead of a lot of writers that who are completely unaware that they're writing rambling dialogue, most of which does nothing to move the overall story.

Find a dialogue scene in a story you're writing that you doubt does much to move your story forward. It gives some background on the characters and it reveals a bit of who they are, but you know that's not enough. Every scene needs to keep the story moving. Now rewrite that scene with one thing in mind—how you can make the dialogue do triple duty: characterize, provide background, and forward the plot. And while you're doing that, keep it lively and full of tension. Not too big of an order, is it?

EXERCISE 5

What if my dialogue sounds stilted and formal and the reader can tell I'm trying to write dialogue rather than just letting my characters talk?

As I mentioned earlier, the key to releasing this fear is to simply relax and not try so hard. You've heard the old advice about how if you try really hard not to think about a banana, guess what you find yourself thinking about. The same is true when it comes to dialogue—the harder you try not to write bad dialogue, the more bad dialogue you write. By bad, I mostly mean dialogue that comes across as less than authentic for the character speaking it. The following exercise is designed to help you focus on relaxing when your characters start talking.

Take what you consider a stilted scene of dialogue from a story you're writing or have written and rewrite it, focusing not on what the characters are saying but on relaxing while you're writing. Decide that it really doesn't matter how your characters sound or what they say—you can fix it later. This could, of course, cause you to plug into one of your other fears—that of your characters sounding stupid. But what we're doing in these exercises is isolating just one of your fears at a time so you can release it and write better.

EXERCISE 6

What if I let my characters start talking and they run away with the scene?

What we often don't understand about our characters is that they're an extension of us, and so if they're saying something we didn't expect or, didn't plan for them to say, we shouldn't try to repress them. We can release this particular fear by letting our characters express their true selves without censoring them. The important thing is to keep writing. There's always the second draft. And the third. We can later fix the dialogue of those characters who might embarrass us in front of our family and friends with dialogue that's too close to the bone, too vulnerable, too out-there.

Take an out-of-control character from a current story you're writing or develop a new one for a story you'd like to write and create a scene for him that has no boundaries. By boundaries I mean your plan for him. Let him go. Let him say whatever he wants to say— to himself or the other characters. Don't try to put words in his mouth and don't try to stop him from saying what he wants to say. Follow him. This could lead you to a completely new story idea, one that's deeper and closer to the "truth." Allowing our characters to be who they are will eliminate our fear of their running away with the scene or—God forbid—the story itself. It's not the end of the world (pay attention to how often I say this in this chapter) to be spontaneous and write the story that emerges with the character. Not only is it not the end of the world, but it indicates your growth as a writer.

EXERCISE 7

What if I don't put in enough narrative or action and the reader can't follow the dialogue? Worse yet, what if I put in too much and slow the dialogue way down?

When is enough enough—of anything? You go by feel. If you don't think you know enough to go by feel, don't worry about it, you will soon enough. The more you do this, the easier it becomes.

Create a scene of bare dialogue with no action, narrative, or identifying tags. When you're finished, go back through the scene and insert bits of narrative and action here and there to expand the scene and create a narrative flow. Be conscious of how much you're putting in. Is it bogging down? Is it just enough? Do you still need more to bring the reader on board with your character's intentions in the scene? When you do what depends on the needs of the story. There are no hard and fast rules.

chapter 3

[THE GENRE, MAINSTREAM, AND LITERARY STORY— THE DIALOGUE MATTERS]

Let's see, I have to get Homer from Point A to Point B by Tuesday afternoon and along the way he has to talk to Amos to see where they stashed the loot. The loot has to be moved by Tuesday evening, so we don't have much time here.

These are Mr. Writer's thoughts as he sits down to write the next scene in his novel.

I'll have him run into Amos in the 7-11. He starts to write:

"So, Amos, hey, man, how's it goin'?" Homer picked up a carton of milk and threw it into his basket. Amos didn't immediately answer, so Homer said, "So do you use Joy or Dove? Let's see, I think I'll get me some cashews for my long evening at home tonight."

"What are you doing tonight?" Amos asked.

"Watching the game, of course. Aren't you?"

"Not sure." Amos grunted. "I met this girl. I might go over to her place. She's pretty nice."

WHO CARES?

Going back to the loot for a moment—we know this is an action/adventure or suspense thriller, so no one cares about the cashews, the game, or Amos's girl. We care about the loot and how they're going to get it moved in time and how Homer is going to get from Point A to Point B.

This chapter is about voice and making sure our voice fits the kind of story we're writing.

Every writer has a unique voice, and nowhere does this show up more than in our story dialogue because whether we want to admit it or not, and no matter how much we think we're beyond this, some part of us is in all of the dialogue we write. If I've had an unresolved fight with my partner in the morning and sit down to write a scene of dialogue in the afternoon, guess what? Suddenly my characters are fighting away.

You've heard writers say that the characters just "ran away with the scene." Well, it doesn't work quite like that. They "run away" because we have some unresolved issues and our characters decide to play these out as we write. I always have to laugh when writers decide to "fictionalize" a true story, believing they're actually hiding the truth from readers. It's like an elephant sticking his head under the bed, thinking no one can see him.

Just like every writer has a voice, so does every story. This is one reason the publishing world has categorized all of our stories for us. The three major categories of story are genre, mainstream, and literary. The genre category includes a few subcategories: fantasy, science fiction, mystery, horror, action/adventure, suspense, thriller, romance, and young adult. These are self-explanatory, but new writers often ask about the difference between mainstream and literary stories.

Mainstream stories are contemporary stories intended for the general public rather than a specific audience. This type of story challenges the reader's belief system, suggests a new life vision, asks provocative questions, provokes introspection, and/or shakes up conventional rules.

Literary stories are avant-garde and experimental stories that incorporate unconventional and nontraditional writing style and techniques. They're often weak on plot and strong on characterization.

With the above in mind, it's only smart marketing sense to get on board and find out where our writing fits and what our category is. Once we do this, we can begin to understand what readers expect from our stories and, more specifically, from our dialogue in that kind of story. As a writing coach, I work with many new fiction writers, and it's clear to me that many of them don't "get" that different kinds of stories call for different kinds of characters, tension, pacing, themes, and dialogue. A fast-paced action adventure needs fast-paced dialogue in every scene to keep the story moving quickly forward. Likewise, a literary story needs the dialogue to match the pace of the other elements in the story—it needs to move more slowly.

Readers pick up certain kinds of stories for specific reasons. Some readers want a magical ride, while others want a scary ride with a lot of unexpected twists and turns. Some read fiction because, and maybe this is on an unconscious level, they want to learn something about themselves. Some just want to kick back and read about someone else's problems for a change. If we don't understand what our readers want, we won't be able to write stories that deeply satisfy readers in our chosen genre. Our characters' dialogue should match the rhythm of the story in every way possible. This chapter is about taking a look at all of the types of stories and the different voices we, as writers, adopt in order to tell these stories.

At the risk of being formulaic, I've put the types of stories into seven categories to help us better understand readers' expectations of our stories and especially the dialogue we create for our characters: magical, cryptic, descriptive, shadowy, breathless, provocative, and uncensored.

MAGICAL

The language of *The Hobbit, Star Wars, The Lord of the Rings, Star Trek,* and *The Wonderful Wizard of Oz* appeals to readers who are looking for the magical. "May the Force be with you" would sound ridiculous in a mainstream or literary novel. Real people just don't talk like that. Readers of mainstream and literary stories know what's real and what isn't.

When writing mainstream and literary stories, we have to go with what is real. Science fiction and fantasy writers can write about what isn't real, but it's not as easy as it sounds. Some of us have the ability to write magical dialogue, and some of us don't. Magical dialogue sounds truly authentic coming from an author like J.R.R. Tolkien. But can you imagine Holden Caulfield telling his sister, "May the Force be with you"? If he had even hinted at it, J.D. Salinger would not be the famous author he is today.

Science fiction and fantasy aren't the only genres where magical dialogue shows up. A good romance writer can also pull it off. Magical dialogue has a lyrical rhythm to it, and fantasy, science fiction, and romance authors should practice until they can write it and write it well. Sometimes magical dialogue seems inherent in writers of these genres—sometimes they even talk in magical dialogue in their everyday conversations.

I don't. I know that about myself. Part of writing dialogue for our stories is knowing who we are and where we fit as storytellers. Do you know if you're a fantasy, science fiction, or romance writer? Have you ever thought about it?

Let's take a look at some of J.R.R. Tolkien's dialogue in *The Lord of the Rings* and see exactly what we're talking about. Do you see yourself at all?

A dozen hobbits, led by Sam, leaped forward with a cry and flung the villain to the ground. Sam drew his sword.

"No, Sam!" said Frodo. "Do not kill him even now. For he has not hurt me. And in any case I do not wish him to be slain in this evil mood. He was great once, of a noble kind that we should not dare to raise our hands against. He is fallen, and his cure is beyond us; but I would still spare him, in the hope that he may find it."

Saruman rose to his feet, and stared at Frodo. There was a strange look in his eyes of mingled wonder and respect and hatred. "You have grown, Halfling," he said. "Yes, you have grown very much. You are wise, and cruel. You have robbed my revenge of sweetness, and now I must go hence in bitterness, in debt to your mercy. I hate it and you! Well, I go and I will trouble you no more. But do not expect me to wish you health and long life. You will have neither. But that is not my doing. I merely foretell."

He walked away, and the hobbits made a lane for him to pass; but their knuckles whitened as they gripped on their weapons. Wormtongue hesitated, and then followed his master.

What makes this scene of dialogue work? What distinguishes it as magical?

It's certainly *dramatic*. For starters, take the phrase, *flung the villain to the ground* in the first paragraph. It's not dialogue, but it could be. It's definitely dramatic. Flung? Villain?

Did you notice that no contractions are used? The language is almost Shakespearean. *"Do not kill me." "He has not hurt me." "I do not wish him to be slain."*

It's *eloquent*. *"You have robbed my revenge of sweetness, and now I must go hence in bitterness, in debt, to your mercy."*

It's *direct*. *"But do not expect me to wish you health and long life. You will have neither."*

If you want to write fantasy or science fiction, you must become a master of magical dialogue. How? Practice. Read lots and lots of stories in the science fiction/fantasy genres. And challenge yourself with the exercise at the end of this chapter.

In a romance, magical dialogue takes on a little different form, but it's still magical in that it transcends the way we talk to each other in normal society in this century. One reason I don't read a lot of romance novels is because many romance writers can't pull off this kind of transcending and magical dialogue. They try, but it comes off as hokey rather than magical. I think Robert James Waller does an admirable job in this passage of dialogue between his hero, Richard, and his heroine, Francesca, in *The Bridges of Madison County.*

> He started to speak, but Francesca stopped him.
>
> "Robert, I'm not quite finished. If you took me in your arms and carried me to your truck and forced me to go with you, I wouldn't murmur a complaint. You could do the same thing just by talking to me. But I don't think you will. You're too sensitive, too aware of my feelings, for that. And I have feelings of responsibility here.
>
> "Yes, it's boring in its way. My life, that is. It lacks romance, eroticism, dancing in the kitchen to candlelight, and the wonderful feel of a man who knows how to love a woman. Most of all, it lacks you. But there's this damn sense of responsibility I have. To Richard, to the children. Just my leaving, taking away my physical presence, would be hard enough for Richard. That alone might destroy him.
>
> "On top of that, and this is even worse, he would have to live the rest of his life with the whispers of the people here. 'That's Richard Johnson. His hot little Italian wife ran off with some longhaired photographer a few years back.' Richard would have to suffer that, and the children would hear the snickering of Winterset for as long as they live here. They would suffer, too. And they would hate me for it.
>
> "As much as I want you and want to be with you and part of you, I can't rear myself away from the realness of my responsibilities. If you force me, physically or mentally, to go with you, as I said earlier, I cannot fight that. I don't have the strength, given my feelings for you. In spite of what I said about not taking the road away from you, I'd go because of my own selfish wanting of you."

Okay, who talks like that? Not anyone I know. That's pretty articulate for an off-the-cuff moment. Pretty articulate and pretty, well, magical. Magical in that all of it makes perfect sense and is said in such eloquent language that we marvel at it while at the same time being fully aware that if left to us, we'd say something banal like, "Nope, I can't hang out with you anymore. If Richard finds out, I'm dead meat." In a romance story, somehow the magical dialogue connects with the romantic in us and we can go there with Francesca. We can believe it.

What makes Francesca's dialogue work so well that we're pulled in at an emotional level? First, it's the *details.* The author paints word pictures. Instead of "*...he'd have to live the rest of his life with the gossip,*" Francesca says, *"…he'd have to live the rest of his life with the whisper of the people here."* This creates an image in the reader's mind, and we can see and feel Richard's pain as the townsfolk whisper to each other about Robert and Francesca.

"If you took me in your arms and carried me to your truck…"

"His hot little Italian wife ran off with some long-haired photographer…"

Magical dialogue also includes *metaphors*. *"In spite of what I said about not taking the road away from you…"* Francesca is talking about Robert's freedom.

Magical dialogue is emotional dialogue. Francesca is able to articulate her longing for what Robert has to offer as well as her compassion for how Richard and her children would suffer if she left them and rode off with Robert into the sunset. She's able to hold those two emotions simultaneously, which tears her in two. It's magical.

Like I said previously, I happen to believe that most writers either have the ability to write this kind of dialogue or they don't. We have to have a mind that thinks in magical terminology, sentences, and phrases. I'm so in awe of those who can write like this, so in awe that most of the time I leave it to them to write. But every once in a while, I try. If you think you have this ability, work to develop it. If not, keep trying. Never underestimate the romantic in you.

CRYPTIC

Much of the dialogue in literary and religious stories deals with abstract ideas and vague concepts and has double meanings that readers can't always immediately decipher. They're not supposed to. Sometimes other novels will have bits of cryptic dialogue when the plot calls for some things to remain hidden or secret. These bits of dialogue plant subliminal messages in the reader's mind that help to communicate the story's theme and will ultimately make sense if the author is able to successfully pull the story off at the end. Some writers are especially gifted at this. Chuck Palahniuk is one of them. Here are three dialogue passages from his novel *Fight Club* that make little sense at the moment, even sounding like the ranting of a crazy person, but when woven into the story build to a satisfying resolution at the end. In the first one, the main character, unnamed because he turns out to be one with his alter ego, Tyler Durden, has just learned that while he was away for a few days, his condo blew up. In the following scene, the doorman is giving the viewpoint character his perspective on the situation.

> "A lot of young people try to impress the world and buy too many things," the doorman said.
>
> I called Tyler.
>
> The phone rang in Tyler's rented house on Paper Street.
>
> Oh, Tyler, please deliver me.
>
> And the phone rang.
>
> The doorman leaned into my shoulder and said, "A lot of young people don't know what they really want."
>
> Oh, Tyler, please rescue me.
>
> And the phone rang.
>
> "Young people, they think they want the whole world."
>
> Deliver me from Swedish furniture.
>
> Deliver me from clever art.
>
> And the phone rang and Tyler answered.
>
> "If you don't know what you want," the doorman said, "you end up with a lot you don't."

We don't completely know what the doorman is talking about because this takes place only forty pages into the story, and we're just beginning to understand that the viewpoint character's major conflict is his disillusionment with an empty consumer culture and his struggle to find an answer. In the next passage, Marla, the viewpoint character's annoying once-in-a-while girlfriend and a constant reminder of what makes our consumer culture so empty, makes a couple of cryptic comments.

> "You know, the condom is the glass slipper of our generation. You slip it on when you meet a stranger. You dance all night, then you throw it away. The condom, I mean. Not the stranger."

A few moments later, after rambling on for a while about her latest Goodwill find and how people dump dead Christmas trees:

> "The Animal Control place is the best place to go," Marla says. "Where all the animals, the little doggies and kitties that people loved and then dumped, even the old animals, dance and jump around for your attention because after three days, they get an overdose shot of sodium phenobarbital and then into the big pet oven.
>
> "The big sleep, 'Valley of the Dogs' style.

> "Where even if someone loves you enough to save your life, they still cas-
> trate you." Marla looks at me as if I'm the one humping her and says, "I can't
> win with you, can I?"

At this point, Marla isn't making many points with us because we don't have a clue as to what she's talking about. Later, it will all make sense and tie in directly to what "Tyler" is dealing with in his life.

In the last example, a police detective has started calling the viewpoint character about his condo explosion. They're on the phone with each other and the detective has just asked if he knows anyone who could make home-made dynamite. "Tyler" is whispering advice over the viewpoint character's shoulder.

> "Disaster is a natural part of my evolution," Tyler whispered, "toward tragedy
> and dissolution."
> I told the detective that it was the refrigerator that blew up my condo.
> "I'm breaking my attachment to physical power and possessions," Tyler
> whispered, "because only through destroying myself can I discover the greater
> power of my spirit... The liberator who destroys my property," Tyler said, "is
> fighting to save my spirit. The teacher who clears all possessions from my path
> will set me free."

It doesn't make a lot of sense at the moment, but later the viewpoint character comes to terms with that part of himself, his ego, that is bent on self-destruction.

What distinguishes cryptic dialogue from other kinds of dialogue is its indirectness, subtlety, and ambiguity. If you want to see a lot of examples of this, amazingly enough, check out Jesus' words in the Bible. That's right— Matthew, Mark, Luke, and John are full of cryptic dialogue. Stories with double meanings. Stories that can be interpreted in many different ways, depending upon what the reader wants to hear.

In order to write cryptic dialogue, you can't be a black-or-white thinker. You have to be able to view the world from more than one perspective. Why? And why is cryptic dialogue so effective in literary and religious sto-ries, and even some mainstream stories? Because these kinds of stories have a message and readers don't want to be preached to, told what to believe, or what to think. But they usually don't mind having their current belief sys-tems challenged. Cryptic dialogue that doesn't come right out and make a concrete statement, that has hidden meanings the reader must discover, honors the reader's intelligence and ability to come to his own conclusions about the story's subject. The reader will be much more receptive to your story's truth when the characters are talking around a subject rather than hammering some moralistic idea into each other's brains.

Practice writing dialogue for your characters that holds back, skirts around the real issues, and can be interpreted in more than one way.

Cryptic dialogue is difficult to do well. If we're not careful, we can end up writing preachy, moralistic, dogmatic junk that can turn off readers in droves. But when done well and woven through the plot, cryptic dialogue can provide the substance that gives meaning to the entire story.

DESCRIPTIVE

The literary, mainstream, and historical story often relies on dialogue for much of its history, background, and description. Or at least it should. Too many of these stories are full of long, boring passages of narrative that the reader has to wade through on the way to the plot. In this kind of story, even once the plot is moving, the author often stops the action with more long, boring passages of narrative. I can appreciate that the author is enamored with the research of her story's time period, but there are more interesting ways to dispense it to us, and for the reader, the most engaging way is through dialogue. The goal of descriptive dialogue is to provide the reader with the information she needs to understand the characters and story line in the context of the setting or time period in which they live. This is the author's goal. The character's goal can't be sacrificed for the author's, and that's where authors often err. Descriptive dialogue can still have tension and suspense and can be inserted into a scene of action so the story doesn't bog down while we're getting the information we need.

Let's look at the following scene of descriptive dialogue from *The Poisonwood Bible* by Barbara Kingsolver. Leah has just put her little sister in the swing outside of their hut in South Africa and is combing her hair when the village schoolteacher, Anatole, comes by. He's trying to explain to Leah, not so successfully, about the state of the Congo at this point in time.

> I drew the edge of the comb slowly down the center of Ruth May's head, making a careful part. Father had said the slums outside Leopoldville would be set right by American aid, after Independence. Maybe I was foolish to believe him. There were shanties just as poor in Georgia, on the edge of Atlanta, where

black and white divided, and that was smack in the middle of America.

"Can you just do that, what they did down there? Announce your own country?" I asked.

"Prime Minister Lumumba says no, absolutely not. He has asked the United Nations to bring an army to restore unity."

"Is there going to be a war?"

"There is already a kind of war, I think. Moise Tshombe has Belgians and mercenary soldiers working for him. I don't think they will leave without a fight. And Katanga is not the only place where they are throwing stones. There is a different war in Matadi, Thysville, Boende, Leopoldville. People are very angry at the Europeans. They are even hurting women and little children."

"What are they so mad at the white people for?"

Anatole sighed. "Those are big cities. Where the boa and the hen curl up together, there is only trouble. People have seen too much of the Europeans and all the things they had. They imagined after Independence life would immediately become fair."

"Can't they be patient?"

"Could you be? If your belly was empty and you saw whole baskets of bread on the other side of a window, would you continue waiting patiently, Beene? Or would you throw a rock?"

The descriptive dialogue in this passage reveals an important part of the setting and the story situation without bogging down the action, which happens when the author uses only narrative to dispense this kind of information. In literary, historical, and mainstream stories, the bantering of descriptive dialogue between characters keeps things moving forward.

You may have a lot of background you need to insert in the story in order for the reader to understand the context of your setting and plot, but if you use only narrative to get it in there, the reader can feel like she's watching a documentary. If you're writing this kind of story, look for ways to *show* the history, description of setting, and/or cultural situation through the characters' conversations with one another so the reader is engaged in the story.

Throughout any passage of descriptive dialogue, you'll want to include narrative thoughts and reactions of the viewpoint character's, of course, but this is so much easier for the reader to absorb when this kind of narrative is woven into dialogue rather than doled out in long, boring paragraphs of exposition.

The pitfall of descriptive dialogue is that sometimes we have our characters going on a little too long because we may have an entire historical situation we want to explain to the reader. Sometimes we get caught up in wanting to dispense all of the research we've done, so we decide to put it all in one passage of dialogue that goes on for pages.

I believe that one of the reasons literary novels are known to have such a small number of readers compared to other kinds of novels is because of the long passages of narrative description. I wonder, if more literary, mainstream, and historical authors used less narrative description and more descriptive dialogue in their stories would they attract a wider audience? You don't have to sacrifice engaging dialogue just to make your novel fit into one of these categories.

Just for Fun

[1] No matter what kind of story you're writing, take the characters out of your story and drop them into another genre, then write three pages of dialogue for them. They might surprise you. You'll get to know them in a way you never intended and maybe never wanted to know them.

[2] Create three characters—one romantic character, one science fiction character, one horror character. Put them in the same scene and write three pages of dialogue.

[3] Challenge yourself to write a short story in a genre in which you've never written. Pay special attention to the dialogue you create for the protagonist.

SHADOWY

The horror and mystery writer's goal is to scare the bejesus out of us, and these authors take their jobs very seriously. Occasionally, a mainstream novel has enough horror and mystery in it to warrant this kind of dialogue.

Getting hold of the purpose of a passage of dialogue will help you write it more creatively because you know it's not just filler. In shadowy dialogue, your character's role is to keep your reader in a suspended state of suspense and a kind of terror, although you periodically tighten and loosen the tension. This is generally achieved with an ominous tone of suspense or fore-shadowing of things to come. Things that are a little more intense than a walk in the park. The kinds of things you find in your worst nightmare: creepy, crawly things that attack, maim, and kill. Shadowy dialogue always has a foreboding threat of danger looming over the protagonist.

Check out the following example from Stephen King's *The Shining.* Here we have Danny, the son of the unsympathetic protagonist, Jack, in dialogue with his imaginary friend, Tony. He has imagined Tony into being to cope with life with his insane father. In "reality" (you never really know what's real and what isn't in a Stephen King novel), Tony is actually Danny in a few years, a suspended character between he and his father, all in Danny's imagination. In this scene, Tony is trying to warn Danny of impending harm to his mother, possibly her death.

> He began to struggle, and the darkness and the hallway began to waver. Tony's form became chimerical, indistinct.
>
> "Don't!" Tony called. "Don't, Danny, don't do that!"
>
> "She's not going to be dead! She's not!"
>
> "Then you have to help her, Danny...you're in a place deep down in your own mind. The place where I am. I'm a part of you, Danny."
>
> "You're Tony. You're not me. I want my mommy...I want my mommy..."
>
> "I didn't bring you here, Danny. You brought yourself. Because you knew."
>
> "No—"
>
> "You've always known," Tony continued, and he began to walk closer. For the first time, Tony began to walk closer. "You're deep down in yourself in a place where nothing comes through. We're alone here for a little while, Danny. This is an Overlook where no one can ever come. No clocks work here. None of the keys fit them and they can never be wound up. The doors have never been opened and no one has ever stayed in the rooms. But you can't stay long. Because it's coming."
>
> "It..." Danny whispered fearfully, and as he did so the irregular pounding noise seemed to grow closer, louder. His terror, cool and distant a moment ago, became a more immediate thing.

One reason the shadowy dialogue in the above passage works is because while Tony seems like a friend, we're not always sure. He's what's known as a shape-shifter, the archetype in Joseph Campbell's *The Hero's Journey,* that keeps the reader in the dark as far as whether the character is really for the protagonist or against him. The protagonist can never quite trust the shape-shifter, so when the shape-shifter speaks in dialogue, we're always questioning him, wondering whether he's speaking truthfully or not. Here Tony is delivering bad news. Should Danny even believe him? Another reason the dialogue works is because it's cryptic, so we have to keep reading to find out what Tony is even talking about. And the last reason it works is because Tony is definitely delivering an ominous threat of something to come that could turn Danny's world upside down and change him forever. Shadowy dialogue's effectiveness is mostly in the tone of the character's words, but you can use setting and action to add to its creepiness.

The purpose of shadowy dialogue, used in mysteries and horror stories, is to keep the story as dark as possible. Horror and mystery readers are interested in the dark and supernatural, preferably both at the same time. The characters are usually somewhere between consciousness and unconsciousness where the darkness is concerned. It's a zone where both character and reader teeter between the light and the dark, between what's real and what's imagined. And we all know scary things go on in our imaginations sometimes. Horror and mystery writers know how to develop those imaginary moments to where they feel more real than reality itself, and therein lies the terror we feel when we read this kind of story. The characters' dialogue reflects this mood.

BREATHLESS

The purpose of this kind of dialogue is to keep the reader on the edge of his chair, turning pages until the wee hours of the morning. The word you want to remember is *suspense*. Breathless dialogue is all about creating suspense, which is what readers are looking for when they buy an action/adventure or suspense thriller. They want every page to be full of spine-tingling, creeped-out, nail-biting suspense. It's your job, as the writer, to give it to them as the characters express themselves to each other in ways that turn up the heat. And turn it up. And turn it up.

Let's look at Michael Crichton's *Jurassic Park* for an example of how dialogue works in suspense thrillers. Here we have three characters trying to get from one side of the lake to the other without the most dangerous of all dinosaurs, the tyrannosaurus, seeing them. But then Lex starts coughing. And coughing.

Lex coughed loudly, explosively. In Tim's ears, the sound echoed across the water like a gunshot.

The tyrannosaur yawned lazily, and scratched its ear with its hind foot, just like a dog. It yawned again. It was groggy after its big meal, and it woke up slowly.

On the boat, Lex was making little gargling sounds.

"Lex, *shut up!*" Tim said.

"I can't help it," she whispered, and then she coughed again. Grant rowed hard, moving the raft powerfully into the center of the lagoon.

On the shore, the tyrannosaur stumbled to its feet.

"I couldn't help it, Timmy!" Lex shrieked miserably. "I couldn't help it!"

"Shhhh!"

Grant was rowing as fast as he could.

"Anyway, it doesn't matter," she said. "We're far enough away. He can't swim."

"*Of course he can swim, you little idiot!*" Tim shouted at her. On the shore, the tyrannosaur stepped off the dock and plunged into the water. It moved strongly into the lagoon after them.

"Well, how should I know?" she said.

"Everybody knows tyrannosaurs can swim! It's in all the books! Anyway, all reptiles can swim!"

"Snakes can't."

"*Of course* snakes can. You idiot!"

Crichton uses this kind of breathless dialogue throughout the novel. If it lets up, it's never for long. I personally believe the dialogue to be one of the reasons for the story's success. These are real folks in real trouble—over and over again. Readers of suspense thrillers and action/adventures demand this kind of tension, so if you're going to write for these readers, you have to be able to give it to them.

When we are facing a difficult situation and have no clue as to the outcome, our breath can become short and shallow as fear, anger, or sadness increases, thus the term *breathless* dialogue. The key to writing effective breathless dialogue is to:

- cut away most of the description and explanatory narrative so the scene is mostly dialogue
- insert bits of action, as Crichton does in the above passage, so the

scene keeps moving forward in a physical way, but not so much that we lose track of the character's speech
- use short spurts of emotional phrases of dialogue rather than long speeches or contemplative verbal pondering
- make clear what's at stake for the reader as he's expressing himself
- hold back just enough information in the dialogue so the suspense is sustained throughout the scene

Is this you? Does this kind of dialogue come easy for you? All dialogue in all fiction, whether short stories or novels, needs a degree of tension and suspense, but for the suspense thriller and the action/adventure, it's at the core.

PROVOCATIVE

The *Nashville Tennessean* wrote of Wally Lamb's *She's Come Undone:* "Wally Lamb can lie down with the literary lions at will: he's that gifted…This novel does what good fiction should do—it informs our hearts as well as our minds of the complexities involved in the 'simple' act of living a human life."

This is actually a very accurate definition of the mainstream and literary story. Lamb's novel is full of pages of dialogue that's *about* something. Not all of the dialogue, of course, in a mainstream or literary story needs to be about something, but a good portion of it does. This is because, unlike most genre stories, which are plot-driven, mainstream and literary stories are character-driven and about something.

As we learned earlier in this chapter, readers of this kind of story want to be challenged in their thinking, provoked to consider other ways of looking at something, and shaken up in their belief systems. They're asking for this when they pick up this kind of story to read.

For a story to be about something, it must be driven by some kind of universal truth, as you'll see in the following excerpt from Harper Lee's *To Kill a Mockingbird*. The universal truth in this novel is that "all men are created equal," and it shows up on just about every page.

Not all writers want to work that hard at writing, to make sure that every line of the story contributes to a larger theme and the story communicates a larger truth of some kind. But some do, and if this is you, you want to make sure much of your viewpoint character's dialogue provokes the reader as much as it does the other characters in a way that could ultimately be transforming. The characters in this kind of story are thinking about something bigger than themselves. They're talking to each other about these bigger things, wondering out loud in dialogue.

Harper Lee challenges the reader on two levels in the following passage from *To Kill a Mockingbird*—racism and injustice—and she does it very effectively through dialogue. Here Atticus Finch is giving his final argument in the case of Robinson vs. Ewell:

> "She has committed no crime, she has merely broken a rigid and time-honored code of our society, a code so severe that whoever breaks it is hounded from our midst as unfit to live with. She is the victim of cruel poverty and ignorance, but I cannot pity her: she is white. She knew full well the enormity of her offense, but because her desires were stronger than the code she was breaking, she persisted in breaking it. She persisted, and her subsequent reaction is something that all of us have known at one time or another. She did something every child has done—she tried to put the evidence of her offense away from her. But in this case she was not a child hiding stolen contraband: she struck out at her victim—of necessity she must put him away from her—he must be removed from her presence, from this world. She must destroy the evidence of her offense.
>
> "What was the evidence of her offense? Tom Robinson, a human being. She must put Tom Robinson away from her. Tom Robinson was her daily reminder of what she did. What did she do? She tempted a Negro."

Atticus goes on for some time in this vein and concludes his argument:

> "...But there is one way in this country in which all men are created equal— there is one human institution that makes a pauper the equal of a Rockefeller, the stupid man the equal of an Einstein, and the ignorant man the equal of any college president. That institution, gentlemen, is a court. It can be the Supreme Court of the United States or the humblest J.P. court in the land, or this honorable court which you serve. Our courts have their faults, as does any human institution, but in this country our courts are the great levelers, and in our courts all men are created equal."

Often, dialogue in the mainstream and literary story will communicate the theme. Atticus is speaking the larger truth of the story to the other characters and to the reader. There is no way we can read this passage and not think about something that is bigger than our daily lives. Provocative story dialogue sometimes makes us squirm, definitely stirs up our gray matter, and often shocks and startles us out of our comfort zones. If you're a mainstream or literary writer, you want to write the kind of dialogue that does this and more.

UNCENSORED

The uncensored dialogue in the young adult story is definitely that of the young person, but that doesn't at all mean that it's full of hip-hop words, slang, and weird phrases. I call it uncensored simply because, while adults most often censor themselves when they speak, teenagers haven't yet learned that skill so their dialogue is more raw, edgy, and honest. The reader of the young adult story expects realism, so keep in mind that your teen characters will not be cleaning up their words before they speak them as so many adults do. What's important about the dialogue in the young adult story, just like in any other story, is that it's authentic. Authenticity isn't more important in this story than in any other; it's just that we have to watch our tendency to create characters that all sound like they just stepped off the planet Way Cool—which isn't any more authentic than if we didn't give them a teen voice at all. This kind of over-the-top teen speak sounds no more real than if we weren't to use any slang. Ann Brashares does a good job of writing uncensored dialogue in her young adult novel *The Sisterhood of the Traveling Pants*. Following is an example from this novel of two teens in conversation, Effie and Lena, neither of whom is from the planet Way Cool, but the dialogue might make some adults roll their eyes, which is what you're after. In this conversation, Effie is trying to get Lena to admit that she's in love with a certain boy. Listen:

> "You are in love with Kostos," Effie accused.
>
> "No, I'm not." If Lena hadn't known she was in love with Kostos before, she did now. Because she knew what a lie felt like.
>
> "You are too. And the sad thing is, you are too much of a chicken to do anything about it but mope."
>
> Lena sank into her covers again. As usual, Effie had summed up her complex, anguished mental state in one sentence.
>
> "Just admit it," Effie pressed.
>
> Lena wouldn't. She crossed her arms stubbornly over her pajama top.
>
> "Okay, don't," Effie said. "I know it's true anyway."

"Well, you're wrong," Lena snapped babyishly.

Effie sat down on the bed. Her face was serious now. "Lena, listen to me, okay? We don't have much more time here. You are in love. I've never seen anything like this before. You have to be brave, okay? You have to go and tell Kostos how you feel. I swear to God if you don't, you will regret it for the rest of your cowardly life."

Lena knew this was all true. Effie had hit the mark so blatantly, Lena didn't even bother refuting it. "But, Ef," she said, her voice belying her raw agony, "what if he doesn't like me back?"

Effie considered this. Lena waited, expecting, hoping for reassurance. She wanted Effie to say that of course Kostos liked her back. How could he not? But Effie didn't say that.

Instead she took Lena's hand in hers. "That's what I mean about being brave."

Why does this dialogue work and why would we call it *uncensored?* Because teens just say what's on their minds. As many times as I've been "in love" in my adult life, when the issue of expressing that to the other person comes up, I have never, would never, say right out loud to a friend, *What if he doesn't like me back?* I might think it. I might feel it. But I'd never be so bold to say it to anyone. I barely want to admit it to myself. And teens are always calling each other out on their "stuff," while adults do their best to be nice. *"You are too much of a chicken to do anything about it but mope."* When's the last time you called a friend out on her stuff? Writing uncensored dialogue can be freeing. We can just write what comes into these characters' minds because most often they blurt out what's in their minds. To write uncensored dialogue is to write the truth, and for the writer, that feels good. You can just relax and write.

Writing category-specific dialogue is not quite this cut and dried. On occasion, the different types of dialogue overlap and cross over from genre to genre. A character in a horror story, for example, may suddenly use descriptive language as he reveals something about another character. In Anne Rice's novels you find both shadowy and descriptive dialogue, and possibly provocative, because she writes mainstream horror. So, just like anything else, we can't and shouldn't try to make our dialogue fit rigid formulas. But I can't overestimate the importance of understanding why your reader might pick up your novel in the first place—because she wants a fast and suspenseful read or a contemplative and thought-provoking story. Delivering dialogue that meets this need is your constant challenge.

Your story's genre will, of course, determine the kind of dialogue you write. This should be one of the first decisions you make after beginning to develop your story idea. You don't want to get too far into the story writing the wrong kind of dialogue for the pace or the characters that have already been determined by the genre.

In the next chapter, we'll look at how to use dialogue to keep the story moving forward so the reader is compelled to turn the pages faster and faster.

EXERCISE 1

Magical. Choose your genre—romance, science fiction, or fantasy—and put two characters, male and female, in a garden. If you've never written a love scene before, hang onto your hat. Well, not too tightly. If it wants to blow away on the magical breezes of your garden scene, let it. Now, we know that a lot of couples don't talk to each other while making love, but your characters do. They say the most amazing words to each other, amazing even to them. Write three pages (or as many as you can stand) of magical dialogue, words you wish you had the courage to say to your own lover or would like him or her to say back to you. The goal is to be authentic, so no corny lines allowed. Remember how magical dialogue feels and sounds in our examples: It's dramatic, formal, eloquent, direct, detailed, metaphorical, and emotional.

EXERCISE 2

Cryptic. A group of characters—four or five individuals in the same family—are discussing another family member who's not present. Someone from outside the family has accused this person of sexual abuse. There is a bigger issue here for the viewpoint character. You decide what it is, and then write five pages of a cryptic dialogue scene that doesn't ever come right out and say what it is they're discussing. You can use metaphors, similes, and hyperbole. They talk about the bigger issue, they talk about their love for their family member, but they don't ever really say what he's been accused of and what it means for the family. Keep in mind that cryptic dialogue is indirect, subtle, and ambiguous; it has more than one meaning.

EXERCISE 3

Descriptive. Two female characters, one a real estate agent and one who's selling her home, are walking through the older Victorian home that the second character wants to sell. They're discussing what will make the house appealing to buyers and what needs a little work. The real estate agent unknowingly keeps insulting the seller, and the tension between them is growing. Choose either of the two women for your viewpoint character and write three pages of tense descriptive dialogue that focuses on bringing out certain details of the property and home. (If you're not familiar with Victorian homes and don't want to do the research, choose another kind of home.) For this scenario, write your descriptive dialogue with a lot of setting and background details woven into the characters' words so the reader gets a sense of place.

EXERCISE 4

Shadowy. Two characters, a father and son, are sleeping in the backyard in a tent when suddenly the father feels an unnatural presence, something he's felt before, more than once, but always when he's been alone. He knows he has to protect his son. Write two pages of shadowy dialogue between this character and his son as the presence becomes more real and darker with every moment that passes. Remember that the emphasis is on the tone in this kind of dialogue. There needs to be an ever-present threat in the dialogue, something the father or son or both can feel but don't know whether or not is real.

EXERCISE 5

Breathless. One character, a female, is calling 911 to report someone breaking into her house. Write two pages of breathless dialogue from this character's viewpoint and make sure we hear both sides of the conversation as well as this character's thoughts as the action and suspense accelerates. What you want to emphasize in this kind of dialogue is the pace and the emotion, whether it's fear, anger, or sadness. Let the short bursts of dialogue carry the scene.

EXERCISE 6

Provocative. Two characters, one male and one female, have just finished a game of golf and are making their way to the club for a drink. Both high school teachers, they're discussing the sexual behaviors of young people today. They've overheard some of the chat between both male and female students and the female teacher, especially, is troubled by the cavalier attitude she's observed in her students. The male teacher is less troubled with more of a boy-will-be-boys-and-girls-like-it kind of attitude. Write a three-page scene of provocative dialogue that challenges both characters and the reader. In this type of dialogue, what's important are the words themselves. This is where the story's message, the theme, what the story is *about* comes through.

EXERCISE 7

Uncensored. Three girls are walking home from school chatting about boys, and two of them suddenly realize they have their eyes on the same boy. They each have stories about his singling them out with some attention, too. The tension starts to mount as each becomes threatened by the other. Use one girl's viewpoint and write three pages of uncensored dialogue, revealing her increasing anxiety. Remember—what you're after in uncensored dialogue is the truth. Let each girl speak from her gut, not her head, because in her gut is where her emotions are, and we all know how close to her emotions the teenage girl is.

chapter 4

[WHEELS OF MOTION — DIALOGUE THAT PROPELS THE STORY FORWARD]

I sighed and put the novel manuscript down. How could this fiction writer really think she was engaging the reader? The two characters were simply sitting at the breakfast table, chatting about their daily to-do lists while eating bowls of cereal. The viewpoint character was crunching her corn flakes and staring out into the field behind her house while saying such profound things as, "I wonder if we should take Ginger in for her distemper shot," and "Do you think *Law & Order* will be a rerun tonight?" Crunch, crunch. How did I nicely tell this writer that her dialogue needed a bit of help?

I decided to ask the students in my weekly novel class what would make this dialogue spark.

"Well, if while the lady is staring into the backyard, a spaceship lands," one student suggested.

"If the lady is rambling on and on about nothing and the husband calmly tells her he's having an affair or wants a divorce or is a cross-dresser. She keeps talking and doesn't even hear him."

"If the lady is talking, taking the day for granted, and doesn't notice that her husband's face is in his breakfast cereal. He's just died of a heart attack."

These were pretty good ideas. I was proud of my class. They understood that dialogue should be *about* something. The dialogue needs to move the plot forward in some way or it's useless.

As a writing coach, I see pointless and useless dialogue all the time. It feels harsh to continually point it out, and writers don't always *understand* why their dialogue doesn't work, but unless it connects to the theme and plot and includes tension and suspense while moving the story forward (a tall order), why bother? Why write a story at all?

DIALOGUE THAT MOVES

Writing a story that stands still will risk your reputation as a writer of artistic fiction. I can't overemphasize the importance of making sure your dialogue moves the plot forward. Dialogue is only a means to an end—it's not the end itself. Dialogue, in and of itself, is simply a fiction element, a tool to be used to move the story forward. That means engaging your characters in conflict and using dialogue to increase their struggle.

As you will see in the examples in this chapter, your characters' struggles are revealed through both your theme and your plot. The first is internal and the second is external. Writers in my classes will often say to me, "Why do I have to have a theme? Can't I just write a nice little story?" Sometimes they even ask that question about plot. "Plot? Why do we need a plot?"

Woe be it unto me to try to convince you that stories need both a theme and a plot. Sure, you can just skip these two elements of fiction—if you want to write stories for yourself, that is. I could be wrong, but I'm going to take a wild guess and assume that if you're reading this book, you most likely are thinking aboutsubmitting your short stories and novels for publication at some point. If that's true, then you need both a theme and a plot in your stories.

Dialogue is one of the fiction elements you can use to propel your plot forward and integrate your theme into each scene. The way you do this is to set your characters up in an animated discussion scene that does any one of a number of things: provides new information to the characters about the conflict, reveals new obstacles that the viewpoint character must overcome to achieve his goal, creates the kind of dynamic between the scene characters that furthers the story's theme, introduces a pivotal moment in the plot that transforms the character(s), sets up the discussion so the character (and reader) are reminded of his scene and story goals, and/or accelerates the emotion and story movement to increase the suspense and make the situation more urgent for the characters.

Yes, this sounds like a tall order—how can you possibly use dialogue to do all of this, and in every single scene? It's not that difficult once you become aware of all of the purposes of dialogue and keep reminding yourself that your dialogue scenes must accomplish something and keep the story moving.

Fixing Your Own Story

What's the criterion for dialogue that moves a plot forward? How do you know whether your dialogue is or isn't propelling the story onward? Ask yourself the following questions to find out:

- If I remove the passage of dialogue that I'm suspecting isn't moving the story, will it be missed? Does the story work just as well without it?
- Does the dialogue characterize to the exclusion of the other important scene elements, like story movement?
- How does the dialogue passage further the story's theme?
- How does the passage of dialogue increase the suspense for what's to come, raising the stakes for the protagonist?
- How does the dialogue make it clearer what the protagonist wants in the story?
- What kind of external and internal obstacles does the passage of dialogue surface for the protagonist?
- What new information about the plot and theme does the dialogue reveal?
- How is the dialogue pivotal in changing the characters—making them more desperate for what they want, causing them to want to give up, bringing them to a place of new determination?

The answers to these questions will help you gauge whether your dialogue passages are pulling their weight when it comes to story movement. Every single scene of dialogue should in some way change the situation for the characters so they are either closer or farther away from their individual goals. When you're clear about your theme, your characters will be discussing only what matters in the immediate story action so the theme can come through a clear and focused channel.

PROVIDES NEW INFORMATION

Recently, I called up a couple of friends of twelve years to thank them for a birthday gift and to ask them when they might like to get together, but before the words were barely out of my mouth, Ellen was saying, "We won't be able to get together. We're breaking up."

Have you ever found yourself relaxed and talking to someone and then suddenly that person inserted something into the conversation that completely threw you, maybe even changed your life in some way?

This is the kind of opening you want to look for in your dialogue passages, those seemingly innocuous moments when you can throw a zinger into the dialogue and completely take the plot in another direction. The viewpoint character receives some new information that causes him to see all of the other characters in a new light or to get a different perspective of the story situation. In Albert Zuckerman's book *Writing the Blockbuster Novel,* he calls this a pivotal scene and says we need at least twelve of them in an average novel. They don't all have to be dialogue scenes, but making a dialogue scene pivotal will ensure that the dialogue is moving the story forward.

In John Grisham's *The Chamber,* the author includes a pivotal passage of dialogue that momentarily upends the protagonist's world. Adam is a young, inexperienced, naïve lawyer who is just learning the ropes, and in his inexperience he's always doing things that threaten the older, more experienced lawyers in his firm. In this passage of dialogue, Adam receives a bit of new information that definitely moves the story forward, creating a crisis that could be a serious obstacle thwarting his goal to get his grandfather a reprieve from his scheduled execution.

"Come in, come in," Goodman said, closing the door as he invited Adam into his own office. He hadn't smiled yet.

"What are you doing here?" Adam asked, throwing his briefcase on the floor and walking to his desk. They faced each other.

Goodman stroked his neat gray beard, then adjusted his bow tie. "There's a bit of an emergency, I'm afraid. Could be bad news."

"What?"

"Sit down, sit down. This might take a minute."

"No, I'm fine. What is it?" It had to be horrible if he needed to take it sitting down.

Goodman tinkered with his bow tie, rubbed his beard, then said, "Well, it happened at nine this morning. You see, the Personnel Committee is made up of fifteen partners, almost all are younger guys. The full committee has several subcommittees, of course, one for recruiting, hiring, one for discipline, one for disputes and on and on. And as you might guess, there's one for terminations. The Termination Subcommittee met this morning and guess who was there to orchestrate everything."

"Daniel Rosen."

"Daniel Rosen. Evidently, he's been working the Termination Subcommittee for ten days trying to line up enough votes for your dismissal."

One character has just announced something to another character that has the potential to short circuit everything he has been working so hard for, which moves the story forward. If his firm terminates him, he loses his power to do anything to save his grandfather's life. It literally is a matter of life and death.

Grisham excels at this kind of thing—throwing obstacles at protagonists in the middle of scenes of dialogue to make their goals more difficult to achieve. If you haven't already, you might want to read some of his novels and study how he does this.

REVEALS NEW OBSTACLES

In dialogue, an obstacle to a character's goal works the same as new information by stopping the viewpoint character in his tracks and creating immediate conflict for him. He may express his discomfort verbally, he may not, but he has to *do something*, so the story is moved forward. If he chooses to express his discomfort verbally, you can create immediate conflict in the scene with the other character who presented him with the obstacle. Whether or not the viewpoint character likes the other character doesn't really matter—he won't like that the other character has presented him with an obstacle to his goal.

In the scene from *The Chamber,* Grisham decides to develop a conflict right in the middle of the dialogue. Adam grows more upset as the scene continues, and his perception of the obstacles begins to increase. Goodman is the voice of reason. When presenting a protagonist with obstacles in the middle of a scene, it's his perception of them that's important. The obstacles may or may not be insurmountable, but if the protagonist *thinks* they're insurmountable, they are, at least momentarily. This is where you want to keep your protagonist much of the time he's in dialogue with other characters because it creates suspense and tension and moves the story forward.

Now, every character will react differently when presented with an obstacle. One character will burst into tears while another character will see the obstacle as a challenge, roll up her sleeves, and get to work solving the problem. Another character will start delegating and another conniving.

Another will start considering the options right out loud in the middle of the dialogue and then look at them forever. Still another character will get scared and want to run away from the problem while still another will get discouraged and give up. Then there's always the character who will get mad and start blaming his mother and father and anyone else who was around when he was being potty trained. As you can see, this is why it's absolutely crucial that you know your characters. It's only in knowing your characters that you'll know how each one will react when presented with an obstacle in a scene of dialogue, which then determines the direction the story wil move.

INCREASES SUSPENSE

As your story is moving forward, you need to keep increasing the suspense for the reader by making everything look worse for the characters. Dialogue works well for this because the characters are in the immediate moment and are suddenly hanging suspended in time while the reader watches the stakes being raised right before the characters' eyes. It's clear to us, and sometimes it's clear to the characters.

Margaret Atwood does this well all through her novel *The Robber Bride.* The main character is Tony, and the antagonist, Zenia, is a very bright and manipulative character who is always catching the other characters off guard with her conniving and scheming. She's always up to something, and it's never good. This is a very character-driven story, and the reader is able to closely watch Zenia's every move. The other characters are only mildly aware of it, as this type of person always acts like she's your best friend, and you don't want to believe you've been taken for a very long ride and she's your worst enemy. Here's one passage of dialogue, which is very typical for Zenia, as she moves forward in her manipulative ways.

> "What would cause you to kill yourself?" says Zenia.
>
> "Kill myself?" says Tony wonderingly, as if she's never thought of such a thing. "I don't know. I don't think I would."
>
> "What if you had cancer?" Zenia says. "What if you knew you were going to die slowly, in unbearable pain? What if you knew where the microfilm was, and the other side knew you knew, and they were going to torture you to get it out of you and then kill you anyway? What if you had a cyanide tooth? Would you use it?"

When Tony finally realizes that Zenia has just stolen her boyfriend out from under her nose, she remembers another conversation she had with her "friend."

> She recalls a conversation she had with Zenia, early on, in the days when they were drinking coffee at Christie's and Zenia was such a friend.
>
> "Which would you rather have?" said Zenia. "From other people. Love, respect or fear?"
>
> "Respect," said Tony. "No. Love."
>
> "Not me," said Zenia. "I'd choose fear."
>
> "Why?" said Tony.
>
> "It works better," said Zenia. "It's the only thing that works."

Look at how much is accomplished in a brief flashback scene. What Zenia is saying is that she wants others to fear her, and if she can get others to fear her she'll be able to manipulate them to get what she wants. This is really what the story is about, how one person is able to do this to many other people and have power over all of them. As long as they don't wake up to what she's doing, she's queen. Because this is a character-driven story, Atwood uses dialogue scenes over and over to create the kind of suspense that shows Zenia's increasing realm of power, moving the story forward with each of these scenes. Tony will eventually wake up, but not until Zenia has done some incredible damage. What I like about the way Atwood does this is that Tony doesn't analyze Zenia after every scene, which would dilute the creepiness of it. She just observes it, wonders about it a bit, feels uneasy, and goes on—until Zenia's next weird question.

Suspense is achieved in dialogue when the viewpoint character gets "that feeling" about the other character in the scene. Or suddenly realizes that things are not as they seem. Or gets some new information which means he isn't going to get what he wants. He may learn that someone else's agenda is different than what he originally thought. He may make a decision right in the middle of the scene that lets us know the plot is now going to turn in a different direction. He may think something in the middle of a dialogue scene that he knows he can't say out loud. Suspense is created in a scene whenever characters are surprised, feel threatened or attacked (it doesn't even matter if the threat is real; if they feel it is real), lose something, interpret events to be unjust—there are a hundred ways to create suspense. As long as the moment of suspense is intricately connected to the plot and theme, you're moving the story forward with the dialogue.

FURTHERS THE THEME

"Sometimes the right course demands an act of piracy." These are the words spoken by Geoffrey Rush's character in the movie *Pirates of the Caribbean: The Curse of the Black Pearl.*

It's not that I amuse myself by going to movies looking for themes and boring my friends by pointing them out in the middle of a crowded movie theater, but I get kind of excited when I hear a character speak a line that is clearly the movie's theme. As a storyteller myself, I get a kick out of observing how other writers do it, whether a novelist or a screenwriter.

When a character announces the story's theme in the middle of a passage of dialogue, it gives the other characters the opportunity to respond and move the action in one direction or another. This can be very effective, because while the reader may not necessarily be able to recognize the theme as the "a-ha" moment in the story as I did in *Pirates of the Caribbean,* subconsciously it registers as a pivotal moment and the reader holds her breath, waiting to see how the other characters will respond.

In Nicholas Sparks' novel *The Notebook,* the author uses a minor character to bring home the theme of enduring love in a character's twilight years. These characters are living in a home for the elderly, and Noah's wife, Allie, has Alzheimer's. Even though his beloved no longer even recognizes him, he keeps going to sit with her. The last time he did, she freaked out and started screaming at him to leave. Immediately, the staff appeared and let him know that the visits to his wife are now over. Here the night nurse catches him sneaking down the hall to Allie's room.

> "Noah," she says, "what are you doing?"
>
> "I'm taking a walk," I say. "I can't sleep."
>
> "You know you're not supposed to do this."
>
> "I know."
>
> I don't move, though. I am determined.
>
> " You're not really going for a walk, are you? You're going to see Allie."
>
> "Yes," I answer.
>
> "Noah, you know what happened the last time you saw her at night."
>
> "I remember."
>
> "Then you know you shouldn't be doing this."
>
> I don't answer directly. Instead I say, "I miss her."
>
> "I know you do, but I can't let you see her."

"It's our anniversary," I say. This is true. It is one year before gold. Forty-nine years today.

"I see."

"Then I can go?"

She looks away for a moment, and her voice changes. Her voice is softer now, and I am surprised. She has never struck me as the sentimental type.

"Noah, I've worked here for five years and I worked at another home before that. I've seen hundreds of couples struggle with grief and sadness, but I've never seen anyone handle it like you do. No one around here, not the doctors, not the nurses, has ever seen anything like it."

She pauses for just a moment, and strangely, her eyes begin to fill with tears. She wipes them with her finger and goes on:

"I try to think what it's like for you, how you keep going day after day, but I can't even imagine it. I don't know how you do it. You even beat her disease sometimes. Even though the doctors don't understand it, we nurses do. It's love, it's as simple as that. It's the most incredible thing I've ever seen."

How does this dialogue move the story forward? It's not terribly profound, but this minor character, a nurse, has observed in Noah his deep abiding love for his wife of forty-nine years, and this scene brings it home to the reader. The novel ends only a few pages later. We've seen this before, certainly, but the nurse puts words to it and is able to turn her back while Noah goes to his wife. The dialogue is a brief summation of the theme—enduring love—and moves the scene and story forward to its final conclusion.

SHOWS CHARACTER TRANSFORMATION

Our characters should be changing, at least in subtle ways, all the way through the story. This is one reason we write fiction—to show how characters become better people. Or worse. I don't think it's particularly easy to create a scene of dialogue that is so transformative that our characters are changed forever and our reader knows it. Our characters have to speak some profound words to each other to make this happen. In the following scene in *The Great Santini* by Pat Conroy, it's more the action rather than the dialogue that really changes Ben Meecham, but the dialogue that follows the action reveals just how big the transformation is. It has truly changed all of the characters in the Meecham family, not just Ben. In this scene, Bull Meecham challenges his son to a game of basketball, planning to easily beat

DIALOGUE

and humiliate Ben in front of the other family members. This is a typical way Bull keeps himself amused on a daily basis, by humiliating others; there's nothing unusual here. What *is* unusual is that this time Bull doesn't win, causing all of the characters, especially his wife Lillian, to stand up to him. And we know that he will never have the same power over any of them ever again.

> Then Bull shouted at Ben, "Hey, jocko, you gotta win by two baskets."
>
> The backyard became quiet again. Ben looked at his father and said, "You said by one."
>
> "I changed my mind; let's go," Bull said, picking up the basketball.
>
> "Oh, no, Bull," Lillian said, marching toward her husband. "You're not going to cheat the boy out of his victory."
>
> "Who in the hell asked you anything?" Bull said, glaring at his wife.
>
> "I don't care if anybody asked me or not. He beat your fair and square and I'm not going to let you take that away from him."
>
> "Get over here, mama's boy," Bull said, motioning to Ben, "and let's you and me finish this game."
>
> Ben moved forward until he heard his mother shout at him, "You stay right there, Ben Meecham. Don't you dare move."
>
> "Why don't you go hide under your mother's skirts, mama's boy?" Bull said.
>
> He was gaining control of the situation again and was entering a phase of malevolent calm that Lillian was having difficulty translating.
>
> "Mama, I'm gonna play him," Ben said.
>
> "No, you're not," his mother answered harshly, with finality, then speaking to her husband, she said, "He beat you, Big Marine. He beat the Big Marine where everybody could see it, right out in the open, and it was beautiful. It was just beautiful. Big Marine can't take it that his baby boy just beat him to death on the basketball court."
>
> "Get in the house, Lillian, before I kick you into the house."
>
> "Don't threaten me, Big Tough Marine. Does Big Tough Marine have to pick on his family the day his son becomes the better man?"

This novel's theme is about a man growing smaller and his family growing larger—on the inside. Ultimately, it's about forgiveness. It's painful to watch, but something inside of the reader cheers when Bull missteps and Ben and the others are given the glorious opportunity to emerge as bigger people. In this basketball scene, Bull continues to taunt Ben, but we know something is different. We can feel it. This is a pivotal scene in the story and Conroy executes the character transformation so well, I think it's my favorite story scene of all time.

REVEALS/REMINDS OF GOALS

The most important element of each scene that you create in a story is to know what your protagonist wants and be able to *show* it through the action and dialogue. The protagonist wants something in the overall story that in each scene he takes steps to achieve. You're moving the story forward in each scene by challenging the protagonist, throwing an obstacle at him, thereby reminding us of his goal and intention in the scene and in the story.

In the following excerpt from *Saint Maybe* by Anne Tyler, Ian, the main character, is trying to confess a perceived horrible sin to his parents. His mother, however, is just not hearing him, choosing instead to focus on her role as a victim. Ian believes he is responsible for his brother Danny's suicide because of something Danny told him shortly before smashing his car against a concrete wall and killing himself. Now Ian has decided to drop out of college and learn to build furniture so he can help his mother with his brother's stepchildren after their mother also dies. He feels he needs to in some way pay for his sin. In this scene, we're reminded of Ian's goal, his intention—penance and forgiveness—and the story moves forward as we see once again what he's really all about.

His mother said, "I don't believe this. I do not believe it. No matter how long I've been a mother, it seems my children can still come up with something new and unexpected to do to me."

"I'm not doing this to you! Why does everything have to relate to you all the time? It's for me, can't you get that into your head? It's something I have to do for myself, to be forgiven."

"Forgiven what, Ian?" his father asked.

Ian swallowed.

"You're nineteen years old, son. You're a fine, considerate, upstanding human being. What sin could you possibly be guilty of that would require you to uproot your whole existence?"

Reverend Emmett had said Ian would have to tell them. He'd said that was the only way. Ian had tried to explain how much it would hurt them, but

Reverend Emmett had held firm. Sometimes a wound must be scraped out before it can heal, he had said.

Ian said, "I'm the only one who caused Danny to die. He drove into that wall on purpose."

Nobody spoke. His mother's face was white, almost flinty.

"I told him Lucy was, um, not faithful," he said.

He had thought there would be questions. He had assumed they would ask for details, pull the single strand he'd handed them till the whole ugly story came tumbling out. But they just sat silent, staring at him.

"I'm sorry!" he cried. "I'm *really sorry!*"

His mother moved her lips, which seemed unusually wrinkled. No sound emerged.

After a while, he rose awkwardly and left the table. He paused in the dining room doorway, just in case they wanted to call him back. But they didn't. He crossed the hall and started up the stairs.

This is a pivotal scene as Ian unburdens his soul to his parents and gets no response whatsoever. We're reminded of his intention in the story when he says, "It's something I have to do for myself to be forgiven." This is what the story is about, Ian working hard to get forgiveness for his "sin." In every scene, you want to remind your reader of the main character's intention, as this is the way you engage your reader and keep engaging her as the story progresses. Using dialogue for this purpose is especially effective because the character is stating his goal out loud. It's coming right from his mouth.

Your protagonist can sit around and think about his intention or you can create a scene of dialogue and action and show his passion about his intention in a scene with other characters. Dialogue shows.

KEEPING YOUR CHARACTERS IN SOCIAL SETTINGS

Dialogue can only keep the story moving when you put more than one character in a scene. When you isolate your characters, there's no one for them to talk to. There's no dialogue. Of course, there is no way to get around putting your characters in scenes by themselves once in a while. But if an isolated character scene goes on too long, the story starts to dry up.

This seems to be a problem with many mainstream and literary stories; the protagonist is too often alone in scene after scene, engaged in self-analysis. The reader will hang in there for a while, but rambling self-analysis slows the story way down, and if it goes on too long, you risk losing the reader. So, when thinking through the scenes you want to create, remember that, for the most part, your reader most enjoys those scenes where two or more characters are engaged in some degree of dialogue and action.

A scene of dialogue must always move the story forward in some way. No exceptions. If you ever find yourself creating dialogue that fails in this purpose, you'll just have to throw it out later, no matter how creative, clever, funny, or brilliant.

Now, have you ever wondered if there's a strategy to bring all three elements of the scene together—dialogue, narrative, and action—so the scene is balanced and focused in its purpose? This is what we'll deal with in the next chapter.

EXERCISE 1

Provides new information. Stephanie and Peter, a married couple, are opening up a new business together, a Greek restaurant on the south side of town. They have had their door open for several hours now and are serving customers. This is a dream come true for this couple. Suddenly someone walks in the door and gives them some information that lets them know this may not be their dream come true after all but the beginning of a nightmare. Write a three-page scene of dialogue that is full of tension and suspense and includes some new information that will take the plot in another direction entirely.

EXERCISE 2

Reveals new obstacles. Imagine the kind of conflict that would make you crazy. (Our best story ideas come from experiences that we ourselves have lived, would want to live, would hate to live, wish we had never lived, etc.) Yes, this is fiction, but in this scenario make yourself the protagonist. Think of a goal that you have in your life and put yourself in a scene with another character—someone who knows you well. Write three pages of dialogue that opens with the other character announcing the obstacle to your goal. How do you feel? What would you say? How would you act in that moment that you know you may be facing an insurmountable obstacle to your goal?

EXERCISE 3

Increases suspense. Every scene in every story should have suspense, but in thinking about a dialogue scene moving a story forward, the suspense needs to connect to the overall plot and theme. Whether the plot is action/adventure, romance, or literary, the dialogue can be used to create suspense. Choose one of the following subjects and write a three-page scene of dialogue that shows the characters in conflict and the suspense intensifying as far as the story's outcome.

- war
- racism
- assisted suicide
- gay parents
- prison reform
- homelessness

EXERCISE 4

Furthers the theme. Choose a subject you feel strongly about, that you could write a story about. Summarize it in a sentence—the conflict or problem and what you see as the resolution, if you have one. Now put two characters into a scene who are on different sides of this issue. It's your story, so the theme that should be evident in the scene is the way you perceive the situation can be resolved. In your three-page scene, show your characters in conflictive dialogue to the point where both of them are thinking a little bit differently at the end of the scene than they were in the beginning.

EXERCISE 5

Shows character transformation. In each of the following scenarios, the protagonist is confronted and challenged to make some changes in her life. The scenario is only a small part of a bigger story about a bigger theme. Write a three-page scene of dialogue that shows the confrontation and the response of the protagonist to the challenge that she needs to look at something within herself.

- A wife finds out her husband (protagonist) is attracted to and beginning to spend time with a single woman who is friends with the couple. She confronts him and gives him an ultimatum.
- A boss tells her employee (protagonist) that she's taking too many coffee breaks and extending her lunch hours, as well as spending too much time on the phone.
- A mother (protagonist) discovers that her twenty-something daughter is a prostitute who plans to continue as long as there is work.

Reveals/reminds of goals. Choose one of the three following scenarios and write a two-page scene from the point of view of the character that feels most passionately about his or her goal. The purpose of this exercise is to make sure that the protagonist's goal or intention is evident in the scene.

- A fourteen-year-old girl wants to go out on a date with a sixteen-year-old boy. This would be her first date, and her parents are against it.
- A man in his thirties loves to work on old cars, then sell them for a profit. He has at least five beaters plus parts laying all over his yard at any one time. The next-door neighbors are growing increasingly anxious over this. They have a perfect house and a perfect yard.
- A young, very aggressive woman tries to sell a harried mother of two some perfume in a store parking lot.

Keeping your characters in social situations. Write a two-page scene of dialogue that starts out with a character alone and in conflict with himself. Then bring another character into the scene and begin to develop the conflict externally as well as internally. Use one of the following settings:

- a mountain trail
- a jail cell
- a hospital room
- a dark alley
- a church sanctuary

chapter 5

[NARRATIVE, DIALOGUE, AND ACTION — LEARNING TO WEAVE THE SPOKEN WORD]

As a new writer, my stories were mostly dialogue. Pages and pages of characters talking. I loved to write dialogue. I don't know that I thought a story needed anything else. I wrote my very first story in fourth grade—a puppet play consisting of nothing but dialogue and a few stage directions. I wrote a lot of skits and plays after that. Dialogue was and always has been my favorite part of writing a story.

Somewhere along the line, I realized there were other elements necessary to telling stories: action and narrative. Description is also part of a story, but it's really just another form of narrative. While dialogue is the element that brings a story and the characters to life on the page, action creates the movement and narrative gives the story its depth and substance. Dialogue is the characters' words, action the characters' physical movement, and narrative the characters' thoughts about everything going on around them, which can take the form of observation of the setting, other characters, or mental musing on the story situation. Stories need all three elements—dialogue, action, and narrative—to create a three-dimensional feel for the reader.

Writing a story means weaving all of the elements of fiction together, just like quilters weave the various patterns of their quilts or ice skaters weave in and out of each other on the ice. When it's done right, weaving dialogue, narrative, and action can create a beautiful tapestry.

WHY WEAVE?

Expert weaving of dialogue, narrative, and action is done unconsciously.

Once we learn how it's done, we don't think about it while we're doing it. We are letting the characters lead us, so we're no more thinking about which element of storytelling we're using than we are thinking about when to use the clutch, brake, and accelerator when we're driving. We just do it. When reading a story, we don't notice whether the author is weaving or not—when it's working. When it's not working, when the author is not doing it, we notice. I can only speak for myself. I notice.

Some talented writers are able to pull off memoirs and novels using mostly narrative and almost ignoring action and dialogue. Many of these books are so well written that we would never even know what's missing unless it was pointed out to us—and even then, we wouldn't care because the story worked for us on some level. Just know that these are the exception. Too many beginning writers, I've noticed, think they're the exception, but most likely they're not.

Certainly, there are scenes in all of our stories that work best using only narrative or only dialogue or only action. The more you write, the more you'll recognize those scenes and why using only one of these three elements is the most effective. In the meantime, it would be a good idea to practice conscious weaving, which we'll focus on in this chapter.

Think for a moment about a "scene" in your life. Maybe you're outside playing with your kids, at the gym, or at work. You're doing (action), you're thinking (narrative), and you're talking (dialogue), often all at the same time. When others around you are doing all three of these things, when do you pay the most attention? Obviously, you don't know when someone else is thinking because you can't read another person's thoughts. Sometimes when others are doing things, we take notice. But if anyone near us is talking about anything interesting at all, we listen. We can't help it. Writers are probably more guilty of this than anyone else. People are always inclined to eavesdrop on the interesting conversations of others. The key word is *interesting*.

We weave because it's life. Our days are full of weaving. We get up, think about a work project, talk to our partner about the day, eat breakfast, take the kids to school, think about a conflict we're having with a neighbor, go to work, think about the stops we need to make on the way home from work, and on an on until we fall into bed at night. This is our life—a series of thoughts, actions, and words that go on all day, every day. We want our fictional stories to imitate life, so we need to show all the dimensions of our characters' lives—at once. Not the boring stuff, of course, but the stuff that matters, the stuff that pertains to and furthers the plot.

Can you imagine a story of only dialogue? Or action? Or narrative? I'm such a fan of dialogue that I'll go out on a limb and say that if you're going to err, err on the side of too much dialogue rather than not enough.

To weave is to blend two or three elements of fiction together so it makes for a smooth ride for the reader. Let's see how that works out practically.

DIALOGUE INTO ACTION

In a scene that is mostly action, bits of dialogue here and there give the scene its three-dimensional feel. Again, this is just like life. When some kind of action is taking most of our attention, we don't completely stop talking, but we probably talk less, depending on the kind of action in which we're engaged and the kind of emotion the action is evoking from us. Too often new writers, when creating an action scene, forget about using dialogue altogether, I'm guessing because they're so focused on trying to get their character from Point A to Point B and they neglect to consider that the character would probably be expressing *something,* even if it's just a word or phrase here and there. Even if he's alone in the scene, you can have him talking out loud to himself, again, for that three-dimensional feel you're after in every scene you write.

Dialogue can be very effective when woven into action scenes that include a lot of characters, such as a crowd or party scene. It can make the scene feel alive and happening while on another level your viewpoint character is having his own private drama separate from the crowd. Especially in crowd scenes, you want to do this because to mimic reality, there is always more than one thing going on with any number of the characters present.

Stephen King does a good job of this in an action scene in his novel *Bag of Bones.* In this scene, King is describing a carnival, and in his magical style, writes the scene so it's part dream, part reality, and the protagonist, Mike, moves between the two in his mind while navigating the carnival. Suddenly he runs into Kyra, the young daughter of the woman he's falling in love with, and for a moment they stand watching the Red-Tops, a singing group, when Kyra notices that a lady on the stage is wearing her mother's dress. Up until this point the scene has consisted mostly of narrative and action. Watch what King does with the dialogue as Mike and Kyra try to make their way out of the carnival.

> "Why is the lady wearing Mattie's dress?" Kyra asked me, and she began to tremble.
>
> "I don't know, honey, I can't say." Nor could I argue—it was the white sleeveless dress Mattie had been wearing on the common, all right.

We watch the action onstage for a few more paragraphs, then:

> The crowd roared happily. In my arms, Kyra was shaking harder than ever. "I'm scared, Mike," she said. "I don't like that lady. She's a scary lady. She stole Mattie's dress. I want to go home."

King moves into a number of paragraphs of narrative and action about the lady on the stage—his usual scary stuff—and then the scene is off and running.

> Right or wrong, I'd had enough. I turned, putting my hand on the back of Ki's head and urging her face down against my chest. Both her arms were around my neck now, clutching with panicky tightness.

King describes another part-dream, part-reality character, then:

> "Excuse me," I said, brushing by him.
>
> "There's no town drunk here, you meddling son of a bitch," he said, never looking at me and never missing a beat as he clapped. "We all just take turns."

Mike and Kyra keep moving, dodging around three drinking farmers, until they're free of the crowd. More dialogue as they head toward the street and home:

> "Almost done, Irish!" Sara shrieked after me. She sounded angry, but not too angry to laugh. "You gonna get what you want, sugar, all the comfort you need, but you want to let me finish my bi'ness. Do you hear me, boy? Just stand clear! Mind me now!"

Mike is carrying Kyra and they begin to move faster.

> On our left was the baseball pitch and some little boy shouting, "Willy hit it over the fence, Ma! Willy hit it over the fence!" with monotonous brain-croggling regularity.

They keep moving.

> "Are we home yet?" Ki almost moaned. "I want to go home, Mike, please take me home to my mommy."
>
> "I will," I said. "Everything's going to be all right."

Each line of narrative I inserted between the dialogue passages is where King has included a few paragraphs of action in the scene. Can you see how the dialogue gives the feel of many things happening at once as Mike passes and runs into the various characters and tries to comfort Kyra, all while trying to get her away from the carnival and home?

Without the dialogue, the scene would feel stagnant, like it's standing still even though there's action and the characters are moving around. The dialogue helps give the scene its momentum as we watch Mike caring in a nurturing way for Kyra while staying focused on getting them out of there. Action without dialogue often lacks substance. Granted, as I said above, there are times in a story when only dialogue or only action or only narrative is what's needed for that moment in the story, but most of the time you want to weave these three elements together.

Fixing Your Own Story

Remember many years ago when the talking heads on television were just that—talking heads? (It's depressing to think about how many people don't remember this—they're too young.) We sat and listened to these talking heads for hours. Somehow at that time it was enough. Rock stars simply stood on stage and sang their songs, well, except for Elvis who moved his hips a tiny bit and freaked everyone out. The singing was enough.

Not anymore. These days, whether we're watching a news documentary or attending a rock concert, those at the center of our attention are moving around. In order to hold our attention, rock stars have to jump up and down, set stage props on fire, and throw things at the audience. The news shows have gotten in on the act, too. No more talking heads. We follow newscasters around as they meet with their interviewees on location and interact with them while engaging in underwater sports or rappelling off a mountain. The reason no one just sits or stands and talks or sings to us anymore? We'd turn to a channel where there's something *happening* or move down the street to a concert where there's some action.

When you're creating a dialogue scene, make sure your characters are doing something. Even in the nondramatic scenes, have your characters engaged in some activity while they're talking about the breakup of their marriage or their wayward teenager. This is what readers are interested in. Dialogue brings characters to life. Action and dialogue combined create characters and a setting that are three-dimensional.

Look for these scenes in your own story—where the characters are simply talking, where you've neglected to use action to create a three-dimensional scene. Insert bits of action into these scenes so that the reader is engaged, not just with talking heads, but with fully alive characters on the page.

NARRATIVE INTO DIALOGUE

Narrative seems to be the favorite element of most writers. I seldom see stories that use too much dialogue, but I often see stories that use too much narrative. Narrative tells, dialogue shows. There's a time for telling and a time for showing. This is the skill in learning to weave—knowing when to do what.

Narrative is the part of the story that does any number of things but show characters talking to one another. It might describe characters or setting, reveal background, flash back to the past, move into a character's mind and reveal thoughts, characterize, and philosophize. In the first person and/or literary story, especially, the story's voice comes through most effectively in narrative, since the story is most often character-driven rather than plot-driven, and the protagonist has a very personal story to share with the reader. In this type of story, the protagonist is developing a more intimate relationship with the reader, gaining the reader's trust and can talk more directly to the reader through narrative.

The problem is this stuff gets boring when that's all there is. The reader will follow an interesting character anywhere, as long as there's plenty of action and dialogue in the story. What you want to do is anchor as much of your narrative as possible within the context of a scene so it's not hanging out there on the perimeter in a vacuum. If there's something important you through narrative, find a way to create a scene and get your characters interacting, then weave the narrative into the scene.

So this time, we're going to approach things from the opposite direction. Instead of weaving the dialogue into the narrative, we're going to weave the narrative into the dialogue. Check out the following scene of dialogue, first without narrative, then with narrative.

Without narrative:

> "Honey, I really think we should stop and ask where Dover Street is."
>
> "Not necessary, sweetheart. I know where I'm going."
>
> "Then why have we been circling this neighborhood for the last 45 minutes? It only took us 20 minutes last time Bob and Sue invited us over for dinner."
>
> "That's because we had written directions in front of us."
>
> "Why are you so stubborn? What's the big deal with stopping at that 7-11 right there and asking where—"
>
> "The people at those 7-11s never speak English, that's one good reason. It's a waste of time."

"And driving around like this isn't?"

"No, because we're getting closer."

"We are—watch out! You just turned down a one-way street, you idiot!"

"There's the house. Told you I'd find it."

With narrative:

"Honey, I really think we should stop and ask where Dover Street is." This is only the third time I'd made this suggestion.

"Not necessary, sweetheart. I know where I'm going."

"Then why have we been circling this neighborhood for the last 45 minutes? It only took us 20 minutes last time Bob and Sue invited us over for dinner." Why did he have to be so stubborn, affirming the stereotype about men not being able to ask for directions? Why couldn't he ever be just a little bit unpredictable?

"That's because we had written directions in front of us."

"Why are you so stubborn?" We passed Elm Street again—the third time now. "What's the big deal with stopping at that 7-11 right there and asking where—"

"The people at those 7-11s never speak English, that's one good reason. It's a waste of time."

"And driving around like this isn't?" Juniper Street again.

"No, because we're getting closer."

Closer. Right. We'd passed this same intersection at least five times now in our scenic tour of Bob and Sue's neighborhood. The truth was I wasn't even sure this was their neighborhood. I didn't know whether to keep arguing with him or let him drive us around until midnight.

"Sure, we are—watch out! You just turned down a one-way street, you idiot!" Was he even awake?

"There's the house. Told you I'd find it."

When you find yourself writing a scene that ends up top-heavy with dialogue and you need to weave in some narrative, simply put yourself into the character's situation and imagine what she is thinking and observing in the moment. You're the actor in a movie and you have to play all the parts. Be aware that any narrative thrown into a scene of dialogue slows it down a bit, so place it strategically in places where the tension isn't affected by a line or two of narrative. In the above scene, we get to know the female character in a way that we don't in the dialogue-only scene.

WEAVING DIALOGUE, NARRATIVE, AND ACTION

Most of the time, we want to balance our scenes using all three elements: dialogue, action, and narrative. This is one reason you want to put your character in a scene with other characters as often as possible. Scenes that are woven engage the reader at an emotional level so much more effectively than scenes that are only dialogue, only narrative, or only action.

Following is an example of a well-woven scene from Sue Monk Kidd's *The Secret Life of Bees.* In the following scene of this literary novel about the civil rights movement, Kidd seems to want to talk to us about the risk of getting "stung" if we want to be true beekeepers. If we want to make a difference in the world, we must take risks, and loving something is enough reason to do it. Rather than "preach" to us through narrative alone, the author blends the scene using dialogue, action, and narrative, pulling the reader in.

> Rescuing bees took us the entire morning. Driving back into remote corners of the woods where there were barely roads, we would come upon twenty-five beehives up on slats like a little lost city tucked back in there. We lifted the covers and filled the feeders with sugar water. Earlier we'd spooned dry sugar into our pockets, and now, just as a bonus, we sprinkled it on the feeding rims.
>
> I managed to get stung on my wrist while replacing a lid onto a hive box. August scraped out the stinger.
>
> "I was sending them love," I said, feeling betrayed.
>
> August said, "Hot weather makes the bees out of sorts, I don't care how much love you send them." She pulled a small bottle of olive oil and bee pollen from her free pocket and rubbed my skin—her patented remedy. It was something I'd hoped never to test out.
>
> "Count yourself initiated," she said. "You can't be a true bee-keeper without getting stung."
>
> A true beekeeper. The words caused a fullness in me, and right at that moment an explosion of blackbirds lifted off the ground in a clearing a short distance away and filled up the whole sky. I said to myself, Will wonders never cease? I would add that to my list of careers. A writer, an English teacher, and a beekeeper.
>
> "Do you think I could keep bees one day?" I asked.
>
> August said, "Didn't you tell me this past week one of the things you loved was bees and honey? Now, if that's so, you'll be a fine beekeeper. Actually, you

can be bad at something, Lily, but if you love doing it, that will be enough."

The sting shot pain all the way to my elbow, causing me to marvel at how much punishment a minuscule creature can inflict. I'm prideful enough to say I didn't complain. After you get stung, you can't get unstung no matter how much you whine about it. I just dived back into the riptide of saving bees.

How did Kidd know when and where to put what? This is largely an intuitive process, and I'm guessing she didn't do a lot of thinking about how she was weaving the elements of fiction as she was writing her first draft. You have to move inside of your characters in order to do this. You can't be thinking about how to do it, at least not while writing the first draft. During the revision process, when reading back through the story, you can see better when a scene is top-heavy with dialogue, narrative, or action. The perfectly balanced scene has a rhythm to it; you'll learn to recognize it when it's there.

And when it's not. The scene heavy with dialogue for too long a period of time can begin to feel unreal, like you're simply listening in on talking heads. Without active images or character observations of setting or mood, it feels like a radio interview with the sound effects missing. Likewise, a scene top-heavy with action can also feel unreal because it's unlikely that characters doing something—anything at all—would not be talking during the activity. Finally, the scene top-heavy with narrative, as we've discussed above, can simply be boring, as it is in real life when a person rambles on and on and on about a subject. Even if it's a subject in which we're interested, the rambling narrative can put us to sleep.

So learn to watch for any scene in which you've used only one of the three elements—dialogue, action, or narrative—and ask yourself if it feels real and emotionally engages the reader.

WHEN NOT TO WEAVE

Having said all that, learning not to weave is as important as learning to weave. Is it ever a good thing to create a scene with only dialogue? Only narrative? Only action?

One reason not to weave is because you want to highlight a particular character trait in your viewpoint character or focus on something specific that the characters are talking about. You don't want the scene cluttered, the reader distracted, or the pace slowed by action or narrative. You know how

Fixing Your Own Story

[1] Choose a scene from your own work or one you want to add to your story. Practice writing the same scene over and over. Use all dialogue the first time. Then use all narrative. Then all action. Finally, weave all three fiction elements for a three-dimensional effect.

[2] Pull a troublesome scene from your own story, one that's mostly or all narrative, dialogue, or action. Which element does it have too much of? Too little of? Consider how you might weave all three elements to make it more three-dimensional.

[3] It could be that you have woven some scenes in your story that you shouldn't have. Maybe one of your woven scenes should be all dialogue or all narrative or all action. Take a look at some of your woven scenes and see if you can speed them up by taking out all of the narrative and using only dialogue. Or slow them down by taking out the dialogue and using only narrative. Maybe a scene should be focused on the action alone, for the sake of moving the external plot forward.

sometimes when someone is telling you a story, the setting, the other people around you, everything just kind of fades away, and you're intent only on what the other person is saying? This is what it's like when you cut away action and narrative and leave only your characters' spoken words.

Picture your characters in a movie and the camera is closing in, coming closer and closer to your characters, their facial expressions, their very beings. You can achieve this same effect with dialogue-only scenes.

Check out this scene in *The Feast of Love* by Charles Baxter. The viewpoint character, Bradley, works at a coffee shop called *Jitters*. His co-worker, Chloe, asks him what's the worst thing that ever happened to him. Up until that time, the author had woven dialogue, narrative, and action into a nicely balanced scene, but it was time to speed things up. Bradley starts to tell Chloe about how he and some buddies were in the cathedral at Notre Dame in Paris. The story's getting long and Chloe tells him to hurry it along. What

DIALOGUE

76

the author wants to highlight here, it would seem, is that Bradley actually thinks the worst thing he's ever done in his life is knock over a bunch of candles in a cathedral. The dialogue focuses on this alone.

> "Let me finish this story... And because my hand was shaking, I reached down to the holder, this freestanding holder or candelabra or whatever of votive candles, and somehow, I don't know how this happened, my hand caused this holder of candles, all these small flames, all these souls, to fall over, and when it fell over, all the candles, lit for the sake of a soul somewhere, there must have been a hundred of them, all of them fell to the floor, because of me, and all of them went out. And you know what the nun did, Chloe, the nun who was standing there?"
>
> "She spoke French?"
>
> "No. She could have, but she didn't. No, what she did was, she screamed."
>
> "Wow."
>
> "Yeah, the nun screamed in my face. I felt like..."
>
> "You felt like pretty bad, Mr. S. I can believe it. But you know, Mr. S, those were just candles. They weren't really souls. That's all superstition, that soul stuff."
>
> "Oh, I know."
>
> "No kidding, Mr. S, you shouldn't be so totally morbid. I thought when you were telling me about the worst thing you ever did, it'd be, like, beating up a blind guy and stealing his car."
>
> "No, I never did that."
>
> "Oscar did, once. You should get him to tell you about it."
>
> "Okay."
>
> "He was drunk, though." She prettily touches her perfect hair. "And the guy wasn't really blind. He just said he was, to take advantage of people. It was, like, a scam. Oscar saw through all that. It's nine o'clock now, Boss. We should open up."
>
> "Right." And I unlock the curtain, and touch a switch, and slowly the curtain rises on the working day. The candles are nothing to Chloe; they're just candles. I feel instantly better. Bless her.

The scene wouldn't have had the same impact if the author had woven action and narrative throughout the dialogue. This is a neurotic character, and this fast-paced scene of dialogue shows the extent of his neurosis, especially compared to Chloe's explanation of the candles being just *candles*.

Because this part of the scene is only dialogue, we get the full impact of his neurosis and how it expresses itself in his life. When you isolate a character's dialogue, if the reader is paying attention, he'll become privy to the character's personality and motives in a way that's not possible in the woven scene just because there's too much going on.

Pacing is probably the most common fiction element to pay attention to when considering when to and when not to weave dialogue, narrative, and action. If you're creating a fast-paced conflict scene between two or more people, you might do well to consider only dialogue, at least for parts of it. Maybe your characters have just entered into an argument and you want to speed up the scene. In Wally Lamb's *She's Come Undone,* the young viewpoint character, Dolores, is fed up with her mother, who has been grieving over the loss of her baby for over four years and acquired all kinds of obsessive-compulsive disorders, the most recent being an obsession with her new parakeet, Petey. Dolores has already been narrating a lot of this, but now it's time for her to act out her feelings. In a scene of dialogue only, the author quickly *shows* what Dolores has taken pages to *tell* us.

> I hated Petey—fantasized about his flying accidentally out a window or into the electric fan so that his spell over Ma would be broken. My not kissing Ma anymore was a conscious decision reached one night at bedtime with the purpose of hurting her.
>
> "Well, you're stingy tonight," she said when I turned my face away from her goodnight kiss.
>
> "I'm not kissing you anymore, period," I told her. "All day long you kiss that bird right on its filthy beak."
>
> "I do not."
>
> "You do so. Maybe you want to catch bird diseases, but I don't."
>
> "Petey's mouth is probably cleaner than my mouth and yours put together, Dolores" was her argument.
>
> "That's a laugh."
>
> "Well, it's true. I read it in my bird book."
>
> "Next thing you know, you'll be French-kissing it."
>
> "Never mind French-kissing. What do you know about that kind of stuff? You watch that mouth of yours, young lady."
>
> "That's exactly what I'm doing," I said. I clamped my hand over my mouth and stuffed my whole face into the pillow.

As you can see, this passage is very effective without a bunch of narrative bogging down the moment. The dialogue *shows* Dolores' true attitude toward Petey, but more importantly, toward her mother. Whereas it can take the protagonist pages to tell us something in narrative, a scene of dialogue can quickly *show* us through that character's own words said out loud. Narrative explains and dialogue blurts out. We'll talk more about pacing in chapter eight.

Obviously, when a character is alone, you can't weave unless he's the kind of person who talks to himself a lot. As I mentioned above, you want to try to create scenes with more than one character in them. It's always more interesting for the reader when characters are interacting than when they're thinking and we're only reading their thoughts.

The same reasons not to weave hold true when writing scenes with only narrative or only action. You want to focus on something in your character's mind or describe something that would only sound contrived in dialogue, so you use straight narrative. Or the action needs to drive the scene forward because it's intense and emotional, and your characters just wouldn't be talking during this time (action). Sometimes, as in real life, there's just nothing to say at the moment. Always, always, always let your characters lead you.

STRIKING A BALANCE

I can't give you any hard and fast rules about when to and when not to weave. To weave well is to find your story's rhythm. There are a few questions you can ask yourself about your story, especially in the rewrite stage, that can help you know which elements are most effective for a particular scene.

- *Is the story moving a little too slowly, and do I need to speed things up?* (Use dialogue.)
- *Is it time to give the reader some background on the characters so they're more sympathetic?* (Use narrative, dialogue, or a combination of the two.)
- *Do I have too many dialogue scenes in a row?* (Use action or narrative.)
- *Are my characters constantly confiding in others about things they should only be pondering in their minds?* (Use narrative.)
- *Likewise, are my characters alone in their heads when my characters in conversation would be more effective and lively?* (Use dialogue.)

- *Is my story top-heavy in any way at all—too much dialogue, too much narrative, too much action?* (Insert more of the elements that are missing.)
- *Are my characters providing too many background details as they're talking to each other?* (Use narrative.)

Whether we're using dialogue, action, or narrative to move the story forward, any or all three of these elements are doing double duty—revealing our characters' motives. To understand a character's motive is to understand the character. In the next chapter, we'll discover how our story's dialogue can reveal motive in a way that's natural and authentic, because whether we're aware of it or not, we reveal our own motives all the time in our everyday lives.

EXERCISE 1

Dialogue into action. Following is a straight action scene with no dialogue or narrative— sort of like a cookie recipe without the sugar. Carson's an outgoing guy, but you'd never know it the way this scene is written. Weave appropriate dialogue that shows his extroverted personality into this scene:

Carson backed his bike up to the curb and climbed off, setting his helmet carefully on the left handlebar. Two muscular bikers in leathers stood by the door, making no effort to hide their disdain for his Honda 450. He ignored them and strode into the tavern, his hands shoved deeply into the pockets of his jeans. They followed.

He made his way up to the bar and ordered a beer. A blonde sitting by herself at the end of the bar motioned for him to join her. He sat down beside her, but then decided to grab an ashtray off one of the tables behind him. He got up and moved toward the table but suddenly found his way blocked by the bigger of the two bikers. He stepped to the biker's right. The biker stepped also.

Carson shrugged and turned around, then felt a hand clamp down on his shoulder. Carson jerked away and before he knew what was happening, a small group of bikers approached him from the front.

He quickly sized up the situation, turned and threw his beer at the biker who had grabbed him, and ran out the door.

Narrative into dialogue. Following is a straight dialogue scene with no action or narrative. Using either of the two characters' viewpoints (but choose only one), weave some narrative into this scene. Watch how it becomes more three-dimensional as the reader has the opportunity to get inside of the viewpoint character's head.

"Hey, man, you got any spare change?"

"No, but I've got the Gospel of Jesus Christ. How about asking Jesus into your heart so you can get off the streets?"

"What? I asked Jesus into my heart one time. That's how I got here."

"I don't think so."

"I do. I'm a pastor, well, used to be. My wife ran off with one of the church deacons and eventually divorced me and I lost everything."

"That doesn't explain how you ended up on the streets. Jesus doesn't put his children on the streets."

"I think sometimes he does. It rains on the just and the unjust—there's a scripture like that."

"Did you turn your back on God when your wife divorced you?"

"Nope. I still go to church down here at the Union Gospel Mission."

"You're an alcoholic, drowning your sorrows in beer and whiskey."

"I buy a beer once in while when I have the money. Today I'd just like a cup of coffee."

Weaving dialogue, narrative, and action. Following are six situations in which a character might find himself. The sentences that follow each situation employ only one fiction element. Add the other two elements to each of the sentences to create a woven paragraph. You can add as many characters to each situation as you want.

Example Situation: In the airport, Sheila watches as a woman trips, dropping her briefcase, which spills out packages of $100 bills.

Action sentence: Sheila's mouth fell open as the woman tripped and her briefcase went flying, spilling out packages of $100 bills.

Dialogue sentence: "Oh my!" Sheila cried. "Let me help you—"

Narrative sentence: Could this be the answer to Sheila's prayers, the miracle she'd been waiting for? What could it hurt? Just one of the packets? The lady would never miss it.

Situation: The dog runs into the ladder knocking it away from the house and Joe, cleaning the gutters, is stuck on the roof. Action sentence: Joe moved carefully to the edge of the roof and looked down.

Situation: Carolyn is stuck in traffic and wants to call home to tell her husband that she'll be late, but she can't get a signal on her cell phone. Dialogue sentence: "Stupid phone!" Carolyn muttered.

Situation: Alison has agreed to go out for dinner with her new coworker, Kyle, but moments before he arrives she receives a call from a reliable source telling her that Kyle is married. Kyle is ringing the doorbell. Narrative sentence: I told myself I'd never go out with a married man.

Situation: Ryan and his wife are getting a divorce. Ryan is throwing a few clothes in his suitcase. His six-year-old son, Aaron, is watching him. Action sentence: I grabbed my golf balls out of my dresser and placed them carefully in the corner of my suitcase.

Situation: Colin has just learned that he has to fire a guy at work, David, who has become a good friend over the last few months. Dialogue sentence: "Janis, would you send David into my office, please?"

Situation: Megan and her friend have just left the mall and are walking to their car when Megan sees a woman repeatedly hitting her small son on the back and then shoving him into her SUV. Narrative sentence: I always wondered what I'd do if I ever encountered an adult abusing a child.

chapter 6

[IN THEIR OWN WORDS— DELIVERING THE CHARACTERS AND THEIR MOTIVATIONS TO THE READER]

I'd been coaching fiction writers for many years when I happened to tune into *Inside the Actors Studio* on Bravo one evening to find host James Lipton interviewing Johnny Depp. When asked who influenced him the most as a young actor, Depp named an acting teacher, now passed on, named Stella.

"She emphasized over and over and over again that we head into every single scene with one thing foremost in our character's mind—what that character wants in that scene. What does my character want? A lot?"

I almost jumped out of my chair. This is what I'd been teaching writers for years, what I'd read so many times in how-to-write books. The most important thing to know about any character is what he wants. A lot. More than a lot—desperately.

If we know our characters well, we know what they want, both in the story and in every scene. There has to be a goal. This is the stuff of fiction. Our task is to let our reader in on what our characters want, as naturally as possible, even when what our characters want is on an unconscious level and they don't even know they want it. We must still let our readers in on it so the story moves forward. Sometimes what the character thinks he wants is the complete opposite of what he really wants, and the plot brings this out.

How does it work? How do we let the reader in on what the character wants, especially if the character is a minor one and we can't go into her thoughts? Well, we have the character's actions, of course, but we also have her words. Human beings always give themselves away with their mouths. Most of us just can't keep our mouths shut, even when we really try. If others are listening closely—and don't worry, they probably aren't because most people are doing more talking than they are listening—they'll tune into what motivates us the minute we open our mouths. The same is true of our characters. So much of writing fiction is just observing human interaction.

The key is dialogue—what a wonderful tool for revealing our characters and their motivations. There are so many ways you can reveal to the reader who these characters are—all through dialogue.

For the last few years, I've been using a tool in conjunction with dialogue to reveal the characters in my stories. It's called the Enneagram, and it has revolutionized my strategy for developing characters. This is how Renee Baron and Elizabeth Wagele define it in their book *The Enneagram Made Easy:*

> The Enneagram is a study of the nine basic types of people. It explains why we behave the way we do, and it points to specific directions for individual growth. It is an important tool for improving relationships with family, friends, and co-workers.
>
> The roots of the Enneagram go back many centuries. Its exact origin is not known, but it is believed to have been taught orally in secret Sufi brotherhoods in the Middle East. The Russian mystical teacher G.I. Gurdjieff introduced it to Europe in the 1920s, and it arrived in the United States in the 1960s.

This is all we really know about the origin of the Enneagram. Personally, I don't need to know any more because since I've been studying it and watching how it works, I really don't need to know anything else. I've tried it and found it to be true every single time I've used it as a tool when wanting to understand where another person—or even myself—is coming from. So many times, when I don't understand my own motivations, I remember that, oh yes, of course, I'm an Enneagram #4, the artist. That explains so much.

I offer the Enneagram as a tool to help you develop your characters. The scope of this particular chapter is to show how using the Enneagram within the context of dialogue can be used to reveal our characters and their motivations to the reader. While there are many ways to develop characters—and I've tried most of them—I've found the Enneagram to be a lot more fun than filling out those ten-page-long character charts to get to who my characters are. Once you learn to identify the different numbers of the Enneagram, you can throw away those character charts forever. All you have to decide is which type of personality you need for a particular character, then go to the Enneagram and find the number. Bingo! You know your character and where he comes from. Your character's dialogue will then come straight from his authentic personality and you can stop wondering if it sounds real or not.

In this chapter, I want to give you a brief overview of each of the nine Enneagram personality types and show how you can create dialogue that fits each of them, thus developing authentic characters who will be true to themselves every time they speak. Each personality type has a label and a number. The definitions after each number are from Baron and Wagele's *The Enneagram Made Easy.*

#1—THE REFORMER

Reformers are motivated by the need to live their lives the right way, including improving themselves and the world around them.

I recently watched a movie that included a young preteen character who was definitely a reformer. She sat in the front row of her classroom, which would be typical of a #1, as this personality type likes to influence others and likes to be seen. In the movie she would be the first to raise her hand every time a question was asked. This character's dialogue clearly showed us where she was coming from—every single time she spoke. Following are just a few sentences of dialogue addressed to her substitute teacher.

"What do you mean you're not grading that assignment? How do we know if we've done it right without a grade?"

"Your unconventional way of teaching is not contributing to a maximum learning situation."

"I've decided I'll need to speak with the principal about what's going on in this classroom."

She's clearly a smart-ass, but also clearly a #1. She knows the *right* way to do something and feels compelled to tell her teacher that his way is definitely *not* the *right* way.

In a scene of dialogue, a reformer is never afraid to speak up for what she believes to be right. Never bashful or shy, this is a character who likes confrontation and sees it as her job to correct the other characters whenever they're doing anything she doesn't agree with. When this character comes onstage in your story, the dialogue you put in her mouth comes from a deep place inside of knowing the right thing to do and making sure she and everyone else around her is doing it.

#2 — THE GIVER

Givers are motivated by the need to be loved and valued and to express their positive feelings toward others. Traditionally society has encouraged #2 qualities in females more than in males.

I have a friend, Jerry, who is always giving me advice. Over the years he's given me many other things, like money and gifts when I was raising my five kids as a single parent, but when we're in conversation, he can't help but give me input, whether or not I ask for it. This is what makes him feel valued and loved. It's what *drives* him because he's a giver. As soon as I figured that out, the unsolicited advice didn't bother me as much.

In fiction, this is what the #2 is doing, whether in action or dialogue. He's *giving*. Sometimes this comes from a pure place, but sometimes this comes as a way to get love and attention from others.

Typical dialogue for a #2 goes something like this:

"Of course, I'll be happy to watch your kids" (even while thinking *Oh, I can't believe she's asking me to watch those brats again*).

Givers are often indirect, finding it difficult to say what it is they really want. They can take on the role of a martyr when doing something they don't want to do and resenting it.

"Sure, I'll be happy to bake cookies for the bake sale." *I'm the only one who really cares about our women's group anyway.*

In dialogue, the giver can often be seductive, using whatever he has to draw another character close to him. This could be sex, money, possessions, counsel, or whatever. When this character appears in your story, he's coming from a place of needing love and attention and the willingness to give whatever he has to get his needs met. This kind of character, when in a desperate place, could sacrifice his soul. Whenever he speaks, whether consciously or unconsciously, he's about giving and receiving. Often, *whether* he's giving or receiving depends on how good he's feeling about himself in the scene of dialogue in which you put him.

#3 — THE ACHIEVER

Achievers are motivated by the need to be productive, achieve success, and avoid failure.

My #3 friends are movers and shakers. They get a lot done. These are the story characters who set goals, schedule their lives tightly, have full calendars, and live their lives by their long to-do lists. Even when engaged in conversation, they're thinking about all of the things they have to do. It's sometimes difficult for the achiever to live in the moment.

In this scene from Sandra Brown's novel *Breakfast in Bed*, Carter and Sloan, a mutually attracted couple who are just getting to know each other, are on the wharf together in San Francisco. Carter is questioning Sloan about exactly how much time she spends working at her bed and breakfast.

"How often do you get out? I mean, for fun and relaxation, not on an errand for Fairchild House." He was unselfconsciously slurping a gooey sundae as they sat at a small round table in the atrium room of the ice cream parlor.

"Not too often," she said dismissively.

"How often?" he persisted.

She fiddled with her candy wrapper. "I'm the sole owner and manager of Fairchild House. Housekeeper, hostess, accountant, chief cook and bottle washer. That doesn't leave much time for fun and relaxation as you put it."

"You mean you never take a day off? An evening off? Never go to a movie? Nothing?"

"You're depressing me," she said, trying desperately to tease him away from the subject. Her life was far from a carnival, she just didn't want him to know how very dull it was.

"Sloan, that's ridiculous." He lay his spoon aside and studied her with embarrassing intentness.

"It's not ridiculous if there's not help for it."

"Hire some help."

"I can't afford it," she snapped. "I told you that earlier."

"You can't afford to hole up in that house and never come out, either," he flared back. When he saw her stricken expression, he lowered his voice. "I'm sorry. It's none of my business, of course, it's just that I can't understand why a beautiful woman like you would hide herself from the rest of the human race."

A beautiful woman like Sloan would hide herself from the rest of the human race because she's a #3, and she's busy working while others are playing. Not only does the above show that she's a #3 because she's obsessed about work but also because she doesn't want Carter to find out just how dull her life really is. Achievers are concerned about their image and how they look to others. What would Carter think of her if he knew she had such a boring life?

In reality, achievers don't have boring lives. They live more interesting lives than many of us, always doing something, always engaged in some exciting activity or new project. They're driven by the need to succeed.

How does this show itself in dialogue? The achiever has to win arguments because she has to succeed, and she can't look dumb or like she doesn't know something. In dialogue, the #3 will be talking fast. Sometimes another character will be talked into something and not know how that happened. The #3 can easily overwhelm the more sensitive #5 (the observer) or #9 (the peacemaker). And the achiever really knows how to "work a room." In group dialogue, the #3 will bounce from person to person, networking, exchanging information, working hard to impress others with what she's capable of.

#4—THE ARTIST

Artists are motivated by the need to experience their feelings and to be understood, to search for the meaning of life and to avoid being ordinary.

As a #4 myself, this Enneagram number is a little difficult to discuss objectively. It seems like I can find something negative about all of the Enneagram numbers but this one. I wonder why that is? I recently asked a friend to tell me something she found annoying about the #4. She knows I'm a #4, but that didn't seem to stop her.

"Oh, it gets old that everything has to be a big drama," she said. "And they're so myopic."

I gulped. "Myopic?"

"They're so focused on themselves, you know, everything's about them."

"Oh yeah…"

"And they can't seem to be happy with what is—they're always missing what they don't have—"

"Okay, that's enough," I told her, feeling depressed.

I found a #4 in Jane Feather's novel *The Accidental Bride*. The protagonist, Phoebe, is definitely a drama queen and quite a handful for her new husband, Cato. It's a marriage of convenience, which makes her feel less than special. And artists need to feel special. In the following scene, Phoebe has just spilled red wine on her wedding gown at the feast after the wedding. When Cato scolds her for the way she's scrubbing at her gown and making the stain worse, her clear and dramatic #4 self emerges.

"I fail to see what difference it could make, sir," she responded acidly. "It's a hideous gown and it doesn't suit me."

"What on earth do you mean? It's an extremely elegant and expensive gown," Cato said, frowning. "Your sister—"

"Yes, precisely!" Phoebe interrupted. "On Diana it was exquisite! On me it's hideous. The color doesn't suit me."

"Oh, don't be silly, Phoebe. It's a very fine color."

"For some people."

Cato had given her only a cursory glance as she'd come up the aisle. Now he looked at her closely. She was looking so flustered and rumpled, with her hair escaping from its elaborate coiffure; even the motherless pearls had somehow become twisted around her neck. Maybe the gown didn't suit her as well as it had Diana, but there was no excuse for such untidiness. She just seemed to become unraveled before his eyes.

Phoebe continued savagely, "But of course new gowns are a frivolous waste of money."

Cato felt unaccountably defensive. "There is a war on, Phoebe. Your father felt—"

"He felt, my lord, that the money should be spent on pikes and muskets and buff jerkins," Phoebe interrupted again. "And if I have to wear this ghastly ivory concoction, then so be it."

"You're making mountains out of molehills," Cato declared.

Exactly. That's what artists do—they love making mountains out of molehills, and they really don't understand how others can just see a molehill when the situation is clearly a mountain. There's a dialogue scene later in the book where Cato is trying to teach Phoebe how to ride a horse and the lesson turns into a disaster rather quickly because of Phoebe's pension for drama. She ends up calling him a "horrid teacher," "a damned tyrant," and tells him quite directly that she wants a different teacher, because no one could learn anything from him. Phoebe's emotional outbursts seem to baffle Cato, but they don't surprise me at all.

Okay, for the #3 or #8 who just wants to get something done, or for the #5 who wants to withdraw and think about things, all of this loud emotion and unnecessary drama could be disconcerting, I suppose.

I probably don't have to tell you how to use an artist in a scene of dialogue. While they are full of creative ideas and relate warmly to others, they're also the ones who are bursting into tears at the smallest thing, blurting out angry words before they can get hold of themselves, expressing fear before there's anything to be afraid of. There's always a kind of flurry of excitement in their corner of the room. Think about how you might use this character in a story; he can be a lot of fun, even though, okay, a little annoying.

›

Just for Fun

Create a family reunion scene for a dysfunctional family—mothers, fathers, brothers, sisters, grown kids, grandkids, aunts, uncles, cousins, etc. This is a very religious family—a long line of staunch Presbyterians (or any religion of your choosing). They're sitting down to dinner and one character announces she's becoming a nun and another character announces he's gay. Write a reactive line of dialogue for nine of the characters at the table, representing each number on the Enneagram.

#5—THE OBSERVER

Observers are motivated by the need to know and understand everything, to be self-sufficient, and to avoid looking foolish.

The observer in your story is not the life of the party and is not the center of attention. She's the one standing off to the side watching, observing, taking notes, reading, thinking, and playing mind games with herself. If someone does engage her in interaction, she chooses her words carefully, so sometimes it takes her a while to form her thoughts and put them into words. In a scene of dialogue, this character can often seem withdrawn, detached, and even arrogant. She is definitely an introvert.

I had a #5 friend who, in a group, no matter what we were discussing, would just sit there and listen and watch. He was a deep thinker and I knew he had something to contribute, but I always had to ask him to do so. And when he did, it was interesting, important, and everyone listened.

In Robin Lee Hatcher's novel *Promised to Me*, I'm guessing Jakob is probably a #5. Here he is, his typical self, in a scene with his wife Karola after their barn has burned down. He's angry and closed off to Karola, not wanting her help and really just wanting her to go away.

> "I don't have time to rest, Karola." He straightened again, this time scowling at her. "You don't have any idea the trouble we're in."

"Then you should tell me."

"I don't want you to worry."

Exasperated, she said, "How can I not worry with you acting this way?"

"You don't understand."

Karola took a deep breath, trying to control her sudden anger. He was being bullheaded. He was pulling away from her again, the way he used to. He was keeping things bottled up inside and excluding her.

She took another deep breath. "I will get a pair of gloves and help you. Two will make the work go faster."

"You can't help me." He motioned with his hand, a gesture of dismissal. "Your skirts might catch fire from a live spark."

"I can tuck my skirts into my waistband."

"No."

"Then I will put on a pair of your trousers."

Jakob shook his head. "Karola, I'd rather be alone."

"But you are not alone. I am with you, and God is with us. Do not shut us out because of this misfortune."

"You and God aren't going to get us a new barn." He slapped a blackened glove against his chest. "I've got to figure out a way to do that."

...

Karola stared at him, heartbroken and furious at the same time. "Jakob Hirsch, have you so soon forgotten what Christ accomplished for you? You have made him too small in your eyes. Do not be arrogant and prideful. Ask him for help. Pray and ask."

"You'll have to do the praying, Karola. You're the pious one in this marriage. I've got to take action."

If Karola comes off as the "pious one," it could be because she's a #1 (the reformer), always pointing out what's right and wrong in her perception. This could be irritating to a #5 who reads and studies and thinks he knows what should be done in a given situation. In the above scene, Jakob thinks it's silly to sit around praying when it's clear what needs to be done.

You can see by this example how you might use an observer in your story. In conversation, they sit back and make observations, thinking things through for what can seem like a long time before offering anything to the subject at hand. Let the other characters draw your #5 out. If she thinks others really want to hear what she has to say, she'll offer her opinions, and once she gets going it can be difficult to shut her up.

#6—THE QUESTIONER

Questioners are motivated by the need for security. Phobic questioners are outwardly fearful and seek approval. Counterphobic questioners confront their fears. Both of these aspects can appear in the same person.

I suspect that most published authors don't have the Enneagram specifically in mind when creating characters for their stories. Still, I think some of this stuff is intuitive because skilled authors create characters who are consistent with the points of the Enneagram. The other day, for example, I was reading Anne Tyler's *A Patchwork Planet* and could clearly see that the protagonist's mother was a questioner. The protagonist is Barnaby, a young unconventional male who was married for a short time to Natalie and with whom he had a daughter, Opal. In the following scene, they've been divorced many years. Opal has come to visit her father and he has taken her on his rounds. He works for a company called Rent-a-Back, Inc., helping old and disabled people in their homes or in nursing homes perform chores they're too feeble to do by themselves. In this scene, he's talking with his mother about a recent visit to a nursing home. He took Opal with him and his mother, the #6, doesn't like this.

> "Barnaby Gaitlin," my mother said, "what could you have been thinking of?"
> "Huh?"
> "Taking a nine-year-old to a nursing home!"
> "So?" I said. "You have a problem with that?"
> "She says there were people in wheelchairs everywhere she looked. Old people! A woman with a tube in her nose!"
> "Geez, Mom," I said. "What's the big deal? We're keeping it a secret there's such a thing as old age?"
> Yes, we were evidently, because my mother threw a meaningful glance toward Opal, who kept her eyes downcast as she stirred the salad. "We'll just let Opal stay with me the rest of the day," Mom said. "I'll take her to see Gram and Pop-Pop."
> "Well, I don't know what you're so het up about," I told her.

Barnaby's mother was so "het up" because she was scared. Of old people? Who knows? We don't often know what a #6 is afraid of. The #6 often doesn't know himself. He just is.

In the very next scene, Barnaby's mother is worried that Opal, in Barnaby's care, isn't eating right.

Mom was miffed when I told her we'd have dinner at a friend's house. "Friend?" she asked. "What kind of friend? Male or female? You might have told me earlier. Is this a person who knows how to cook? Who'll give her fresh vegetables, and not just a Big Mac or whatnot?"

"It's someone who'll serve all the major food groups," I assured her.

"Well, I want you to know that I'll hold you to blame if Opal gets a tummyache," Mom said.

A few scenes later, when Barnaby's new girlfriend remarks to his parents, "You must be very proud to have raised such a caretaking person," his mother shows her surprise and says:

"Why, thank you, Sophia," my mother told her. "That's sweet of you to say." She glanced down the table to Dad. "It's not as if he hasn't caused us some worry, in times past."

Questioners are *always* worrying and are skeptical of any kind of encouragement or kind words, not really believing in the sincerity of the words. I sense that maybe Barnaby's mother doesn't believe Sophia when she tells her what a caretaking person Barnaby is and how, as his mother, she's raised him to be that way. Hmmm, maybe Tyler does use the Enneagram to develop her characters.

In any case, when the questioner speaks, it's out of a place of either fear or skepticism, especially if he's feeling insecure. This kind of character can be a lot of fun to develop in a story because in a scene of dialogue he's jumpy and questioning everything the other characters are doing or saying, never accepting things at face value, always suspicious of everyone's motives. The questioner's fear is endless. In any one scene of dialogue, he could be fretting about everything from earthquake preparedness to nuclear war to, like Barnaby's mother, if someone is eating right.

#7 — THE ADVENTURER

Adventurers are motivated by the need to be happy and plan enjoyable activities, contribute to the world, and avoid suffering and pain.

A typical conversation with a #7 might go something like this:

"It looks like it's going to rain again."

"Oh, that's wonderful." (Runs to get umbrella and boots.) "We need the rain. I love the rain. It always makes everything smell so fresh and keeps every-thing moist, you know?"

"The Snohomish is about to overflow again. Remember how it overflowed last week and flooded all of those homes?" (Maybe a #6 [the questioner] here?)

"Yeah, I saw on the news where neighbors were meeting each other, and families were spending time together, you know, because they had to use their boats just to get around the neighborhood. Very touching, wasn't it?" (Sniffs.)

"You're nuts.'

"Sometimes the worst situations can become exciting adventures, you know? It gives everyone a chance to pull together. I'm planning a mission trip to Africa, did I tell you about that? Well, that's after I color code my files and make scrapbooks of my vacation to Israel."

Adventurers can make the rest of us dizzy with their many projects and adventures. Sometimes, I'll watch someone on the *Oprah Winfrey Show* or some other talk show chatter on about everything she is doing, and I'll get all down on myself because I'm doing so little to save the world, but then I'll remind myself, "Oh, yeah, that's the chatter of a #7, and I don't have to be like that person to feel okay about myself."

When you put your #7 into a dialogue scene, she chatters away, like the above, about the many projects she's working on or issues about which she feels strongly. She's in her head a lot when in conversation and often needs others to help her get down to her heart, to stop and feel her feelings.

In a dialogue scene, the main thing to know about an adventurer is that he will always come from a place of positive thinking. He doesn't want to see anything negative and will either ignore those who do put a negative spin on life events, or in his personal life, pretend negative or difficult events aren't happening when indeed they are. These characters can be funny in a story because they're always off in some fantasy that doesn't relate to the here and now. They can really annoy the characters for whom the here and now is vitally important, like the #9 (the peacemaker).

#8—THE LEADER

Leaders are motivated by the need to be self-reliant and strong and to avoid feeling weak or dependent.

Leaders are also often overprotective and will fight hard for social justice as is evidenced in the following excerpt from *The Street Lawyer* by John Grisham. In this scene, a man, clearly a #8, is holding a bunch of rich lawyers hostage, drilling them about how much of their money they're giving away versus keeping for themselves. Study his dialogue, as this is what's important to leaders.

> He slowly shook his head. "And how much for the poor people?"
>
> "Total contributions of one hundred eighty thousand."
>
> "I don't want total contributions. Don't put me and my people in the same class with the symphony and the synagogue, and all your pretty white folks clubs where you auction wine and autographs and give a few bucks to the Boy Scouts. I'm talking about food. Food for hungry people who live here in the same city you live in. Food for little babies. Right here. Right in this city, with all you people making millions, we got little babies starving at night, crying 'cause they're hungry. How much for food?"
>
> He was looking at me. I was looking at the papers in front of me. I couldn't lie.
>
> He continued. "We got soup kitchens all over town, places where the poor and homeless can get something to eat. How much money did you folks give to the soup kitchens? Any?"
>
> "Not directly," I said. "But some of these charities—"
>
> "Shut up!"
>
> He waved the damned gun again.
>
> "How about homeless shelters? Places we sleep when it's ten degrees outside. How many shelters are listed there in those papers?"
>
> Invention failed me. "None," I said softly.
>
> He jumped to his feet, startling us, the red sticks fully visible under the silver duct tape. He kicked his chair back. "How 'bout clinics? We got these little clinics where doctors—good decent people who used to make lots of money—come and donate their time to help the sick. They don't charge nothing. Government used to help pay the rent, help buy the medicine and supplies. Now the government's run by Newt and all the money's gone. How much do you give to the clinics?"

Leaders are into justice. They feel protective of their environment and will crusade for causes. In the above scenario, the antagonist has gone over the edge in his crusading and is willing to kill others to make his point.

A therapist friend told me once that a lot of leaders end up in prison because they simply get swept away by their fierce drive to protect their loved ones and their environment. This isn't all that an #8 is, of course, but this is largely what motivates him. Some Enneagram books identify this number as not the leader but the boss.

The Enneagram isn't a cut-and-dried method of putting characters in categories. For example, in the movie *Heat*, both Robert DeNiro's and Al Pacino's characters are clearly leaders. One is a professional criminal and one is a cop. Go figure.

Human beings are complex and made up of many elements. But if you need a character in your story who is driven to fight for a cause, who needs to be in charge, who likes to be close to others but who often drives them away because of his aggressive personality, choose the #8. In dialogue, this character comes across aggressively—not always as aggressively as the antagonist in Grisham's novel, but there's never any doubt as to what he wants and when he wants it. Watch out or he'll take the scene away from the other characters. He's bigger than life and, by the way, has a gentle soul and can be a loving, caring presence in your cast of characters if he's working on himself and hasn't gone over the edge like the antagonist in *The Street Lawyer*.

#9—THE PEACEMAKER

Peacemakers are motivated by the need to keep the peace, merge with others, and avoid conflict. Since they, especially, take on qualities of the other eight types, peacemakers have many variations in their personalities, from gentle and mild mannered to independent and forceful.

The peacemaker's dialogue is usually soft-spoken and meant to please the listener, not always having a lot to do with the #9 herself. She often seeks to hear and understand what everyone else wants and forgets to listen to her own heart's needs. A typical #9 in your story will do anything to avoid conflict, putting all of her energies and efforts into calming everyone down in a crisis and denying the seriousness of a situation if it looks like drama or conflict is on the horizon. With this character, it's "peace at any price," and sometimes it's a heavy price, as in the sacrifice of her goals.

I'm writing a novel at the moment with a #1 (the reformer) protagonist who is dead set on revenge. Someone killed her daughter and she's obsessed with making sure the killer comes to justice. I knew I needed her husband to be a peacemaker, as this would provide the maximum conflict for her. If she were married to a #8 (the leader), he'd simply come alongside her in her goal, possibly even stabbing the dude himself in a dark alley some night. Or a #3 (the achiever) might strategically go about the goal of bringing this guy to justice as well. Either of these Enneagram numbers would most likely agree with my #1 protagonist, but not a #9. He just wants the entire situation to go away. He's not interested in a prolonged fight with anyone, not even in court. In his grief, he simply goes inward and despairs rather than fights. This drives my protagonist crazy and allows for a lot of verbal conflict between her and her husband throughout the story.

A typical conversation between them might go something like:

> "What is taking the cops so long to find that monster?" Linda said for the hundredth time since this nightmare began two months before.
>
> "Well, it's probably not their only case," Dan said quietly. He never knew exactly what to do with Linda when she got like this. "I mean, I'm sure they're doing the best they can—"
>
> "The best they can?" she screeched. "How can you say that? Half the time when I call, I have to explain all over again who I am. They're idiots."
>
> "I'm sure they're frustrated, too. They want to find the guy who did this, I'm sure—"
>
> "Why do you always take their side?" she cried. "It's like you don't even care—"
>
> That's when he shut down. How could she say he didn't care that they'd never see their 19-year-old daughter alive again? It was too much for him to bear, that's all. He sunk deeper into the chair and closed his eyes.

Dan can't cope with his aggressive reformer-wife. He feels hopeless and helpless and overwhelmed and her ranting and raving simply puts pressure on him to fix a problem that can never, ever be right again. Peacemakers like to roll up their sleeves and fix problems, but when they can't, their enthusiasm turns to despair.

USING THE ENNEAGRAM IN STORIES

The best time to wonder about which Enneagram numbers you need in a particular story is before you begin writing—if you're writing a plot-driven or idea-driven story. If you're writing a character-driven story, the character's Enneagram number may only emerge for you after you've begun to

Fixing Your Own Story

Go through a story you've written and identify each character's Enneagram number. Then, with a clear understanding of each character's motivation, revise your dialogue according to who each character is on the Enneagram.

write the story and come to know the character a bit.

For example, if you're writing a plot-driven murder mystery, neither the sleuth nor the murderer is probably a #2 (the giver) or a #9 (the peacemaker). This is simply because these Enneagram characters don't have enough aggression to go after criminals or to be criminals. You could have a #2 or #9 who could be assisting the sleuth or criminal. That would work, but these folks just don't tend to take charge.

So, depending on what kind of story I'm writing, and I usually write character-driven stories, I sit down and think through which Enneagram number I need for each character I'm planning for my story. Then I write first-person character sketches where I let the character *talk* to me in his own words. It almost feels like channeling the character. What's most important to know about any character from the very start, before anything else, goes back to what Johnny Depp's acting coach taught him—what the character *wants*. Your character's Enneagram number will determine this, then you're off and running. Your character's Enneagram number will drive that character's action in the story. You'll never have to wonder who she is or where she's coming from if you've studied who she is on the Enneagram. You'll *know*. And this one thing alone can make writing your character's dialogue a lot of fun.

You've read enough now to know whether this is a tool that might work for you in developing fictional characters and their dialogue. As I mentioned before, this is only one of the many tools available to us as fiction writers, but I hope you'll find it as helpful as I have. In this chapter I've just begun to scratch the surface of all there is to know about the Enneagram. If you want to become a serious student of the Enneagram, you can do an Internet search and pull up dozens of sites for more information. Or you can go to any bookstore and find any number of books on the Enneagram. In a well-written story, everything is connected: dialogue, characterization, viewpoint, plot, theme, and as we've seen in this chapter, motivation. In the next chapter, we'll see how *setting* can be woven into our characters' dialogue naturally and authentically so the reader has a sense of *who* our characters are based on their backgrounds as well as *where* they are in any given scene.

EXERCISES

Scenario: A man and woman are intent on scamming an elderly woman (or man) in the parking lot of a bank. Using the victim's point of view, write a one-page scene of dialogue for each Enneagram number, using the following focus:

#1 – begins to lecture the couple about the moral value of scamming people in parking lots

#2 – wants to help, eager to be scammed (not knowing she is)

#3 – begins to instruct the couple on a better approach for their scam, one that would be more successful

#4 – makes a scene, screaming for security

#5 – watches and listens and waits and wonders while the scammers persuasively chatter away

#6 – is suspicious and skeptical; asks lots of questions of the scammers about their approach

#7 – puts a positive spin on the encounter or pretends it's not happening

#8 – takes over the situation or gives the couple a lecture about what they should be doing with their lives

#9 – doesn't want any trouble; is kind and can't say no

chapter 7

[THERE IS A PLACE — USING DIALOGUE TO REVEAL STORY SETTING AND BACKGROUND]

Of all of the elements of fiction, setting has always been the most difficult for me to incorporate into my stories because, while I'm an observer of human nature, I forget to notice my environment. I take walks with a certain friend on occasion and she is forever stopping because she hears the chattering of a flicker (what's that?) and wants to interact with it. Or she might pass a certain tree or bush and stop to touch it. Without her by my side, I notice none of these things.

What I do love is to listen to people talk. To eavesdrop. Dialogue is my favorite element of telling stories. When I learned—I can't remember how—that I could use dialogue to reveal setting in my stories, I was thrilled. No more long narrative descriptions where I was trying to describe things I never "saw" in the first place. All I had to do from now on in the way of setting was notice what my characters noticed. That was easy enough because the characters I was used to creating weren't all that different from myself.

This may not be your problem. You may love to describe your story's setting and can easily go on for pages doing so. But that's a problem of another kind. Unless you're writing literary fiction, pages of description aren't usually what a reader is looking for, and he will often skip over it. It depends on the kind of story you're writing, of course. Literary and mainstream fiction are sometimes setting driven, but in the other genres, setting is most often simply the story's background. And dialogue is a useful tool for revealing it.

In order to reveal it through dialogue, of course, you have to first know your characters.

KNOW YOUR CHARACTERS

Just as we want our characters to speak authentically out of who they are, we also want our settings to be authentic, so that when we plunk our stories down somewhere we can bring our readers in and know that all of our props and background characters are for real. The very first thing we can do to ensure that this happens is to know our characters. It's only when we know our characters and how they feel and relate to the settings in which they find themselves that we can create authenticity in a scene. We have to know them so well that when we create dialogue for them that's connected with their setting, we're not surprised at how they feel about where they are.

For example, if your character, John, finds himself in the middle of a crowded street fair on a blind date and he's claustrophobic, he isn't going to take his time at a booth admiring the leather belts. You might want to mention the leather belts, though, to show that John is a biker. This is your story setting, and you have an opportunity here. Rather than let the need to establish setting drive the scene, go for authenticity and let John's claustrophobic, biker self drive the scene through dialogue.

> "Yeah, cool belts," John said, nodding at the owner of the booth and nudging Lori along. "I only have ten belts now." An older man bumped into him and John swore. "It's sure hot, isn't it?" He pulled his kerchief out of his back pocket and tied it around his head. "I bet it's twenty degrees hotter in this crowd than it is out there." He looked longingly through the crowd to the empty sidewalk a few feet away.

You get the idea. You want to weave the setting details into the dialogue, integrating action and narrative. You're looking for a three-dimensional feel.

It's important to know your character. Would a character who lives in Seattle even notice the Space Needle on his way to work in the morning? I live in Seattle, and I can tell you that I see it sometimes because it stands by itself and it's so tall, but most of the time I don't really *see* it. Oh, except on New Year's Eve and the Fourth of July when fireworks are shooting out the top of it—then everyone in Seattle notices it, if they're outside.

When you're on vacation, how often do you and your family and friends sit around and have a lively discussion about the hotel room you've rented for the weekend?

When at work, do you and your co-workers have regular animated discussions about your office building, the color of the walls, the way the desks are arranged, the drab carpet, etc.?

When taking your kids or grandkids to the park, are your eyes on the elm trees or your kids? On the ducks in the pond or your grandkids? If you were to strike up a conversation with a stranger, also with kids, would you most likely talk about the playground equipment or your kids?

You can see where this is going. Getting setting details into a scene is a little tricky because people/characters don't sit around discussing place.

However, setting isn't just about concrete place details. Setting isn't just a house or a beauty salon or a park. Setting can be an industry, a profession, or an organization. Whether or not your characters are sitting around discussing place, there are many opportunities to get setting details into scenes of dialogue if you are fully confident of your setting and you know your character.

Let's go back to John for a moment. You want to give the dialogue scene a three-dimensional feeling, so you have John saying, *"Wow, look at these cool garden decorations. Oh, and hey, here's a booth with homemade kitchen towels."*

John the biker? I don't think so. I hate to stereotype any group of people, but if this biker is into garden decorations and homemade kitchen towels, you better set this up before we get to the street fair so we'll believe you. And there better be a good reason, too.

No, John is more likely to say, *"Hey, babe, there's the beer garden,"* grab his old lady's hand and pass right by all of the booths full of garden decorations and homemade kitchen towels.

Know your character so you'll know what he might notice at a street fair, a circus, or the grocery store. Know what he might notice and what he might say about what he notices. What he would notice and not say anything about. Know him very well so your dialogue scenes will ring true, which is always more important than anything else.

ESTABLISHING SETTING

A written story is like a movie, where we see the characters on a screen acting out their scenes. As writers, we don't want our readers to have to work hard at *seeing* our characters, at visualizing the setting where the characters are in dialogue with each other. This means we need to make sure to establish the setting in the beginning of each scene of dialogue. If you open a scene with dialogue, integrate some setting details as quickly as you can so the reader can begin to picture the characters and the atmosphere in which the dialogue takes place. This is one way to make the scene three-dimensional so your characters aren't talking to each other in a vacuum.

Use only those details that will further the story situation, your theme, or your character's conflict. Once the setting is established for the dialogue, you can relax a bit, but continue to feed setting details into the scene so the reader can continue to visualize where the characters are in relation to their physical surroundings.

Fixing Your Story

Take a hard look at a troublesome dialogue scene that has setting as at least part of its focus. What's bogging it down? Following are some questions that you can ask that will help you get to the root of the problem and fix it.

[1] Is it that you can't seem to get the setting details into the scene in a natural way? How could you revise the scene to make it more natural?

[2] Is it that you're not confident about your character's description of the setting because you've never been there and you don't yet have the picture in your mind? What can you do to write your character's dialogue with more confidence? Do you need to visit this setting or one like it?

[3] Is it that you don't know your character well enough to know what he would notice and how he might express his observations? Do you need to do more work on your character sketch?

TOO MUCH TOO SOON

When writing dialogue, there's something we can keep in mind that will help us immensely. The story's dialogue shouldn't be that different from real-life conversation. With that in mind, when was the last time you or another person engaged in conversation that focused on setting to the exclusion of just about anything else?

"Oh and here we are at the circus. Just smell that popcorn, would you, and well, my favorite is the cotton candy, but I can't wait to see the clowns. As a child, they were my favorite part, and the sawdust on the ground feels so crunchy."

"I know what you mean. Here come the elephants with their pretty riders in pink outfits matching the elephants' neck ruffles. Don't you love how the trapeze artists are always in such good shape? They must work out for hours every day."

"Okay, I'm counting eleven clowns that have climbed out of that Volkswagen now. How do they do that?"

In case you haven't noticed, this isn't working. The author (that would be me, hate to say it) is trying to acclimate us to the setting by throwing all kinds of setting details into the dialogue. While dialogue is a great way to introduce the setting, it's not effective to dump it all on the reader at once. The above is called an "info dump," and it never works. It's contrived and unnatural, not the way people really talk. So let's say you want to give the reader the authentic feeling of being at the circus, but in a natural way, weaving it into the dialogue. Everything depends on the story situation you're developing in the scene. No matter what your agenda as the author, you can't let *your* agenda drive a scene. The characters' needs should always drive the scene. So, let's say a married couple on the verge of divorce has arrived at the circus for one last date together with their four-year-old son. Let's use the mother's first-person voice. The action is your primary focus, but you want the setting to feel authentic. You *don't* want an info dump.

"Cotton candy, Mom?" Jason turned to me, his eyes wide with wonder at everything around him.

"Sure, honey." She stepped up to the cotton candy man and gave him two dollars. "One, thanks."

"I want one, too." Aaron looked at me, and I remembered how much he loved cotton candy.

The sawdust crunched under our footsteps as we made our way to the auditorium. "Remember when circuses were under a tent?" Aaron said as he led the way past the cages of tigers and lions.

He said that every time we'd gone to a circus for the last ten years.

A clown on stilts passed us, smiling down at Jason and stopping to shake his hand.

"Tall man, Mom," he said.

I'd never understood why he directed all of his comments to me rather than Aaron. Was it because Aaron seldom interacted with his son?

I think it's clear why this circus scene works better than the previous one. The setting details in the first scene feel contrived, like the author's goal is to make sure the setting comes through. In the second scene, the setting is the scene's backdrop and the details are integrated into the story situation. It feels much more natural this way.

There's nothing wrong with wanting to get the details into a scene as soon as possible. This is good because when characters start talking, the reader needs to know where to picture them.

IT'S ALL IN THE DETAILS

Whether you're writing dialogue, action, or narrative, vivid details are what cause a reader to be able to see, hear, touch, taste, and smell—in short, to be able to experience your story on a sensory level.

Now, in dialogue, we have to remember that characters don't necessarily talk using rich details to describe another character's appearance, a building, or anything else. Most of us are actually quite uncreative when it comes to using sensory details. So above all, you want your characters to sound real.

As I emphasize so often in this book, everything depends on the kind of story you're writing and the characters that inhabit it. Anne Rice, because of the voice she uses in her vampire novels, can get away with some pretty heavy descriptive details in her dialogue passages. Let's look at one in *Interview With the Vampire*. The vampire, Louis, is telling a boy about a journey he took with his daughter, Claudia. In this particular passage, he describes their approach to a monastery. *Listen* to the richness of the detail in this short paragraph, which is only a small part of the setting.

> "In moments we had found the gap that would admit us, the great opening that was blacker still than the walls around it, the vines encrusting its edges as if to hold the stones in place. High above, through the open room, the damp smell of the stones strong in my nostrils, I saw, beyond the streaks of clouds a faint sprinkling of stars. A great staircase moved upward, from corner to corner, all the way to the narrow windows that looked out upon the valley. And beneath the first rise of the stair, out of the gloom emerged the vast, dark opening to the monastery's remaining rooms."

This passage appeals to the reader's sense of sight and smell. The reader can see the *great black opening, the vines encrusting the edges,* and *the sprinkling of stars.* Can't you *smell* the damp stones?

Rice doesn't stop there. She continues with the sensory details, putting them into Louis' mouth as he goes on with his story. She appeals next to the reader's sense of hearing.

> "There was only the low backdrop of the wind... I could see a flat stone there, and it sounded hollow as she gently tapped it with her heel."

Claudia stops to listen and asks Louis if he can hear what she hears.

> "It was so low no mortal could have heard it... Just a rustling now, a scraping, but it was steady; and then slowly the round tramping of a foot began to distinguish itself... The tramp of the feet grew louder, and I began to sense that one step preceded the other very sharply, the second dragging slowly across the earth."

In the middle of all of this emphasis on sensory sound, the author throws in the sense of touch, as well.

> "Claudia's hand tightened on mine, and with a gentle pressure she moved me silently beneath the slope of the stairway... I could feel the fabric of my shirt against me, the stiff cut of the collar, the very scraping of the buttons against my cape."

Would that we could all tell stories that were so suspenseful and employ the kinds of sensory detail that causes the reader to hold her breath and intensely feel every moment of the scene.

Again, the author can get away with this because of the voice she uses in her vampire novels. You probably wouldn't be able to reveal this level of detail in the dialogue of a character who's a gangster or a plumber. The level of detail might be the same, but the way it's expressed would be different.

When creating setting details for your character to express through dialogue, you don't want to go overboard and clutter the dialogue with a lot of unnecessary minutia. Include only those details that enhance the mood you're trying to create, get across the emotion the character is feeling, or move the plot forward in some way. Actually, the fewer the details, the more each one will stand out. And the sharper the detail, the more the setting will come into focus.

Setting contrasts are another way to make details stand out. In the above passage, one reason the *streaks of clouds* and *sprinkling of stars* stands out is because the author already established in our minds the *black* walls and opening into the room.

If you find that the dialogue in your story suffers from a lack of detail when you're trying to establish your story's setting, try a visualization exercise. Imagine yourself as your character in the story setting:

- What do you see before you?
- What do you smell in this particular setting?
- What can you reach out and touch?
- What do you hear all around you?
- Can you taste anything? What?
- How are some of the sensory details contrasted?

DIALOGUE DESCRIPTION

Writers use a variety of techniques to describe their story settings:

[1] omniscient narrative description as a character appears in a particular setting

[2] a character's thoughts about the setting in which he finds himself

[3] moving the characters into action and throwing in setting details as the characters are chasing each other and interacting in every way possible

[4] dialogue

Setting details can often feel static in narrative description (1), and many readers can easily get bored after a few paragraphs that describe a house's furnishings or a town's main street. The same thing happens if a character stands in the middle of a setting looking around and thinking, *Ugh* (2). Yet this is what seems to come to us to do first when considering how we might present setting. Action (3) works well because the writer is dispensing details as the characters move, so it's just a few here and there.

But what about using dialogue to get your setting across to your reader? If you do it in a lively and intriguing style, putting words in the mouths of characters the reader cares about, this can work nicely.

In Terry Goodkind's novel *Wizard's First Rule,* one of the characters, Kahlan, is explaining the setting to another character, Richard, in such a way that even includes suspense for the future, because this is a setting they're going to have to understand if they're going to navigate it and get where they want to go in the story.

> Kahlan stared into the fire. "The boundaries are part of the underworld: the dominion of the dead. They were conjured into our world by magic, to separate the three lands. They are like a curtain drawn across our world. A rift in the world of the living."
>
> "You mean that going into the boundary is, what, like falling through a crack into another world? Into the underworld?"
>
> She shook her head. "No. Our world is still here. The underworld is there in the same place at the same time. It is about a two-day walk across the land where the boundary, the underworld, lies. But while you are walking the land where the boundary is, you are also walking through the underworld. It is a wasteland. Any life that touches the underworld, or is touched by it, is touching death. That is why no one can cross the boundary. If you enter it, you enter the land of the dead. No one can return from the dead."
>
> "Then how did you?"
>
> She swallowed as she watched the fire. "With magic. The boundary was brought here with magic, so the wizards reasoned they could get me safely through with the aid and protection of magic. It was frightfully difficult for them to cast the spells. They were dealing in things they didn't fully understand, dangerous things, and they weren't the ones who conjured the boundary into this world, so they weren't sure it would work. None of us knew what to expect." Her voice was weak, distant. "Even though I came through, I fear I will never be able to entirely leave it."

Using words like *the underworld, death, curtain, rift, wasteland, magic, spells, and dangerous,* the author brings this setting to life even though we're not quite there. We anticipate getting there because now we know it's an exciting place fraught with all kinds of scary things.

The use of dialogue to convey setting is effective here because we trust Kahlan. She speaks with authority and confidence and we know that she knows what she's talking about. We believe her. We're actually in Richard's point of view in this scene, and one reason we believe her is because Richard believes her, and he's a trustworthy character.

Once again, when using dialogue to describe, you have to know your characters so you know what kinds of details they would mention in their description of a place. As you can see, Kahlan is the kind of character who goes psychologically deeper when describing place than many characters would. She doesn't just describe the physical appearance of the boundary or the underworld. She goes into the wizards casting spells and what it all means, which is much more interesting than just physical details.

STAY IN VOICE

Sometimes I see fiction manuscripts from my students who use dialogue to describe setting and the characters begin to sound like those time-share salespeople: "And over here in this corner we have a gas fireplace with a marble hearth and mantle and strobe lights on the ceiling above." What you want to remember when using dialogue to describe setting is to stay in your character's voice. If you have a character in your novel who's into hip-hop, then, "Hey, man, it's yo mama's blue rag on the floor there," and well, you know what I mean. Joyce Carol Oates handles this pretty well in her novel *Middle Age*. Roger and his fifteen-year-old daughter, Robin, are in the car together discussing a dead uncle. While the setting they're discussing doesn't play a huge part in the story, it's important for the characterization of Uncle Adam.

> She said hesitantly, "Mom was telling me, she'd heard from some friends there, Mr. Berendt had—some things?—people were surprised to find?—in his house?"
> "What things?"
> "Oh, I don't know."
> "What kind of things?"
> "It's just gossip, you know Mom. She'll say anything people tell her."
> "Honey, what kind of things? I'm Adam's estate executor, and I know."
> "Mom was saying she'd heard Mr. Berendt had, like, lots of money hidden away? In boxes? Like, buried in the cellar of his house? Millions of dollars?" Robin was watching him closely. Seeing his grimace, she said, "I never believe it, why'd Uncle Adam hide money like that, if he had it? If, like, anybody had it? You'd put it in a bank, right? I told Mom that. She's so credulous."

They discuss the ridiculousness of this idea for a moment, and then Robin continues:

> "I was in Uncle Adam's cellar, a few times. When we were there visiting. I must've been, like, ten. A long time ago."
> "Were you?"

"The cellar was old. It was sort of creepy. Uncle Adam said maybe there'd been dead people buried there, a really long time ago? Like, if they'd been murdered in the tavern, that the house used to be, they were buried in the cellar. Was that so?"

Oates uses the setting details to show the eccentricity of Robin's Uncle Adam. We learn that he may have hid money in the old house and told his niece stories about possible dead people buried in the cellar. Robin talks about her uncle and his creepy house and cellar. But note how she phrases so many of her remarks as questions. This is how she talks throughout the story and how so many teens typically speak, raising their voices at the end of their sentences in a question.

When your character is describing place, be sure to remember who's talking and stay in voice.

DIFFERENT STORIES, DIFFERENT SETTINGS

There are all kinds of stories, settings, and characters, and when certain characters in certain kinds of stories talk about certain settings, they mention certain things that other characters in other kinds of stories would never think of mentioning. The following are three very different characters from three very different kinds of novels speaking about three very different kinds of settings.

In this first excerpt from J.K. Rowling's *Harry Potter and the Sorcerer's Stone,* Mr. Dursley, Harry's uncle, is listening to the news. This is how the local newscaster and weatherman describe one aspect of the story's setting on this particular day in Britain:

When Dudley had been put to bed, he went into the living room in time to catch the last report on the evening news:

"And finally, bird-watchers everywhere have reported that the nation's owls have been behaving very unusually today. Although owls normally hunt at night and are hardly ever seen in daylight, there have been hundreds of sightings of these birds flying in every direction since sunrise. Experts are unable to explain why the owls have suddenly changed their sleeping patterns."

The newscaster passes to the weatherman and the dialogue continues:

"Well, Ted," said the weatherman. "I don't know about that, but it's not only the owls that have been acting oddly today. Viewers as far apart as Kent, Yorkshire, and Dundee have been phoning in to tell me that instead of the rain I promised yesterday, they've had a downpour of shooting stars!"

Owls and shooting stars mark Harry Potter's arrival at the Dursley's. And J.K. Rowling came up with a rather creative way to describe the setting in this fantasy novel, through the evening news.

The next excerpt is taken from *The Lords of Discipline*, a mainstream novel by Pat Conroy. The protagonist, Will, is telling Abigail, an old friend, how he feels about the Corps, which is the story's primary setting, comparing it to how she feels about her roses.

"I used to think that the Corps represented sameness. We all dress the same, we look the same, we live by the same rules, everything. But each one of us is different. When I walk into this garden each rose looks about the same to me, and you go to a parade at the Institute and all two thousand cadets look exactly the same to you. But if you look at them carefully, Abigail, the same thing happens to those cadets as to your roses. Each one is different, with his own surprises, his own miracles."

Keep in mind that this is a mainstream novel so the dialogue, the description, and even the action should make some kind of universal statement to the reader that connects ultimately to the story's theme. Will is describing the setting as he speaks, but he's doing it in such a way as to also make a statement about what he believes to be true about human beings. As you can see, the voice is very different than the newscaster's in the Harry Potter novel.

Finally, the following is an excerpt from *Fried Green Tomatoes at the Whistle Stop Cafe* by Fannie Flagg. This is a literary novel, and in this scene Evelyn Couch and elderly Mrs. Threadgoode are sitting in the visitor's lounge at Rose Terrace where Mrs. Threadgoode, now that she has an ear she can bend, is going on and on and on about her life. Understandably, her voice is very different from the newscaster's in *Harry Potter and the Sorcerer's Stone* and Will's in *The Lords of Discipline*.

"The railroad tracks ran right across the backyard, and on summer nights that yard would be just full of lightning bugs and the smell of honeysuckle that grew wild, right alongside the tracks. Poppa had the back planted with fig trees and apple trees, and he had built Momma the most beautiful white lattice grape arbor that was full of wisteria vines...and little pink sweetheart roses grew all over the back of the house. Oh, I wish you could have seen it."

Since most of the story is a flashback, this is a creative way to introduce the setting to us before we even get there ourselves. We begin to get a feel for the town of Whistle Stop through the aged voice of one of its most prominent citizens.

WEAVING NARRATIVE SETTING INTO DIALOGUE

In an earlier chapter, we discussed how to weave narrative into dialogue. Now we're going to discuss how to specifically weave narrative setting into dialogue. If done right, we can keep unfolding the setting throughout the scene as it moves. This is how it should be done—otherwise, the action and dialogue will begin to feel like it's taking place in a vacuum. We want our scenes to be visual. We don't want to create a bunch of talking heads; the reader needs to be able to picture our characters somewhere.

Weaving also gets us away from the tendency to create info dumps, those large paragraphs full of background, characterization, and setting details that are boring to write—we know they don't feel quite right—and worse yet, boring to read. So as much as you can, try to throw setting details into the actual dialogue as the scene moves forward.

The following example from Lorna Landvik's novel *Your Oasis on Flame Lake* will give you a small example of how this is done.

> Darcy *was boogying around to "Love the One You're With," playing air* guitar like the maestro she is, and I was laughing, *trying to screw a fixture into its socket,* when *Sergio blasted through the door* like a gas explosion.
>
> "It looks fantastic," he said, *twirling around like the little plastic ballerina inside a jewelry box* I once bought Lin. Even if *I hadn't been high up on the ladder,* I wouldn't have been able to watch him—he just made me too damn dizzy.
>
> "Wow," said Franny, who had followed Sergio in. *She plopped down on the couch and hugged a pillow to her chest.* "It looks just like a nightclub."
>
> Darcy's air guitar vanished *and she flung herself on the couch* next to Franny.

Obviously, the words in italic are the lines I want you to pay special attention to. This isn't heavy on setting, and you could do a lot more if you had to. For example, if you wanted to show that the characters were affluent, instead of just screwing a fixture into a socket, the viewpoint character could be changing the lightbulb in a crystal candelabra. You could describe the couch as a *mammoth black leather sofa with a mink afghan hung over the back.* You could go the other way and describe a *25-watt bulb hanging from the ceiling* and a *ratty red futon with an old blanket that smelled like a dog bunched up in one corner.* How you use a dialogue scene to describe the setting always depends on what you're trying to get across about the characters or the story.

INTEGRATING YOUR SETTING

The most effective way to integrate setting into a story is to use all three of the fiction elements at your disposal: dialogue, action, and narrative. This causes setting to simply form a background for the story. It's always there, almost like another character. It takes a gifted writer to be able to pull this off and make it feel natural.

Katherine Dunn is such a writer. In her shocking novel *Geek Love* (and I do mean shocking—and it takes a lot to shock me), Dunn is able to pull off just about everything in one scene. This is a story about a family of carnies. The main characters are the parents and their five children: Arturo, better known as Aqua Boy because he has flippers for arms and legs; Electra/Iphigenia, Siamese twins joined at the hips; Olympia, the hunchbacked protagonist; and Fortunato, who can move objects around rooms. Lil Binewski, the mother, ingested drugs—insecticides, arsenic, radioisotopes, anything to make her babies more "special"—so she and her husband could make a living with them in the carnival, which was their home. In this scene, the father is telling his children the by now very familiar story about how he came by the idea of creating the Binewski freak show using his own children as the stars of the show. The story is told in Olympia's first-person voice.

> "It was in Oregon, up in Portland, which they call the Rose City, though I never got in gear to do anything about it until a year or so later when we were stuck in Fort Lauderdale."
>
> He had been restless one day, troubled by business boondoggles. He drove up into a park on a hillside and got out for a walk. "You could see for miles from up there. And there was a big rose garden with arbors and trellises and fountains. The paths were brick and wound in and out." He sat on a step leading from one terrace to another and stared listlessly at the experimental

roses. "It was a test garden, and the colors were... designed. Striped and layered. One color inside the petal and another color outside..."

...The roses started him thinking, how the oddity of them was beautiful and how that oddity was contrived to give them value. "It just struck me—clear and complete all at once—no long figuring about it." He realized that children could be designed. "And I thought to myself, now that would be a rose garden worthy of a man's interest!"

We children would smile and hug him and he would grin around at us and send the twins for a pot of cocoa from the drink wagon and me for a bag of popcorn because the red-haired girls would just throw it out when they finished closing the concession anyway. And we would all be cozy in the warm booth of the van, eating popcorn and drinking cocoa and feeling like Papa's roses.

I love the way the author moves between dialogue, narrative, and action as well as between the past and the present to give a sense of the story's setting, while at the same time turning the key to unlock the door to the story's theme. Brilliant. If you can ever pull this off, you, too, will fall into the category of brilliant.

In the Fundamentals of Nonfiction workshop I teach for Writer's Online Workshops, there's a line about settings I particularly like to use: *Description in action beats static description.* I would say the same is true of dialogue. Description in dialogue beats static description. Don't ever use narrative to describe your setting when you can have a viewpoint character interacting with the setting in a lively discussion with another character. That's really the whole point of this chapter.

You've learned how to move the story forward through dialogue, how to weave dialogue, narrative, and action, how to use dialogue as a characterization device, and in this chapter, how to use dialogue to reveal your story's setting. In the next chapter, we're going to discuss how dialogue can help with the pacing of a scene or story. You can use it to speed things up or pull back to slow things down. Read on to discover how you can get better control of your stories.

EXERCISE 1

Know your characters. Jerry is a computer geek who is accompanying his wife to her company picnic at a large park near a reservoir. She works for the Sanitation Department.

Write a two-page dialogue scene that focuses on setting. What would Jerry notice about the setting and what would he say out loud?

Establishing setting. Write a two-page scene of dialogue between two characters in one of the following settings or a modified version. Focus on integrating setting details into the scene from beginning to end. And remember, the details can come through the character's observations of the setting, through dialogue, or through action.

- a rock concert
- an AA meeting
- a corporate office
- a shopping mall
- the inside of a car

Too much too soon. Your characters are entering a winter wonderland. It's their first date and they've decided to leave the city behind and drive up to the slopes for the day to go skiing. One of the characters is from California and has only seen snow once before, as a small child. Describe the setting from her point of view as she describes it to her male partner in the car. The goal is not to info dump but to let it gradually emerge—not too much too soon.

It's all in the details. In the heart of downtown Seattle, we have a place called Pike's Place Market. It's an outside array of food booths and shops full of tables of homemade clothing, jewelry, leather goods, and anything else you could think of. In one area, the vendors throw fish back and forth to entertain the customers. You can buy any kind of fish imaginable here. It's a place full of life and energy, a sensory heaven. Create a one- or two-page scene of dialogue between two characters who are visiting from out of town. Use all five senses in your descriptive dialogue of this setting.

EXERCISE 5

Dialogue description. A character, Janie, is taking her blind friend, Darcy, to Las Vegas for the first time. Janie lives in a small town in Iowa where she's a teacher's assistant for a second grade class. She's only been to Vegas once before. Using Janie's third-person voice, write a one-page scene of dialogue for Janie as she describes the sights and sounds of the city. Use as many descriptive, active, and specific verbs and nouns as you can.

EXERCISE 6

Stay in voice. Write a one-page scene of dialogue describing a Harley-Davidson convention from any or all of the following characters:

- a Buddhist monk
- a Ninja motorcycle enthusiast
- a small child
- a mental hospital escapee
- a political candidate

EXERCISE 7

Different stories, different settings. If you haven't already, identify the kind of story you're writing—genre, mainstream, or literary—and write a one-page scene that shows your character in dialogue with another character, describing the setting and staying with the voice of the kind of story you're writing. If you're not currently writing a story, choose a type of story and create a protagonist for that story who is talking to another character about the setting. Or choose one of the following:

- romance – the female protagonist describing a beach in Hawaii to her male antagonist
- horror – two characters in an empty warehouse rounding a corner and finding it not so empty after all
- action/adventure – one character describing the setting of his next crime spree to another character, in an effort to get him to join in
- science fiction/fantasy – one character describing an otherworldly setting to another character
- suspense thriller – two characters discussing an area of town where bodies keep turning up
- mystery – a character describing a suspicious looking house to her friend

- literary – one character flashing back in her mind to a time on her grandmother's farm and telling another character about it
- mainstream – a corrections officer telling a friend about how the system works against the inmates

EXERCISE 8

Weaving narrative setting into dialogue. Write a one-page dialogue scene for the following settings, weaving narrative details into the characters' dialogue:

- a dingy bar on the edge of town
- a candy store in a beach town
- a vacant lot
- a cross-dresser's closet
- a zoo

EXERCISE 9

Integrating your setting. A father has taken his ten-year-old son on a vacation to his childhood hometown. Using his thoughts, words, and actions, write a two-page scene of descriptive dialogue.

chapter 8

[BRAKES OR ACCELERATOR—DIALOGUE AS A MEANS OF PACING]

"Let's see," the small-town, slow-talking cop said as he stood outside my window.

It doesn't matter if he was slow talking, fast–talking, or a deaf mute—cops intimidate me.

"Looks like you were doing about sixty-seven in a fifty-five mile-per-hour zone. Well, I suppose I'll have to write you up."

Whatever. Just hurry up so I can get back on the road and out of this humiliating moment sitting here in my car hanging out with you.

I can't believe it, I grumbled to myself as he returned to his patrol car to write me up. Almost twenty years without a ticket and here I am. I mean, really, I would have hit the twenty-year mark in another year or so.

"Okay, I'm just gonna make it sixty-five instead of sixty-seven so it'll bring your fee down a bit."

"I haven't had a ticket in almost twenty years," I told the cop, thinking this bit of trivia might make him swell with pride for me, resulting in a torn-up ticket. "Isn't that something?"

"That's something, all right," he said as he handed me the ticket. "You gotta be careful around here because, you know, us small-town cops don't have nothing else to do but sit out here and catch folks like you hightailing it through our town like you got somewhere to go."

This is a true story; I'm still feeling the pain of the $75 ticket. The point? I might have been speeding, but the minute I ran into Mr. Small-Town Cop, my true story slowed right down. We weren't going anywhere fast. And that's simply because he wasn't in any hurry. You can't speed up a slow character; he moves in two speeds—slow and reverse. The same is true with a fast character—fast and fast forward. So it pays to know your characters because who they are determines how slowly or quickly they talk.

PACING YOUR STORY

Every story has its own pace. Most literary and many mainstream stories move slowly, easily, from opening to conclusion. Such a story may ramble on about the characters' philosophies and life strategies, and on occasion the author will even use dialogue to achieve the slow pace—if the author knows what he's doing. Reading slow-moving dialogue is preferable to reading lengthy passages of philosophical narrative.

Genre stories generally move quickly, employing more dialogue and action and less slow-paced narrative, because they are generally plot-driven rather than character-driven, like literary and mainstream stories. The emphasis is on the action that keeps the plot moving rather than the narrative that keeps the character growing.

Whatever kind of story you're writing, you want to be conscious of the pacing. It makes sense that a character-driven literary story will move more contemplatively than an action suspense story. Dialogue generally speeds things up, but of course there are exceptions, as there are exceptions to everything in fiction. For example, you might have a slow talker who, every time he appears in a scene, causes the action and other characters to just kind of come to a stop. But that's the exception, and we want to look at the general rule—that dialogue normally speeds everything up. A story is woven, using both fast and slow-paced scenes, to achieve a rhythm that works for the kind of story you're writing.

Let's say you're writing a suspense thriller and you need to keep things moving. The focus of your story will be on your fast-paced dialogue and action scenes, and the narrative will be woven in only if and when you need it. The characters in a suspense thriller don't do a lot of thinking other than moments of wondering how to get out of the scrapes in which they find themselves. These nondramatic scenes are placed strategically every so often so the viewpoint character can catch up with himself. Other than that, the story keeps moving. And dialogue makes up the bulk of a fast-paced story.

What you want to learn is how to control the pace of your story through dialogue. Without knowing how to do this, you have no sense of whether you're putting your reader to sleep or keeping her wide awake and turning pages as fast as she can. By the way, you can keep your reader quickly turning pages in a literary or mainstream story, too, if you can learn to write dialogue that has some substance.

The only thing standing in the way of our being able to pace our stories is plain and simple unconsciousness. We're just not thinking about pacing as we're writing, so my challenge to you in this chapter is to start to think about it. Not after you've completed the story and while reading it to your critique group happen to notice the yawns and blank stares. Most stories are paced not too fast, but too slow. The time to think about pacing is while you're writing your first draft.

My goal in this chapter is twofold: (1) to get you to think consciously about pacing your story, and (2) to teach you how to use dialogue as a pacing tool.

CREATING MOMENTUM

A story gathers momentum as it moves. That's not to say we should start our stories out slowly, hoping things will pick up as we write. We can't afford that luxury. We situate our characters in the scene's setting, introduce the conflict, create some emotion, all while the characters are moving into dialogue with one another. In real life, conversation can take many twists and turns, and sometimes you're left wondering how you even got into a particular conversation. Dialogue has its own momentum and is driven by—guess who—the characters. We have to trust our characters enough to let them talk to each other about what they need to talk about. This isn't always easy because as writers we have agendas, and it's so easy to impose our agendas on our characters. When we do that, the characters start making speeches and going off on all kinds of tangents that aren't theirs but ours.

In the following scene from John Kennedy Toole's comedic novel *A Confederacy of Dunces,* the protagonist, Ignatius Reilly, is visiting a ladies' art show trying to sell some of his hot dogs. The scene starts off slowly as Ignatius approaches some of the paintings, then gathers steam as he starts to comment quite candidly on the artwork.

> The Alley was filled with well-dressed ladies in large hats. Ignatius pointed the prow of the wagon into the throng and pushed forward. A woman read the Big Chief statement and screamed, summoning her companions to draw aside from the ghastly apparition that had appeared at their art show.

> "Hot dogs, ladies?" Ignatius asked pleasantly.
>
> The ladies' eyes studied the sign, the earring, the scarf, the cutlass, and pleaded for him to move along. Rain for their hanging would have been bad enough. But *this*.
>
> "Hot dogs, hot dogs," Ignatius said a little angrily "Savories from the hygienic Paradise kitchens."
>
> He belched violently during the silence that followed. The ladies pretended to study the sky and the little garden behind the Cathedral.

The author now inserts a narrative paragraph where Ignatius abandons his cart for a moment to scrutinize the ladies' paintings of flowers—critically.

> "Oh, my God!" Ignatius bellowed after he had promenaded up and down along the fence. "How dare you present such abortions to the public."
>
> "Please move along, sir," a bold lady said.
>
> "Magnolias don't look like that." Ignatius said, thrusting his cutlass at the offending pastel magnolia. "You ladies need a course in botany. And perhaps geometry, too."
>
> "You don't *have* to look at our work," an offended voice said from the group, the voice of the lady who had drawn the magnolia in question.
>
> "Yes, I do!" Ignatius screamed. "You ladies need a critic with some taste and decency. Good heavens! Which one of you did this camellia? Speak up. The water in this bowl looks like motor oil."
>
> "Let us alone," a shrill voice said.
>
> "You women had better stop giving teas and brunches and settle down to the business of learning how to draw," Ignatius thundered.

What causes a dialogue scene to gather momentum and really begin to move is when one or more characters begin to express emotion or strong opinions. It happens when your characters' agendas begin to collide, when one character can't get what he wants from the other characters. In the above scene, Ignatius, in rare form, is actually minding his own business, but then true to his nature, he can't keep his mouth shut and his opinions to himself. Of course, the scene speeds up the minute he opens his mouth and begins to express just how appalled he is at the atrocities he sees in front of him in the name of art. And of course, the ladies just want him to leave and stop attracting so much negative attention to their artwork.

You want your story to go somewhere. You know you need to pick up the pace a bit so that it does. Dialogue does this because, of all of the fiction tools at your disposal, dialogue is the one that most quickly puts your characters and your reader in the present moment.

SPEEDING UP

Letting a scene drag is one of the worst mistakes a writer can make. There is no excuse for this. Bringing two or more characters together and letting them chat on and on about nothing is inexcusable. The problem is many writers aren't even aware that their characters are doing this, even when it's in front of their noses. They're sitting right there writing the story and fail to see that they're boring their reader to death with going-nowhere-fast dialogue.

There are many reasons dialogue scenes bog down. The main one is that we clutter them with so much added narrative and action that the reader has to muddle his way through and the going becomes a little clunky. Sometimes, the scene is weak when it comes to tension and suspense, and the reader is yawning big time. Our characters are just talking about nothing. For a very long time. Like this:

"Hi Mom," Dolores spoke loudly into the phone. Her mother was hard of hearing.

"Dolores, is that you?"

"It's me, Mom, how are you?"

"Fine, I'm fine, my back's been acting up again."

"Have you been to the doctor?"

"Oh, yes, he can't do anything, just writes out more prescriptions. I'm so drugged up now, I can hardly even stay awake."

"How have you been sleeping?"

"Oh, fine, just fine."

"Do you need anything?"

"Need anything? You mean, like milk or eggs or---"

"Anything at all. Do you need me to bring you anything?"

"Oh, no, I'm fine. How's the boys?"

"They're fine, growing like weeds."

"How's Bill?"

"He's fine. He got laid off his job."

"That's nice, dear, well, thanks for calling."

"Bye, Mom."

"Bye, Dolores."

I see scenes written like this all of the time, more often than I care to admit. Long and slow and boring. No tension. No drama. No suspense.

As I mentioned above, dialogue by its very nature is an accelerator, metaphorically speaking. When a story or scene needs to move, get people talking. The faster you get them talking, the faster the scene moves. Cutting out any extra narrative or action sentences causes your story to speed along. You can even cut out descriptive tags so your dialogue comes down to the bare bones. Also, the more emotion you put into a scene, the faster it moves.

The reason emotion speeds things up is because it heightens the tension and suspense. Characters expressing emotion are unpredictable and often out of control. Anything can happen, so the stakes are up.

Do you ever notice how, when you're watching a fast-paced movie and the stalker is closing in on his victim, you start shoveling your popcorn into your mouth at breakneck speed?

That's where your reader is when you include the kinds of emotional dialogue scenes that move so fast that the characters are stumbling over their own words. Whether the emotion is fear or anger (closely connected) or sadness, it gives the dialogue a power surge and propels the scene forward. In this scene from Anne Tyler's *Ladder of Years*, the protagonist, Delia, a wife and mother, has run away from home. Her sister, Eliza, has come to visit her, possibly to talk some sense into her.

> "Sit down," she told Eliza. "Could I offer you some tea?"
>
> "Oh, I...no thanks." Eliza took a tighter grip on her purse. She seemed out of place in these surroundings—somebody from home, with that humble, faded look that home people always have. "Let me make sure I'm understanding this," she said.
>
> "I could heat up the water in no time. Just have a seat on the bed."
>
> "You are telling me you're leaving us forever," Eliza said, not moving. "You plan to stay on permanently in Bay Borough. You're leaving your husband, and you're leaving all three of your children, one of whom is still in high school."
>
> "In high school, yes, and fifteen years old, and able to manage without me fine and dandy," Delia said. To her horror, she felt tears beginning to warm her eyelids. "Better than with me, in fact," she continued firmly. "How are the kids, by the way?"
>
> "They're bewildered; what would you expect?" Eliza said.
>
> "But are they doing all right otherwise?"
>
> "Do you care?" Eliza asked her.
>
> "Of course I care!"

Things start out slowly with long sentences and paragraphs as Eliza is getting settled in the room. But when she starts to accuse Delia, things start to speed up. Delia feels the tears warming her eyelids, and the scene surges forward with short sentences and paragraphs. We're in the emotion now and everything feels more urgent.

Pumping up the emotion doesn't necessarily mean using a lot of exclamation points. It could mean shortening the sentences and paragraphs or cutting out any and all narrative and action sentences. It could mean having your characters shooting short phrases of dialogue back and forth at a rapid pace. This can be very effective when done well and not overdone.

Just for Fun

A married couple, Marilyn and Robert, are going to garage sales, one of their favorite pastimes. Well, until recently. Marilyn has been tiring of this twenty-year hobby and has recently taken up gardening. They are presently going through someone's junk at a garage sale, and a conflict ensues when Marilyn decides she's ready to go home. Using either Marilyn's or Robert's viewpoint, write a two-page fast-paced scene and then a one-paged slow-paced scene taking these two through their conflict.

SLOWING DOWN

As I mentioned earlier, often the problem with our stories is that that they move too slowly. But if they move too quickly, the reader can't catch her breath and the story often feels fragmented, kind of like it's running away with the characters. Both characters and scenes feel undeveloped, causing the whole story to kind of derail. While too much dialogue is usually not the problem in a story that's not working, every once in a while, someone gives me a story to evaluate where the writer has decided that the characters will just talk away. And away. And away. Just as we can learn how to use dialogue to gather momentum in a scene, we can also learn how to control our scenes by slowing them down.

But if dialogue is a device used to speed stories up, then how can dialogue be used to slow them down?

It's true that to use dialogue is most often to step on the accelerator. But if the story is running away with you in the middle of a dialogue scene and you need to put the brakes on, there are a few ways you can do it.

You can weight the scene down with narrative, description, and background, or you can bring slow-talking Harry onstage and everything will come to a screeching halt. Harry just isn't in a hurry.

When everyone in the scene is running on at the mouth and things are heating up but the point has been made and now you want to slow things down, a slow-talking character can bring the other characters, as well as the reader, back into the moment. Use some hems and haws and uhs along with long, rambling sentences to show the slow pace. You can add bits of action—slow action—to show Harry kind of moseying his way through the conversation. Picture an old guy on a porch sitting next to his friend talking about fishing. That's Harry.

Another way to slow the scene and/or story down using dialogue is to move your characters into a rational conversation where there's less action and emotion and more cerebral logic concerning their situation. Note I said less action and emotion, not less tension. Tension is something that needs to be present in every scene of dialogue no matter how slow or fast. But dialogue that focuses on the intellectual side of a conflict or problem simply moves more slowly and methodically than dialogue where the characters are emoting and arguing.

Following is an example of this from John Steinbeck's novel *East of Eden*. The younger brother, Charles, is insanely jealous of his father's love for his older brother, Adam. In this scene, Charles has just unleashed his rage on Adam and beaten him to a bloody pulp. The scene moves at high speed through the fight, slows down just a bit as Adam makes his way home, then speeds up again as the boys' father demands to know why Charles beat up his older brother.

> Cyrus stumped over to him and grasped him by the arm so fiercely that he winced and tried to pull away. "Don't lie to me! Why did he do it? Did you have an argument?"
> "No."
> Cyrus wrenched at him. "Tell me! I want to know. Tell me! You'll have to tell me. I'll make you tell me! Goddam it, you're always protecting him! Don't you think I know that? Did you think you were fooling me? Now tell me, or by God I'll keep you standing there all night!"
> Adam cast about for an answer. "He doesn't think you love him."

The father's heightened emotion keeps the scene moving quickly because people in a heightened state of emotion are unpredictable. You never know what they're going to do next. But once Adam tells his father this, his father immediately turns away, walks out the door without another word, and the boys' mother begins to rationally explain away her younger son's behavior, slowing the scene down.

> "He doesn't think his father loves him. But you love him—you always have."
> Adam did not answer her.
> She went on quietly, "He's a strange boy. You have to know him—all rough shell, all anger until you know." She paused to cough, leaned down and coughed, and when the spell was over her cheeks were flushed and she was exhausted. "You have to know him," she repeated. "For a long time he has given me little presents, pretty things you wouldn't think he'd even notice. But he doesn't give them right out. He hides them where he knows I'll find them. And you can look at him for hours and he won't ever give the slightest sign he did it. You have to know him."

I did mention above that you could slow a scene down by adding bits of narrative, description, and background to your dialogue scene. In the next chapter, we see Adam again, after spending four days in bed recovering from his brother's beating. This scene is very brief but shows how you can use narrative, description, and background to make a scene move more slowly, even though there's dialogue in the scene.

> Into the house, into Adam's bedroom, came a captain of cavalry and two ser-geants in dress uniform of blue. In the dooryard their horses were held by two privates. Lying in his bed, Adam was enlisted in the army as a private in the cavalry. He signed the Articles of War and took the oath while his father and Alice looked on. And his father's eyes glistened with tears.
> After the soldiers had gone his father sat with him a long time. "I've put you in the cavalry for a reason," he said. "Barrack life is not a good life for long. But the cavalry has work to do. I made sure of that. You'll like going for the Indian country. There's action coming I can't tell you how I know. There's fight-ing on the way."

Can you see how just a little bit of narrative, background, and description can make a scene of dialogue move more slowly? There's little emotion in the above scene, only the glistening of Adam's father's tears. But his words are matter-of-fact. We get the background first, then his father simply offers a half-baked explanation for why he's doing what he's doing, and the scene is over.

GAINING CONTROL

Pacing your dialogue is about gaining control of your scenes so they don't run away from you or drag to the point that even you can't stay awake while writing them.

What exactly causes us to lose control of our stories and therefore the pace of our dialogue?

Losing control happens for a number of reasons and again, when we're conscious of this, it's easier to stay in control. Of course, the very act of losing control is an unconscious one. By definition, that's what losing control is, whether in real life or in storytelling. To lose control is to lose consciousness. During the act of writing a story, what causes us to lose consciousness so the dialogue suddenly begins to speed out of control or painfully drag along?

I think we often underestimate the personal connection we have to the stories we write. We think we're writing about characters we've made up. After all, this is fiction, isn't it?

Yes and no.

When our dialogue begins to take our characters to places we hadn't intended faster than we intended to go there, we need to pay attention. Most writing books will tell you that when this happens, you need to go back to where you began to lose your way and fix the dialogue right there, to pick up the thread where you lost it and start over.

This isn't necessarily true. Losing control of our dialogue at certain points simply means we're finally feeling the freedom to say those things we've always wanted to say to whomever we've wanted to say them. They're our words rather than our characters' words, and at this point, if we recognize what's going on, the story may turn out to be about something we hadn't intended at all. You may think you're writing about a young man landing his first job and then discover you're really writing about a young man thrust into adulthood before he feels ready. Maybe this is your story, after all, one you've never told. When you realize this, you have a choice. You can keep following the real story or you can go back to where you lost your way and get the dialogue back on track with the story you started out to tell. If you choose the second option, that's fine, but at some point you should consider writing the real story as well, because you can count on it being the most authentic one. The one that's inside of you crying to get out.

A sudden change in pace when we're writing dialogue can signal to us that we need to pay closer attention to what the scene is bringing up for us personally. Sometimes the dialogue will speed up and we'll lose control because, yes, we've touched on a theme in our real life. But instead of going ahead and writing authentic dialogue, we become uncomfortable with the *feelings* connected to the dialogue and so quickly, go off on some tangent to get away from them. Again, awareness is what gets us back on track.

When a dialogue scene slows way down so that it drags, and this doesn't happen as often, the reasons for it are the same as when it speeds up too fast. When our characters start talking to each other again, it can happen that we come upon a personal theme that we unconsciously decide to explore, and we have to slow down in order to fully follow where it seems to be leading us. We may start weighing it down with actions of the other characters or too many of the protagonist's thoughts. We're really into this before we realize it has nothing to do with the original topic of dialogue.

We always have a choice. We can follow the tangent and see where it leads us or we can arrest the dialogue we're writing, set the real story aside for later, and continue.

We always hear about how being a control freak is such a negative thing. But maybe, in the world of writing, our efforts to gain control of our dialogue, and therefore our stories, means that we're control freaks in a good way because we're trying to write the most authentic story possible.

IS IT WORKING?

How do you know if your dialogue is paced well? This is often something you can't know until you've finished the story. When reading through the entire story, you'll be able to see where you need to speed a scene up here, slow a scene down there, add a bit of setting here to keep things steady, and a bit of narrative there to momentarily let the reader breathe again.

You want a combination of slow and fast-paced scenes, alternating them so you don't either wear the reader out or put her to sleep. In Jack Bickham's book *Scene & Structure,* he instructs us to write both scenes and sequels. The scenes move more quickly while the sequels are often more nondramatic moments in the story where both character and reader catch

Fixing Your Own Story

When you realize you've lost control of a scene of dialogue, ask yourself the following questions to help know whether you want to gain control of the original story or tell another, possibly more authentic, story.

[1] Where did I begin to lose my way in this dialogue scene?

[2] Why did I speed the dialogue up faster than it needed to go? Or why did I slow the dialogue down, making it suddenly drag?

[3] Is the original direction the way I still want to take this story?

[4] Should I be listening to the new direction these characters seem to be leading me through their dialogue, and where do I think they might be taking me?

[5] Do I trust these characters enough to follow them into the kind of dialogue discussion I hadn't originally planned for them?

[6] Which direction—the original or the new—is the most authentic dialogue and therefore the most authentic story?

[7] Can I give up control of the dialogue that I think I want to write so in the end I will gain control of my most authentic story?

Go through your novel or short story and find the scenes that move either too slowly or too quickly and rewrite them, adding bits and pieces of narrative and action, or taking it away, so that every scene is in balance with the rest of the story and effectively pulls its weight.

up with themselves. There are no hard and fast rules. Certainly there will be times where you'll need two or three fast-paced scenes in a row to move your plot along. But just be conscious of when you're doing what so you stay in control of your story.

Don't worry too much about pacing while you're writing. Just get the story down. Then put on your editor's hat and with a purple or green pen (it's a new day—no red pens anymore), go through the story and mark the places where you want to speed things up or slow them down. Following are some questions you can ask about your viewpoint character to try to discover if a dialogue scene is moving too slowly or too quickly.

• Is he talking too fast, not giving the other characters time to answer?

- Is he avoiding the subject and rambling on about nothing that has anything to do with what the story's been about so far?
- Is he thinking too much and not talking enough? Or is it the other way around?
- Are there too many tags and other identifying actions so his words become lost in the clutter?
- Is he making speeches instead of interacting with the other character(s)? (You may want him to make speeches in order to slow things down; just be aware that you're doing it and make sure that the speeches further the plot.)
- Is he too focused on observing the other characters in great detail or describing the setting to himself, sacrificing the kind of dialogue that would create tension and suspense in the scene?
- Do you, as the author, keep intruding on the scene with your own observations and descriptions that interrupt the flow of dialogue between the viewpoint and the other characters?

You can never completely know when you're going over a hair into dialogue that moves too slowly or hanging back a hair with dialogue that doesn't move quite fast enough, but the above questions will get you close enough. As always, awareness of pacing your dialogue is what will eventually get and keep you on track.

Seeing dialogue as either brakes or accelerator will help you stay in control of your story so it doesn't leave you in the dust like a runaway stagecoach or move at a snail's pace. You're the one who can press hard on the gas to propel the dialogue into motion or hard on the brakes to slow it way down. Every story has its own rhythm and motion, and pacing your dialogue to pace your story will give your reader an easy and smooth ride.

The next chapter is closely connected to this one in that it, too, is about controlling your dialogue so it's always full of tension and suspense, ensuring that your reader will keep turning pages from beginning to end.

EXERCISE 1

Pacing your story. Focus on just one scene in a story you're writing. Now answer the following questions as honestly as you can:

- Is this a slow-paced or a fast-paced scene? Or neither?
- In relation to the entire story, what kind of pace do I want this scene to have?
- What is making this scene move so slowly (or quickly)?
- How much dialogue have I used in this scene, as compared to action and narrative?
- Using more or less dialogue, how can I adjust the pacing of the scene.
- Are the scenes on either side of this one slow or fast-paced?
- How much dialogue have I used in the scenes on either side of this one? Do either one of them need more or less dialogue to make them move better, so they're in rhythm with this one?

Now rewrite the scene so it moves at the pace you want it to.

EXERCISE 2

Creating momentum. Choose one or all three of the following scenarios. Start the scene out slowly and then, through dialogue, gather momentum as you write. You also may want to do this with a scene or scenes in your own story.

- A father and his daughter are stuck in rush hour traffic. She's fiddling with the radio, and he's talking on his cell phone. Suddenly the phone goes dead and the girl's favorite radio station won't come in. They have to talk. Write this scene from either the father's or the daughter's viewpoint, or try one of each.
- A man and woman are having an affair, but up until now, it's been only physical. One of the two decides the relationship needs to be taken to the next level. Write a sex scene that turns out to be more about talk than sex.
- Two homeless men, strangers to each other, end up under the same freeway overpass for the night. They ignore each other at first, but then one of them starts to talk and can't seem to quit.

EXERCISE 3

Speeding up. Take the scene about Dolores under the subhead Speeding Up and rewrite it so it moves. You can add narrative or action or delete lines, anything that will make the scene move and contribute to a story that's going somewhere.

BRAKES OR ACCELERATOR

Slowing down. Steve and Jennifer are a happily married couple, well, most of the time.
Jennifer is a little uptight and anal, always needing to be on time wherever they go. Steve
is just the opposite. He really doesn't get why everyone is in such a hurry all of the time,
especially his wife. In the following scene, you'll find only the bare dialogue between
Steve and Jennifer. When a scene includes only dialogue, it moves quickly. Your task is to
slow this scene down by adding narrative, description, background, and bits of action
here and there.

"I'm ready to go, Steve."

"Coming."

"When?"

"Right now, right now. I'll be right down."

"It's 4:15, Steve."

"Yeah, it sure is. I just looked at the clock."

"Mom is going to be so upset if we're late to pick her up."

"Yeah, she gets like that, all right."

"Steve!"

"Huh?"

"C'mon!"

"I'm coming, honey, just putting on my socks."

"I'm going out to start the car."

"Don't forget to open the garage door—don't want to asphyxiate yourself."

"Are you coming?"

"I'll be right down."

chapter 9

[TIGHTENING THE TENSION AND SUSPENSE—DIALOGUE THAT INTENSIFIES THE CONFLICT]

"Please take one," I instructed my writing class as I passed a box of rubber bands around the room.

Once everyone had a rubber band, I said, "Now, take your rubber band and stretch it a few times in your hand."

I took my own rubber band and pulled it back and forth, across and under my fingers. The writers in the room followed my example.

"This is tension," I told them. "Now, stretch it across your fingers and aim it at your neighbor."

It took a moment, but soon everyone had a rubber band aimed at someone near them.

"We've turned the tension up a notch," I said, smiling at the wincing and cringing individuals in front of me. "This is what you need a lot of in every scene of dialogue you write."

The tension created by a rubber band is weak compared to the kind of tension you want to create in your scenes of dialogue. Tension, suspense, and conflict should be at the core of every one of your dialogue scenes. No, this doesn't mean the characters need to be shouting at one another, fighting and raging, throwing things and brandishing weapons. Not at all. If this kind of tension and conflict is what your story calls for, of course, go for it. But the kind of tension, suspense, and conflict we're talking about here can range from one character subtly disagreeing with another character to such tightly strung words in a character's mouth that if he lets go, the force will do a thousand times more damage than letting go of a wimpy rubber band.

The horror writer Dean Koontz once wrote that most of the manuscripts he'd seen from new writers suffered from a lack of action more than anything else. I have always echoed that, but the more I coach writers, I'd have to now say that the absence of tension, suspense, and conflict is what I see manuscripts suffering from most. These are three different things, yet they can be lumped together because of their close association—they give movement to a scene. Dialogue without these three things is flat, one-dimensional, and boring. And as you know, no writer can afford to be boring. Not ever. Not even for one line of dialogue.

TENSION—THE KEY TO EFFECTIVE DIALOGUE

Readers live vicariously through the characters you create for them. Some stories inform our lives to the degree that we have made life choices based on them. How many attorneys have been inspired by Atticus Finch in *To Kill a Mockingbird?* Mathematicians by John Nash in *A Beautiful Mind?* Prep school dropouts by Holden Caulfield in *The Catcher in the Rye?* Okay, let's hope not. But you get the idea. Storytellers throw their characters into external and internal conflicts, then throw impossible obstacles at them, and readers are inspired as they turn page after page to see how these characters resolve their conflicts. Conflict is what stories are all about, and dialogue is the expression of that conflict. Without conflict, there's no story. Without dialogue, there's no expression of that conflict. How interesting would it be to read an entire novel with a character simply thinking about his conflict? Or moving around by himself to try to resolve it without talking to anyone else?

As things heat up for the viewpoint character in your dialogue scenes, you can present one, two, or three types of conflict, or all three at once: mental, verbal, or physical. The characters can play mind games with each other and harbor hateful or tormenting thoughts (mental). They can exchange heated and/or tense words (verbal). Or they can engage in violence or sex (physical). When conflict escalates to its peak, all three can take place in one scene. In this chapter, we'll give most of our attention to the verbal kinds of conflict where words are used as weapons.

IN SCENE OPENINGS

When opening a scene, and especially when opening a story, you want to insert tension as soon as possible because tension is what will engage your

Just for Fun

If you want practice writing dialogue with tension, try putting characters in tense scenes and letting them express their fear and anxiety. Write one or two pages of dialogue for all of the following:
- two characters on the edge of a cliff fighting—verbally and/or physically
- four characters at a card game
- two characters painting a room

reader most quickly. Tension and dialogue are the perfect combination because you have people in conflict. Pit your characters against each other right away in some kind of tense scene of dialogue and reader interest is assured.

In the opening scene of *Phantom* by Susan Kay, the author shows the viewpoint character delivering a baby, but not a normal baby. The story starts out with narrative that's tense, but the dialogue increases the tension even more as Madeleine begins to express her horror upon seeing her child for the first time. Here, Father Mansart is trying to comfort the new mother after her initial horror.

> "My dear child," he said compassionately. "Do not be deceived into believing that the Lord has abandoned you. Such tragedies as this are beyond all mortal understanding, but I ask you to remember that God does not create without purpose."
>
> I shivered. "It's still alive...isn't it?"
>
> He nodded, biting his full underlip and glancing sadly at the cradle.
>
> "Father" –I hesitated fearfully, trying to summon the courage to continue—"if I don't touch it...if I don't feed it..."
>
> He shook his head grimly. "The position of our Church is quite clear on such issues, Madeleine. What you are suggesting is murder."
>
> "But surely in this case it would be a kindness."
>
> "It would be a sin," he said severely, "a mortal sin! I urge you to put all thoughts of such wickedness from your mind. It is your duty to succor a human soul. You must nourish and care for this child as you would any other."

It's tricky to open a scene with dialogue because the reader needs some idea of the setting and who the characters are as they start talking. Once all

135

of that's established, the dialogue can take off and be the catalyst for all kinds of tension between the characters. *Phantom* begins with narrative. Madeleine, the viewpoint character, has just given birth to a freak of nature and is understandably upset.

When you begin a scene, any scene, you want to establish your character's intention right up front. You can do this either through narrative, action, or dialogue. Clearly, the viewpoint character's intention in this scene is to separate herself from her freakish newborn as fast as she can, and the only way that immediately comes to her is to simply neglect "it" and let it die. She puts her thoughts into words, which horrifies the priest at her side. Things are already tense as she realizes what she's produced, but the tension accelerates as Father Mansart heaps guilt on her for even allowing herself to think such a thought. When the tension in the dialogue accelerates, the reader knows things are really going to take off.

DEGREES OF TENSION

In fiction, when we speak of tension or conflict within the context of dialogue, our minds begin to immediately think of fighting, arguing, and verbal sparring, and yes, all of that can happen in a passage of tense dialogue. But it doesn't have to. There are degrees of tension, and when a character falls silent in the middle of a conversation, that can be as tense, maybe even more, than if the characters start shouting at each other. You know how they say that it's calm before the storm? Before certain people go over the edge, sometimes they're eerily quiet.

If you know your characters, you know which of them would exhibit this trait—the more tense a situation becomes, the more stressed out the character is and the more likely he is to grow quiet until he cracks. In a dialogue passage, you could show one character growing quiet by accelerating the dialogue of another character. This contrast would actually make the silence of the other character very loud, if you know what I mean. Whenever you want to emphasize something, put the opposite of whatever it is in the near vicinity.

When turning up the volume on your characters' voices as well as moving them into physical conflictive action, you're going over the top and you probably can't suspend this kind of tension for a long time, so keep it short. Excuse the graphic example here, but I recently heard that it took only ten minutes for a dog to kill a young woman in San Francisco. Ten minutes seems like such a short time when we think about an entire day or week. If we think about our entire lives, what's ten minutes? And can we even imagine the kind of tension in a real-life scene like this? I can't imagine anything worse, honestly. But if you're writing a similar scene in a story, comparatively speaking, you wouldn't want to go on and on with either dialogue or description. You would want to speed it up to the max, let it peak, and then bring it back down just as fast. Every once in a while, Stephen King can get away with pages of tension for one single dialogue scene, but, well, he's Stephen King.

The more you do this, the better you'll get at how much for how long. Check inside every so often and try to *feel* the scene the way the characters would. If the tension *feels* too drawn out, it probably is.

On the other hand, you don't want to cheat your reader out of the action, especially if you've been building up to it, so make sure the scene is long enough.

CONFLICT—THE CENTER OF TENSE DIALOGUE

At the center of every passage of dialogue should be some kind of conflict for the viewpoint character. This is often how you know whom to use as your viewpoint character—the one with the major conflict in the scene.

The conflict can be external or internal, but the reader must be able to feel the tension when the viewpoint character speaks. Ideally, this character is experiencing an internal conflict that he's unable to keep from expressing externally to another character. If he'd like to keep his thoughts to himself and can't, this alone creates tension.

When it comes to tension, you have to be careful that you don't have characters overacting to each other just because you know you need tension in the scene. I happen to see this quite often in the manuscripts of writers I work with. They have characters fighting just for the sake of fighting.

Above, I mentioned that story conflict can be verbal, physical, or mental. In the most intense conflictive scenes, the writer employs all three. There's no order that works best, although the physical would most often come last. It's true that some psychotic people can physically attack and then rant and rave for a long time after the attack, both playing with their victim's mind as well as berating him with words. But most often conflict between two people starts with words that can then become mind play and sometimes finally escalate into a physical attack.

The conflict at the center of a passage of dialogue doesn't have to be overt. The characters don't have to be arguing or beating each other up—with words or fists. There simply has to be something at stake for the viewpoint character, something to risk or lose, some kind of internal torment or crisis, some problem to resolve, an agenda that opposes the other characters, a decision to be made. The viewpoint character can struggle externally or internally or both.

I've worked with many writers who not only don't get the need for tension in their dialogue or even in their overall story, but they don't want to get it. They don't seem to want to work that hard at writing to make sure their stories not only grab but also keep the reader. Tension grabs and if sustained, doesn't let go. You want to be the kind of writer who is willing to rewrite as often as it takes to make sure each scene of dialogue can be just as tense and have as much suspense as possible. Don't you? Then you have to be willing to throw your characters into conflict after conflict.

I run into fiction writers quite often who seem to resist putting their characters in conflicts, and if they can be made to do it, the kinds of conflicts they finally come up with aren't really much for the reader to worry about. I sense that this is because these writers don't really want to create pain for their characters or hurt them in any way. They're basically nice folks who just want to write nice little stories where the characters have little minor problems to resolve. I tease the students in my fiction classes, telling them that if they want to write good fiction, they can't be too nice. It's too difficult for nice people to create problems for their characters. Fiction is about conflict and resolution. Characters resolving problems. The more serious, the better. The more desperate the character is to resolve his conflict, the more the reader is engaged in the story.

You're not too nice, are you?

TECHNIQUES TO TIGHTEN TENSION

When you're in control of your dialogue (chapter eight), you can release and tighten the tension at will. So the first goal is to always get in control. If you feel like you have control, here are some useful techniques to increase the tension when your characters are interacting.

Fixing Your Own Story

Take a look at all of the scenes in your story that end in dialogue and see if they're as full of tension as they can be. Ask yourself the following questions:

- What have I left open-ended in this passage of dialogue?
- Do I have my viewpoint character making the last statement and/or how does the last line of dialogue affect my viewpoint character?
- Have I pumped up the emotion in the last line of dialogue enough so the tension is palpable?
- Have I successfully showed in this passage of dialogue the collision of my characters' agendas?
- Have my characters' words to each other raised the stakes for my protagonist and created as much tension as possible?

Silence

As I mentioned earlier, one way to show tension during a passage of dialogue is to have your viewpoint character drop out of the conversation for moments here and there to evaluate the moment and how he feels about it. If he's thinking things he's not saying, for whatever reason, tension increases. Is he afraid to speak his real thoughts? Why? What will happen if he says these things out loud? You want to show the action continuing while the viewpoint character is silent, so let the other characters play out their parts, whether it's action or dialogue. Previously, we discussed contrast. It works. The louder the other characters are and the more they move around, the more tension you'll create by leaving your viewpoint character silent.

Anxiety

Consider what happens to your voice when you're anxious, afraid, nervous, excited, angry, or momentarily insane. Okay, first, you have to admit to these states of mind in order to observe your voice and demeanor in conversation. Most of us can acknowledge all but the last one. Who wants to admit to any kind of insanity, even momentary? Only the bravest soul, that's for sure. Momentary insanity is simply anxiety, fear, nervousness, excitement, and anger at their extremes. No big deal.

Anyway, let's take a look at human behavior, for that's always where we find the most authentic dialogue. In the following scene from *Postmortem* by Patricia Cornwell, the protagonist, Dr. Kay Scarpetta, is standing by as Sergeant Marino is interviewing a woman named Abby about her recently murdered sister. Watch how Abby's anxiety peaks as the scene progresses.

> "When was the last time you saw her?"
>
> "Friday afternoon." Her voice rose and caught. "She drove me to the train station." Her eyes were welling.
>
> Marino pulled a rumpled handkerchief out of a back pocket and handed it to her. "You have any idea what her plans for the weekend were?"
>
> "Work. She told me she was going to stay in, work on class preparation. As far as I know, she didn't have any plans. Henna wasn't very outgoing, had one or two good friends, other professors. She had a lot of class preparation, told me she would do the grocery shopping on Saturday. That's all."
>
> "And where was that? What store?"
>
> "I have no idea. It doesn't matter. I know she didn't go. The other policeman in here a minute ago had me check the kitchen. She didn't go to the grocery store. The refrigerator's as bare as it was when I left. It must have happened Friday night. Like the other ones. All weekend I've been in New York and she's been here. Been here like this."
>
> No one said anything for a moment. Marino was looking around the living room, his face unreadable. Abby shakily lit a cigarette and turned to me.
>
> I knew what she was going to ask before the words were out.
>
> "Is it like the other ones? I know you looked at her." She hesitated, trying to compose herself. She was like a violent storm about to break when she quietly asked, "What did he do to her?"
>
> I found myself giving her the "I won't be able to tell you anything until I've examined her in a good light" response.
>
> "For God's sake, she's my sister!" she cried. "I want to know what the animal did to her! Oh, God! Did she suffer? Please tell me she didn't suffer..."

Abby's pretty much losing it by the end of this scene—understandably. Any time your character encounters the kind of situation that sends her up the wall, you can count on increased tension. So, especially in mysteries or suspense thrillers, you want to keep moving your character from tense situation to tense situation, especially ones that involve other characters so the anxiety can be expressed in dialogue. Keep the anxiety up.

Strategic tagging

You can increase tension in small ways by stringing your sentences of dialogue out and inserting your tag in the middle of the sentence. *"I came looking for you," he whispered huskily, "never imagining I'd find you here."* Check out the difference between that sentence and the next two: *He whispered huskily, "I came looking for you, never imagining I'd find you here."* Or, *"I came looking for you, never imagining I'd find you here," he whispered huskily.* Can you see the difference? Say them out loud and hear how the rhythm adds tension to the first sentence that the next two don't have.

Pacing

We talk about the how-tos of pacing in other parts of the book, so I just want to mention here that to pace a scene of dialogue is to increase its tension. For example, if your character is in an agitated state and suddenly begins to talk slowly, it could mean he's gone over some edge. The opposite is also true. If a character is rambling on in his dialogue and suddenly becomes agitated and starts speaking very quickly, the edge is probably near, as well. Tension increases. Of course, there always has to be a reason for a sudden shift in the pace of dialogue. You can't just shift into either high or low gear for no reason.

Suspense

When you create suspense in a scene of dialogue, you automatically pump up the tension. The way to create suspense is to plant thoughts or ideas in the reader's mind that point to a future event or situation.

Here's a scene from *Garden of Lies* by Eileen Goudge. Watch the tension increase as Rachel tells David what her plans are if he doesn't do what she wants. He's her boyfriend, but he's also a doctor and she wants him to perform an abortion on her—to abort *their* baby. He's just basically told her she's crazy, that she needs a "shrink."

> "...That's what you need, baby. Yeah. You've really gone over the edge this time."
>
> "Maybe," she said. "But that doesn't change anything. We're still in this together, one way or another."
>
> "What do you mean?" His eyes were narrowed, suspicious.
>
> "I mean that if you won't perform the abortion, there won't be one. I'll have the baby."
>
> "Are you threatening me?"

"No." And she meant that too. "I'm just telling you what's possible for me. What choices I can live with. Having your friend Kelleher do a nice neat D and C on me isn't one of them."

Having the baby, of course, is no better than getting an abortion in David's eyes, maybe even worse. So what will Rachel do? And how will David react? Goudge successfully engages the reader with a few lines of suspenseful dialogue that point to a future event. If you can use your dialogue to do this all the way through a story, you'll never lose your reader—not for a moment.

IN SCENE ENDINGS

You can use a character's words at the very end of a scene to create the kind of tension that will compel the reader to keep turning the pages, no matter that it's the end of a chapter and he had planned right then to turn out the light and go to sleep. The trick is to leave things open-ended. Too often, we think the end of the scene or chapter is the place to neatly tie things up. Nothing could be further from the truth. You want to do the exact opposite. You want to leave things hanging. As many things as possible.

Also, if your viewpoint character makes a statement that increases the tension and causes another character or the reader to gasp, you don't need to let the other character respond and then include the moral and everything else to bring things to a tidy ending. You always want to end a scene with either a statement by your viewpoint character or one that will affect your viewpoint character. A statement that is suspenseful and will compel the reader to keep reading into the next chapter to see what happens. Sometimes a question works. Or a reaction just left hanging.

In real life, when someone makes a startling or shocking statement and no one says anything, the words are suspended in air and are much more powerful and influential than when others around that person begin to fill in the emptiness with their own words or reactions.

Rita Mae Brown is an expert at this in her novel *Venus Envy*. The story is about a woman, Frazier, who goes into the hospital thinking she has cancer and "comes out" to everyone that she's gay, then finds out that someone made a mistake and she doesn't have cancer after all. Now she has to live and deal with the mess she created by coming out. Without even knowing the events of each chapter, let's just look at the dialogue Brown uses to close some of her chapters.

- "I can see I'm getting nowhere with you. You won't be content until you ruin this family. Why? So you can be queer?" Libby was ripshit. "The only people who are queer are the people who don't love anybody. That means you, Momma. You are incapable of love!" Frazier slammed down the phone so hard she scared the cat.
- "...Maybe every human being has only one question to answer—" Carter, listening intently, interrupted: "What's that?" "Do you want to live or do you want to die?"
- Frank sighed. "What this town needs is an enema."
- As Kimberly left, Sara and Frazier sat for a moment. "Sarah, I get the feeling people would have preferred that I died. It would be better than having to face things. Or maybe saying that they want me dead is too strong. Maybe they just want me to get a pink slip, you know, so I could be excused from life."

The author clearly knows the effectiveness of this technique, which is why she uses it so often and so well. I'm guessing she really gave her chapter endings a lot of thought to come up with a tense line that would create enough suspense so the reader has to keep turning the pages. And notice how she doesn't go on to the other characters' reactions. She just leaves us with the one shocking line of dialogue.

Sometimes it can be difficult to leave our characters' words hanging, but it works wonders for suspense and tension.

Is there anything that creates more drama, more suspense and tension, than people's feelings? Feelings create wars between individuals and nations, and at the same time create mutually loving relationships. In the next chapter, we'll explore how dialogue can convey our characters' feelings so as to engage our reader at an emotional level.

EXERCISE 1

Scene openings. Go through some of the novels on your bookshelf—preferably the ones you've read—and study the scene and chapter openings. How hard did the author work to grab the reader with dialogue to get the action rolling and bring the characters to life? Choose at least five scene or chapter openings and rewrite them, using dialogue that will pull the reader into the scene or story. Go over the top and be as outrageous as you can. Doing this exercise will free you to think out of the box. Now go through any of the stories you're in the middle of writing and see if you can write more compelling scene openings using dialogue.

Conflict—the center of tense dialogue. Write two pages of tense dialogue for each of these conflictive scenarios:

- a character who is keeping a secret from another character, while trying to make small talk
- a character who is being forced to go against her value system in a job setting; she's in dialogue with her boss
- a male character who has just discovered that his best friend has slept with his (the first character's) girlfriend; the two friends are at a bar playing pool

Techniques to tighten tension. Write one page of dialogue for each of the five techniques we discussed earlier in this chapter:

- Silence – Put a character in a scene that creates such intense feeling for him that he doesn't trust himself to speak. Show the other characters around him chattering away.
- Anxiety – Put a character in a scene that creates such anxiety for her that she begins to feel out of control on the inside and the more she talks about it, the more anxiety she feels.
- Strategic tagging – Rewrite the following sentences so as to string them out and increase the tension; put the tag in the middle of the sentence:

"I'm not sure I can do the job unless there's something in it for me," he said.

She looked at him and said, "I love you, but I'm not free to start another relationship right now."

"If you do it quickly and carefully, they'll never hear a sound," she said.

- Pacing – Put a character in a situation that is increasing in tension and let his dialogue match the increasing tension.
- Suspense – Put a character in a scene of dialogue in which she's trying to find a

way to tell another character about something that's going to happen in the future.

Scene endings. Now go through the novels on your bookshelf—again, preferably the ones you've read—and study the scene and chapter endings. How hard did the author work to write dialogue endings, or even narrative endings, that were tense and suspenseful? Choose at least five weak endings and rewrite them, ending each with one final line of startling dialogue. Then, if you're in the middle of writing a short story or novel, check out your scene endings and see if there's a line of dialogue you can tack on that will startle the reader and compel her to read on, even though she has to get up early the next morning.

chapter 10

[IT WAS A DARK AND STORMY NIGHT—USING DIALOGUE TO SET THE MOOD AND FACILITATE THE EMOTION]

"I'd rather be working at Taco Bell!" I told my friend as I climbed out of her car after a heated discussion about my current editorial job. Nothing wrong with Taco Bell, you understand—that's not the point. The point is I was over-the-top tired, angry, frustrated, disappointed, and done with my job. I spoke those words with so much emotion that they haunted me for days and I eventually quit my job.

The words that you say, scream, or whisper to others with the most emotion are the ones you remember. The words that others say, scream, or whisper to you with the most emotion are the ones you remember.

We want our stories to be memorable for our readers. We want to create characters who are unforgettable. In order to do this, we must write dialogue that is full of emotion. It doesn't matter whether the emotion is fear, sadness, joy, or anger. What matters is that our characters are emotionally engaged with the situations and conflicts we've created for them, and that they're conveying their feelings to one another through dialogue that is charged with emotion. Charged and super-charged. Turbo-charged. The more emotion, the better.

I didn't say melodrama, I said emotion. There's a difference. We're not writing soap operas. The emotion in a scene of dialogue is what draws your reader into your characters' situational conflict and makes her care about the problems facing the character. Every bit of dialogue in your story must convey some kind of emotion. What you have to decide is what kind. This is determined by the kind of story you're writing and what is going on for the characters in any one particular scene.

I see new writers make a lot of mistakes when it comes to writing emotional dialogue. This usually comes from trying too hard:

- characters cracking jokes and laughing uproariously when the jokes aren't funny
- characters crying and sobbing all over each other to the point that the reader is watching, going, "Yeah, yeah, get on with it."
- characters who are full of fury when the situation amounts to something like a stubbed toe or a broken fingernail

We create characters that go over the top and are inappropriate in the expression of their emotions because we (1) are not able to access our own emotions and therefore act inappropriately ourselves, or (2) we're trying to make a point in our story and think extreme emotion is the way to do it.

More often, I see the other extreme. Writers that underplay the emotion:

- A character loses her husband, whether to an affair or death, and goes to her Bridge Club the next night, the main concern on her mind getting the recipe for the cranberry cucumber salad.
- A female character hears a noise, and with no fear, grabs a baseball bat and runs down the dark basement stairs to confront the burglar.
- A character loses his job only to tell his wife when he gets home that he knows he deserved to be fired—no anger, just acceptance.

We create characters who deny and repress their emotions because we deny and repress our own.

As a writing coach, I'm often frustrated that I can't help writers with this aspect of their storytelling. I joke that writers need therapy to be able to write well, but somewhere down deep, I think I really believe that.

Whether or not you get therapy is up to you. In the meantime, there are some practical things you can do to make sure your dialogue is full of the kind of emotion that grabs readers and makes your characters memorable. In this chapter, we'll take a few common emotions and see how dialogue can be used to show these emotions through your characters. But first, let's talk about how the use of emotion can establish your story's mood.

SETTING THE MOOD

"I hate you!"

"I don't want to live…"

"I won!"

"Don't you dare move—"

These are strong statements. When we, as real-life people, are emoting, we express ourselves in a variety of physical ways. We may punch a wall, grit our teeth, or clap our hands—any number of physical movements. But at some point, we talk. To ourselves or someone else. One of the most effective ways to reveal our characters' emotions is to let them talk. Out loud, whether whispering or yelling. Interwoven with action and narrative.

Cartoonists have it made. They can simply draw a mad, sad, happy, or scared face on their cartoon figures and we know immediately what's going on with the characters in the present moment. Likewise, scriptwriters have real actors to work with. The audience will see the frowns, the tears, the smiles, and the eyes wide with fear.

Writers don't have these luxuries. Our only tool is words and we must put those words in our characters' mouths so our reader will know what our characters' emotional states are at each present moment. The only way to connect with our reader on an emotional level is to first connect with our characters. The way we do this is to make sure our characters connect with themselves.

This isn't a self-help book on the psychology of human emotions, but many of us don't slow down enough to feel our feelings on a moment-by-moment basis. However, whether or not we know how we feel, we are continually giving off signals to others. The same is true of our characters. While they may not be able to tell you how they feel unless another character asks them, their behavior and words will give them away. You'll know, no matter how they try to hide their feelings. We can only hide our real feelings for so long.

The feelings of anger, sadness, joy, and fear are primary, although we might have a range of other more minor feelings that come and go: jealousy, confusion, frustration, etc. These other minor feelings are more states of being, so in this chapter we'll deal with the primary feelings and learn how we can use dialogue to set a mood in our story.

LOVE

Regardless of what you think of *The Bridges of Madison County* (some read-

Just for Fun

Do you want your reader to know what your character is feeling? Use dialogue. When your character opens her mouth and speaks, she immediately reveals her emotional state of being, which is very powerful and very effective. You can use the following exercises to practice using dialogue to show your character expressing emotion. They all involve at least two characters so you can use dialogue as the primary vehicle to show the specific emotion. Write a one-page scene of dialogue for each scenario. Feel free to modify any of the scenes to fit your own needs.

[1] Your character and his best friend are driving down the freeway minding their own business when an older vehicle sideswipes your character's brand-new SUV and then keeps driving. What are the first angry words out of his mouth?

[2] Your character and her boyfriend are out to dinner at an upscale restaurant. The boyfriend has just told your viewpoint character that he wants to break up, that he doesn't love her anymore. Without using tears, let your character express her shock and sadness through dialogue.

[3] Your character has just landed his dream job. He will be doing work he loves and getting paid more than he ever imagined. He's sitting in the office of his future employer. He can hardly contain himself, he's so excited. He blurts out how he feels.

[4] Your character and her boyfriend have been hiking since early in the morning. It's now dusk and they realize they are hopelessly lost. Your viewpoint character is growing increasingly anxious on the inside. Suddenly she's terrified and expresses it out loud.

[5] Your character has just learned that his emotionally unavailable father has died. He's in his therapist's office, and feeling numb. When he asks him what he'll miss most about his father, suddenly he's no longer numb and has a lot to say.

ers loved it, many hated it; personally, I'm a sucker for mushy love stories), there's an effective bit of dialogue in the middle of a love scene between Francesca Johnson and Robert Kincaid. I even heard Oprah read this bit of dialogue on her show when the author, Robert James Waller, was her guest.

The story is about a man who waltzes into a woman's life for four days and waltzes back out again, taking her heart with him and leaving behind a part of his own. That's basically it. Well, I doubt that's the synopsis Waller turned into his agent or editor, but it's pretty close. The following line of dialogue was spoken as Francesca tried to get Robert to understand why she couldn't just leave her husband and kids to follow him across the backcountry roads of Iowa and off into the sunset. It was about responsibility.

> Robert Kincaid was silent. He knew what she was saying about the road and responsibilities and how the guilt could transform her. He knew she was right, in a way. Looking out the window, he fought within himself, fought to understand her feelings. She began to cry.
>
> Then they held each other for a long time. And he whispered to her: "I have one thing to say, one thing only, I'll never say it another time, to anyone, and I ask you to remember it. In a universe of ambiguity, this kind of certainty comes only once, and never again, no matter how many lifetimes you live."

Women readers swooned over this line in the book. Is there a woman anywhere in the world who wouldn't give anything to hear that special someone say those words to her? To be thought of as that special?

But what specifically makes these words connect with readers so effectively? And how can you create the kind of emotional dialogue that can convey a character's feelings of love in a tone that's both genuine and authentic?

You might be writing a love scene or coming to that point in your story where your character is full of feelings of love—for another character, an animal, a setting. How can she express herself without sounding corny, melodramatic, or like a character in a novel, which, of course, is exactly what she is?

One reason the above passage works so well is because there is both conflict and resolution. These two people want what they can't have, what they can't make happen. So they're both torn, even though deep down they both know that Francesca will do the *right* thing because that's who she is. It's all right there in those two paragraphs. And we can identify with the certainty that Robert is talking about. We've felt that way.

As human beings, we are afraid of intimacy with other human beings. And love is very intimate. So what's important to remember when creating a love scene between two characters, whether it leads to sex or not, is that your character is simultaneously feeling both fear and love. To make the scene feel authentic, you have to capture both feelings at once in the same character—sometimes in both characters, since it takes two to tango, or tangle, as the case may be in a love scene that leads to sex.

How is this done? By practicing. The more comfortable you are with real love scenes, the more comfortable your characters will be. You may have to put your characters in a number of love scenes and various settings to come up with one that works. Keep in mind that a love scene doesn't always mean a sex scene. What we're after is a feeling of love. That could be between parent and child or between friends just as easily as it could be a romantic feeling between a man and a woman. Sometimes jumping to sex between a man and woman is to actually short circuit the feeling of love that is surfacing for the couple. If you really want to develop a love relationship between two characters, take your time and reveal it gradually through the dialogue as they grow closer.

ANGER

The emotion of anger expresses itself in many different ways. Watch what makes you angry so you can access your anger and authentically use it in your dialogue scenes. You also want to watch what makes others angry and how they express it, which will often be very different than how you do.

Let's look at a passage from Michael Dorris' novel *A Yellow Raft in Blue Water.* Here we have a character whose mother abandoned her ten years before, leaving her with her grandmother. She's just a little upset about that. Her mother, who doesn't quite have her head on straight, is also angry. When people are angry, they blame, defend, say things they don't mean, and say things they do mean. The words usually rush out without much thought given to them. Here, the viewpoint character, Rayona, is finally taking advantage of the opportunity to blast her mother for abandoning her so many years before.

> I'm so used to being Mom's daughter, I defend myself.
>
> "I meant to get in touch," I say.
>
> "You meant to, you meant to!" Mom pulls the sash of her robe tight and ties it in a knot. "That's just great. Here I am, sick as a dog, and you're off..."
>
> "I was working at Bearpaw Lake State Park."

"Having fun!" Mom shouts. "At some park."

"But you left first."

"That's right, blame me." Mom turns to Dayton. "It's my fault she walked out on her grandmother. Of course."

"Now don't get yourself all upset," he says. "When you calm down, you're going to be glad to see Ray."

"I thought something happened to you!" Mom screams at me. It's the worst thing yet she's said.

"A lot you cared." I've got my second wind. "You could come for your box of pills from Charlene, but not for me."

That stops her. "How did you know it was pills?"

"And all that time, here you are, not ten miles away. Don't tell me about leaving."

"She has no heart!" Mom appeals to Dayton. "She wants to hurt me, sick as I am."

"You tried that on Dad and it didn't work." I'm mad beyond the bounds of what's fair. "You're not sick."

But of course she is. I see it the minute the words are out of my mouth. In some part of my brain it has been registering every since the car stopped. She's ragged, pale. There are new wrinkles in the skin of her forehead, thin lines that stretch like threads above her eyebrows. Her cheeks are hollow but her waist has thickened.

"You're just like him," she says to me in a voice tied to a rock. "In every way."

What makes this dialogue scene work so well is that it feels so real. Angry people in conversation don't often make a lot of sense, and the train of thought in a conversation can't often be followed because there really isn't one. They're just throwing out whatever they can to hurt each other and to defend their own position, all the while not wanting the other to see their raw underbelly.

Most often, when your characters become engaged in anger, you want to speed the scene up. Use shorter sentences and paragraphs, less narrative. An angry slower-paced scene works, too, and is often even scarier because it could mean an explosion is on the horizon. See the second bullet below, the slow burn. Carie is holding it together, but if this scene was to continue, and Matt was to keep arguing with her, this character would inevitably erupt in angry threats and accusations.

For example, the words "I hate you" may be spoken loudly and with one's body shaking. The words "I hate you" may also be spoken softly and coldly and with one's body tense. Hatred is not a feeling—it's a state of being. Anger is the feeling. And we get angry for a myriad of reasons, less often as we grow older, I've been pleased to discover. How much anger we hold inside of us all depends on how much we work on ourselves during our lives, expressing that anger and dealing with the root causes. This is one reason it's important to create a character chart before writing your story so you know your character well enough to know what will make her angry. As I mentioned above, the same things do not make the same people angry. You know how we tell each other not to talk about religion or politics because of the strong feelings these subjects evoke in us. Well, the truth is, you can talk politics all you want, and I won't even feel one tense muscle. But if you start in on religion, you'll be taking your life in your hands talking to me. This is the kind of thing you want to know about your character. What causes her anger—at every level? What frustrates her? What peeves her? What can create the kind of internal rage that causes her to lose control of herself in a matter of moments? Do you know?

This is one step toward knowing your character from the inside out. But you must also know your character from the outside in. Once feeling that anger, how does she express it physically and verbally? Some of us become unnaturally quiet. Others of us immediately vent our anger on whoever happens to be nearby. Few of us, it seems, understand how to be angry and take responsibility for that anger without blaming someone for the cause of the anger. Many of us try to deny we're even angry because we're not comfortable with this feeling. Which is it for your character? You'll want to know this about her before putting her in a situation in which her buttons are pushed. Let's look at three different ways a fictional character might express his anger in the exact same situation. As a young couple, Matt and Carie are saving for their first home so they can start a family, and Carie has just learned that Matt has gambled away their savings.

• Denial.

> "We have that appointment with the mortgage broker tomorrow, remember."
> Carie spooned some mashed potatoes on her plate.
>
> "Why bother? The money's gone." Matt's voice was flat.

"You couldn't possibly gamble away that much money—that was more than $20,000. You wouldn't do that. We've been saving for five years." Matt wouldn't do that. He must have been drinking and it felt like he was spending it all. How could he even get access to all of their savings in one night? "It's just not possible, that's all." Carie shook her head. "It can't be gone, not all of it. We've been saving. All of these years we've been putting away money every single week—out of our paychecks. Going without things we really needed. No, I know you like to gamble, but you must have figured wrong."

Matt just sat there staring at his plate. The silence in the room was deafening.

- The slow burn.

"You what?" Carie spooned some mashed potatoes on her plate. "You didn't say what I just thought you said."

"You heard right." He ducked his head. "The money's gone. That weekend I went to Vegas for that business trip? I was winning... I started off the night winning and well, before I knew it—"

"Get out." Carie stared at her plate. "Get out right now before I throw you out."

"Huh? What do you mean get out? This is my home, too—"

"Not any more it's not." Her voice sounded far away, even to her. "This is the last time. I'm filing for divorce tomorrow. You'll never do this to me again."

- The explosion.

"We have that appointment with the mortgage broker tomorrow, honey. This is it. We're finally going to be able to do it. After all these years of saving. I'm so excited—"

"It's gone..."

"What?" Carie stared at Matt, her forkful of mashed potatoes halfway to her mouth. She let it clatter to her plate. "What did you say? What's gone?"

"The money. That night in Vegas—that business trip I took. I started out winning. I don't know what happened. Before I knew it—"

"What?" she cried. "You're telling me all of our money, twenty thousand dollars, is gone?"

"That's what I'm saying. You catch on quick."

"No! Omigod! Are you out of your mind? How could you do that?" She was standing now, towering over him, grabbing her fork, raising it above her head.

He looked up at her with that sheepish grin she used to love. "This is how it's going to end? Our marriage? You're going to stab me with a fork?"

She looked up at her fork, then slumped back into her chair and dissolved into tears.

Matt rose and stood beside her, putting a hand on her shoulder. "Honey—"

"Don't touch me!" she said, shaking off his hand. "I hate you! I can't believe I married such a loser. You've always been a loser, I just couldn't see it." She was screaming now. "Leave! Now!" She stood to face him, his face inches from hers. "Get out of this house and out of my life!"

FEAR

Showing the emotion of fear in a character is again a matter of knowing your character so you know what she'll do and say when scared. I remember standing in the airport with a bunch of my friends on the day of my very first airplane ride. I couldn't even talk, I was that scared. It's funny because other times when I'm scared, I chatter on endlessly. So it also depends on the situation. One thing for sure in a passage of dialogue where you want to indicate a character's fear—there's tension. Fear creates tension, not just in the person who's afraid, but also in everyone in that person's energy field.

Mystery and suspense thriller writers must become masters of revealing this emotion in their characters because that's what readers of this kind of story are looking for. Mary Higgins Clark has written a large number of novels with the emotion of fear at the core of each story. Following is a passage from *While My Pretty One Sleeps*. Note especially the pace of the scene.

The door to Sal's showroom was open. She ran in and closed it behind her. The room was empty. "Sal!" she called, almost panicked. "Uncle Sal!"

He hurried from his private office. "Neeve, what's the matter?"

"Sal, I think someone is following me." Neeve grasped his arm. "Lock the door, please."

Sal stared at her. "Neeve, are you sure?"

"Yes. I've seen him three or four times."

Those dark deep-set eyes, the sallow skin. Neeve felt the color run from her face. "Sal," she whispered, "I know who it is. He works in the coffee shop."

"Why would he be following you?"

"I don't know." Neeve stared at Sal. "Unless Myles was right all along. Is it possible Nicky Sepetti wanted me dead?"

The author weaves the dialogue and action so you get a picture of a scared character. Read the scene again and pull out the actions: She's running into the room, grasping his arm, and the color is draining from her face. She uses short sentences, which always make a scene speed up:

"I think someone is following me."

"Lock the door, please."

"I know who it is."

"Is it possible Nicholas Sepetti wanted me dead?"

The emotion of fear speeds everything up and makes it all stand still at the same time. The protagonist's thoughts, words, and actions are accelerated while the story stops for just a moment as the reader assimilates what's going on in the scene and feels the danger, whatever it is.

Fixing Your Own Story

Choose the character in your story that seems the most flat and one-dimensional. You've tried to get to know him, but he's not coming through the way you'd like him to. The problem could be that the emotions he needs to express in the story are ones you yourself are uncomfortable with.

Decide that you're going to let go of this character for just one scene. Let 'er rip. Undo the leash and let him say anything he wants. If that means screaming, throwing things, crying, even killing someone, let him do it. Give him full reign and see if he comes to life for you. If you need a little help, here are three possible scenarios you could use to bring out his emotion:

- He's at a Little League game with his ten-year-old son when the umpire makes a bad call. (anger)
- He has just realized he's in love with the heroine in your story. They're in bed together, and he wants to tell her. He's overcome by emotion. (love)
- The phone is ringing and he picks it up to hear a representative from the IRS identifying herself, telling him they're planning an audit. He cheated on his income tax this year. (fear)

JOY

For a new writer, getting something published is a big deal. I know of no writer who would dispute that. Over the years I've seen a variety of joyful responses. One writer might happen to mention to a friend, "Oh, my story came out in *The Atlantic Monthly* last week," while another might make twenty-five phone calls and carry her published story around in her purse to show everyone. I spotted my very first published article in a magazine on the newsstand, grabbed it and ran around to all the store clerks, holding it up and shrieking like a crazy woman.

Joy, like fear and anger, shows itself in a variety of ways. A character who's normally introverted and quiet may simply share her joy in a few brief sentences of peaceful contentment, while the more extroverted character may shriek and cry out her excitement while jumping up and down, eyes lighting up and hands flailing—like I did when I saw my article in the magazine. What do you do when feeling joy?

In the following passage from Iris Ranier Dart's novel *Beaches,* you'll find a combination of emotions. It's especially effective when you can combine positive and painful emotions in the same passage of dialogue, giving the reader one wild emotional roller coaster ride. The author does this so well in this passage as Cee Cee and Bertie, two best friends, are sharing an incredible moment—a very happy event for Bertie while the same event is destroying Cee Cee.

> They walked silently again for a long time until Bertie broke the silence again.
>
> "Cee Cee," she said. "I did it."
>
> Later, when she thought about the conversation, Cee Cee remembered that the minute Bertie said those words, she knew exactly what Bertie had done and with whom, but she was hoping (God, are you listening?) she was wrong.
>
> "Did what?" Cee Cee asked, and she stopped walking.
>
> "Got laid. By John."
>
> Cee Cee couldn't speak. It was a joke. Now Bertie would say, "It's a joke, Cee. You didn't believe me, did you?"
>
> "Oh, boy, I didn't mean to blurt it out like that," she said instead. "To say I got laid—which is really an awful way to put it, because it wasn't like that. We made love. I mean, we really made love, and it was so neat, Cee Cee, not like it probably would be with someone my own age. He was so gentle and sweet.

And you want to know the funny thing?"

"Yes," Cee Cee managed to say. Oh, God, yes, she wanted to know the funny thing. Let the funny thing be that this was a lie, and that everything she was picturing now that was making her feel weak wasn't true.

"The funny thing is that I don't feel guilty, and I don't feel dirty, and I'm not the least bit in love with him. You know the old myth about the man you give your virginity to being the first man you fall in love with. Well, I'm not. And I think that's really great."

But I am! Cee Cee screamed inside. Outside, she just stood there, looking at the ocean, unable to look at Bertie. Beautiful Bertie. With John Perry.

"I'd never tell another soul, Cee," Bertie said hastily. "I mean, I'm not embarrassed or ashamed, because he's a wonderful person and everything, and I'm glad it could be with him my first time, but I had to tell you."

A chill came over Cee Cee and she wished she'd brought a shawl.

Because we're in Cee Cee's point of view, this passage may feel like it's more about sadness and jealousy than it is about joy. But Bertie's pretty thrilled about what just happened. She's excitedly telling her friend about something that she's been wanting for a long time. When showing a character's happiness or excitement through dialogue, you don't want to rely on the exclamation point to convey the emotion. You'll notice there are no exclamation points in the above passage. The dialogue is worded in such a way that we can feel Bertie's thrill about her news as well as Cee Cee's sadness. This scene would have been interesting in Bertie's point of view, too, but there's more suspense with Cee Cee's viewpoint as she's thinking a lot of sad thoughts she can't possibly say out loud.

What makes this scene work so well is the way the author alternated Bertie's words and Cee Cee's thoughts so we get the feeling of both happiness and sadness simultaneously.

SADNESS

The emotion of sadness is often the most difficult to show in a scene of dialogue only because it's so easy to slip into melodrama. I once read that "if your character cries, your reader doesn't have to," and it seems to be true. Once characters start shedding tears, for some reason the reader seems to want to resist the emotion. So you want to try to show your characters' sorrow using something besides tears. Dialogue is good just because a character can talk about what's going on in his life in a way that moves the reader, but without melodrama, because the truth is, when it comes time for most of us real folks (as compared to fictional characters) to emote about our lives, we tend to hold back rather than to break forth with tears or angry words or even admit that we're scared of something. We just don't want to make ourselves that vulnerable to others.

In the following scene from the novel *Terms of Endearment* by Larry McMurtry, the prevailing emotion is sadness. These two little boys, Tommy and Teddy, are losing their mother, who is dying of cancer. Everyone is trying to remain strong, and they all have their own way of doing so. But we can feel the intense sadness in the way they talk to each other.

> Teddy had meant to be reserved, but he couldn't manage. His feelings rushed up, became words. "Oh, I really don't want you to die," he said. He had a husky little voice. "I want you to come home."
>
> Tommy said nothing.
>
> ...
>
> "Well, both of you better make some friends,' Emma said. "I'm sorry about this, but I can't help it. I can't talk to you too much longer either, or I'll get too upset. Fortunately we had ten or twelve years and we did a lot of talking, and that's more than a lot of people get. Make some friends and be good to them. Don't be afraid of girls, either."
>
> "We're not afraid of girls," Tommy said. "What makes you think that?"
>
> "You might get to be later," Emma said.
>
> "I doubt it," Tommy said, very tense.
>
> When they came to hug her Teddy fell apart and Tommy remained stiff.
>
> "Tommy, be sweet," Emma said. "Be sweet, please. Don't keep pretending you dislike me. That's silly."
>
> "I like you," Tommy said, shrugging tightly.
>
> "I know that, but for the last year or two you've been pretending you hate me," Emma said. "I know I love you more than anybody in the world except your brother and sister, and I'm not going to be around long enough to change my mind about you. But you're going to live a long time, and in a year or two when I'm not around to irritate you you're going to change your mind and remember that I read you a lot of stories and made you a lot of milkshakes and allowed you to goof off a lot when I could have been forcing you to mow the lawn."
>
> Both boys looked away, shocked that their mother's voice was so weak.
>
> "In other words, you're going to remember that you love me," Emma said.

"I imagine you'll wish you could tell me that you've changed your mind, but you won't be able to, so I'm telling you now I already know you love me, just so you won't be in doubt about that later. Okay?"

"Okay," Tommy said quickly, a little gratefully.

Nobody's crying in this scene, and there's even some anger being expressed. But it's incredibly sad because this mother is dying and trying to redeem in this one last encounter with her sons every moment she's been a less than perfect mom. When your dialogue is poignant and honest enough, you don't need to get your characters crying to indicate just how sad they are. I remember how moved I was when I first read these words from a mother to her son: *"... I'm telling you now I already know you love me, just so you won't be in doubt about that later."* What incredible love—that she would contain her son's love for her when he couldn't speak the words himself. This would protect him from later guilt and shame over not being able to say the words himself when he had the opportunity. In that sense there is both amazing love and incredible sorrow in the same passage of dialogue. What an emotional ride for the reader.

PEACE

Showing a character at peace with himself is to show a state of being, but it's also to show an emotion in that it's a calmness exhibited by a character who has resolved or is resolving the issues in his life that have caused him so much confusion and stress. The challenge is to put him in a scene of dialogue that includes tension, because a character at peace isn't often a character with much drama. And drama is what readers require.

In the following scene from *The Prince of Tides* by Pat Conroy, Tom Wingo is telling his mistress (and therapist, but that's beside the point), Susan Lowenstein, that he's finally decided to go back to his wife. He's at peace with his decision, but you can imagine how she feels.

Over wine I asked, "What do you feel like eating tonight, Lowenstein?"

In silence, she watched me for a moment, then said, "I plan to order a perfectly lousy meal. I don't want to have anything like a wonderful meal on the night you say goodbye to me forever."

"I'm going back to South Carolina, Lowenstein," I said, reaching over and squeezing her hand. "That's where I belong."

...

"What happened?"

"My character rose to the surface," I said. "I didn't have the courage to leave my wife and children to make a new life with you. It's just not in me. You'll have to forgive me, Lowenstein. One part of me wants you more than anything else in the world. The other part of me is terrified of any major change in my life. That's the strongest part."

"But you love me, Tom," she said.

"I didn't know it was possible to be in love with two women at the same time."

"Yet you chose Sallie."

"I chose to honor my own history," I said. "If I were a braver man, I could do it."

...

"I've got to try to make something out of the ruins, Lowenstein," I said, looking into her eyes. "I don't know if I'll succeed, but I've got to try."

...

"Have you told Sallie about us, Tom?"

"Yes," I said.

"Then you used me, Tom," she said.

"Yes," I said. "I used you, Susan, but not before I started loving you."

"If you liked me enough, Tom..."

"No, Lowenstein. I adore you. You've changed my life. I've felt like a whole man again. An attractive man. A sensual one. You've made me face it all and you made me think I was doing it to help my sister."

"So this is how the story ends," she said.

"I believe so, Lowenstein," I answered.

"Then let's make our last night perfect," she said, kissing my hand, then slowly kissing each one of my fingers as the building swayed in a strong wind from the north.

Some of the tension in this scene comes from Tom and Susan being in two different places. He's going back to his wife and she's having a difficult time letting go of him.

The other part of the tension is Tom's admission that he's torn. He cares about Susan and wants her, but he also wants his wife. And he knows he's a man of character and so he could never leave his wife and kids without tremendous guilt, which would be toxic to his relationship with Susan anyway.

In this scene, Lowenstein continues, making sure that he's sure:

"...on the night you say good-bye to me forever."

"But you love me, Tom."

"Yet you chose Sallie."

"Then you used me, Tom."

"If you liked me enough, Tom."

He continues to answer her, confident in his decision, although he's still able to acknowledge what he's losing:

"That's where I belong."

"My character rose to the surface."

"I chose to honor my own history."

"I've got to make something out of the ruins."

The above lines of dialogue reveal where both of these characters are. As the protagonist, Tom is at peace about his decision, but the other emotion that comes through here is sadness, although no one ever uses the word, and Conroy himself doesn't use it in the narrative. But the dialogue creates the sad feeling in us because we're watching two people who love each other but can't be together.

COMPASSION

Like peace, the emotion of compassion, sympathy, or empathy is often a fairly nondramatic one, so it's your job to find a way to bring some drama to it. I honestly had a difficult time finding a published passage where compassion was the prevalent emotion, leading me to believe that maybe compassion doesn't make good drama.

Anne Tyler is one of my favorite writers because she's so good at creating all kinds of emotion in her characters, but in a subtle, matter-of-fact kind of way, it kind of hits you in the gut. The following is a scene from her novel *Breathing Lessons*. The protagonist, Maggie, is sitting in a hospital waiting room with two strangers—another woman and a man in coveralls. Suddenly, from a nearby room comes a nurse's voice as she talks to a patient.

"Now, Mr. Plum, I'm giving you this jar for urine."

"My what?"

"Urine."

"How's that?"

"It's for urine."

"Speak up—I can't hear you."

"*Urine*, I said. You take this jar home twenty-four hours! You bring the jar back!"

In the chair across from Maggie, the wife ⟨…⟩ deaf as a doorknob," she told Maggie. "Has to hav⟨…⟩ all and sundry to hear."

Maggie smiled and shook her head, not knowing h⟨…⟩ Then the man in coveralls stirred. He placed his great, furry⟨…⟩ He cleared his throat. "You know," he said, "it's the funniest t⟨…⟩ that nurse's voice all right but I don't understand a single word s⟨…⟩

Maggie's eyes filled with tears. She dropped her magazine and⟨…⟩ her purse for a Kleenex, and the man said, "Lady? You okay?"

She couldn't tell him it was his kindness that had undone her—such⟨…⟩ cacy, in such an unlikely looking person...

Maggie is so moved by this man's compassion as he pretends not to hear what the nurse is saying, in order to save a complete stranger, the patient's wife, from humiliation. Now, the man in coveralls isn't the viewpoint character so we can't feel the compassion from inside of the character speaking, but we can certainly feel it through his dialogue and Maggie's fearful response. One line: *"I can catch that nurse's voice all right but I don't understand a single word she's saying."*

Sometimes it doesn't take much. One line.

Setting a mood and conveying a character's emotions through dialogue is one of the most effective ways to bring your story to life on the page. Creating tense dialogue is one thing, but creating tense dialogue that is also full of a character's fear, or sorrow, or joy is another. This is the stuff that moves readers so that they engage with your characters on an emotional level. And once you are able to accomplish that, you're home free. The reader will stay with you until the last page.

Now that you know how to show a character expressing emotion, it's time to consider those characters who talk just a little bit differently than the rest of us. How can we use dialogue to characterize them so that their speech mannerisms sound real?

ws his father's days

eyes. On a rare occa-

EXERCISE 1

left Carl alone in the house

attic and comes across a box

Love. Follow old tackle box, a bunch of snap-

express ackyard, climbing a tree, taking

expre of love and gratitude for his father.

irs to tell his father. Something.

in

born daughter in her arms. Her first baby.

s that wash over her. She begins to talk to

oing out with Marisa for over a year. Recently, he

usual warmth in his heart whenever he's with her. And he

em to get enough of her. He's never been in love before, so has no frame

of reference. One night as they're sitting on her front porch, he's overcome with

that warm feeling again, and it's too much for him. He turns to her.

w else to respond.

fist on his knees.

ing. I can catch

e's saying."

groped in

deli-

EXERCISE 2

Anger. Have you ever felt betrayed? Or betrayed someone? Write a dialogue scene where one character confronts the other about the betrayal. Write two pages of dialogue from the betrayer's point of view and then rewrite the same scene from the viewpoint of the character who was betrayed.

EXERCISE 3

Fear. Write a two-page scene of dialogue that shows a viewpoint character whose fear is accelerating as the action progresses. This could mean the other character giving the protagonist new information or making immediate threats against the protagonist.

EXERCISE 4

Joy and sadness. Write a three-page scene that contrasts joy and sadness. First, write from the sad character's point of view, then rewrite the same scene from the happy character's point of view. This can be two characters breaking up, one character being offered another character's job, or a brother and sister learning what's in their recently deceased parent's will. You get the idea.

EXERCISE 5

Peace. Write one passage of dialogue that reveals a character at peace but still includes tension. Some possible scenarios:

- a character who has accepted her doctor's cancer diagnosis, but whose family members are going nuts
- a character on death row being led to his execution
- a character facing off with a bear in the wild

EXERCISE 6

Compassion. Create a scenario between two characters who are arguing and trying to get their points across. They're conflictive and defensive, but one finally makes a statement that causes the protagonist to feel compassion. Go inside of the protagonist for the emotion and then carefully craft his response.

chapter 11

[THE UHS, ANDS, AND ERS—SOME HOW-TOS OF DIALOGUE QUIRKS]

Earlier in this book, I mentioned that I once had a Marine boyfriend with a bit of a speech problem. I was attracted to his dark looks and muscular build the moment I met him at a friend's party, but then he spoke.

"Would you like to go for a walk?" he asked. "To the thore? Ith's cold outthide, but you can wear my jacket."

"Okay…"

"Let me thee if Richard needsth anything at the thore."

Aaargh! How could this good-looking guy have such a horrible lisp? As much as I tried to get over it, every time he came home on leave and showed up on my doorstep, I just couldn't cope. As I reflect on that time in my life now, of course, I feel terrible that it even mattered to me. But I was seventeen and needed a perfect boyfriend to show off to my friends. The point is, as much as I hate to admit it, and though I wasn't aware of it at the time, the lisp was a deal breaker for me as far as feeling attracted to this man. That's how important speech can be in a story, too. It can make or break relationships and business deals, and it certainly affects how seriously we take a character.

Most people speak fairly normally—if there is such a thing as normal. But every now and then, someone opens his mouth and something distinctive comes out. It could turn us off or it could turn us on, but what it does do is mark that person. In the '80s television show *The Nanny*, the main character had this nasal voice and really, really nasal laugh. It was horrible. No matter what she said, we were laughing, just because of her voice.

The quirkiness of a character's speech should be something we think consciously about. It should rise organically out of who the character is and what his purpose is in the story. You don't want to just have a character stuttering or talking ninety miles an hour for no reason. Remember—with dialogue you're not just trying to find something to use to characterize your cast, you're creating a story that needs to hang together and connect on all levels to communicate your theme to the reader.

With that in mind, let's look at a few ways of speaking that will distinguish your character from the rest of the cast in your story while at the same time *show* us who he is and how his way of speaking will enhance his role. The challenge for us as writers is to find a way to *show* our characters' speech on the printed page. Sometimes we can do it by formatting our words and sentences in a certain way; other times we need to use tags to indicate that the dialogue is being said in a certain way. For the sake of example, let's use my boyfriend's sentence above, "Let me thee if Richard needsth anything at the thore."

THE TWISTED TONGUE

Let's start with this one—which would include my boyfriend's lisping problem. But there's also the stutterer, which in real life can be painful to listen to because you keep wanting to help the speaker get the words out. "L-l-let me see if R-R-R-R-Richard needs anything at the s-s-store."

This is something you don't want to overdo. When a character has a speech impediment, you want to just show it once in a while, throwing in a line or two of lisping or stuttering so we remember how this character talks. Use it too much and the reader begins to find reading the story a rather annoying journey. And remember, there needs to be a good reason for giving a character a speech impediment. Characterization isn't enough; it needs to have something to do with the plot so it's part of the piece of art that eventually becomes your novel.

THE ROCKET

This character is off like a rocket every time he gets a chance to talk.

"LetmeseeifRichardneedsanythingatthestore." This could be one way of showing the speed at which this character talks. Of course, if this is a major character in your story, it could be annoying to read much of his dialogue.

Also, this could simply indicate not necessarily speed but that this character runs all of his words together.

You could simply describe the pace at which he speaks the first time he appears and then just allude to it occasionally after that. This is sometimes the most effective way to work with speech patterns of all kinds—make sure the reader gets it the first or first few times, then simply indicate it here and there after that so it doesn't take over the story or be so difficult to read that the reader puts your story down.

What's important with all speech patterns is what's underneath. In some cases, like a stutter or lisp, it could be something physical, though I've learned that these particular disabilities can be corrected through therapy because they are often acquired in childhood when someone is traumatized.

But most often, the way we talk emerges out of who we are. I can personally speak about the "rocket" because this is me a lot of the time. Unless I'm consciously trying to talk slowly, I'm off like a rocket. I just get so excited about whatever it is I'm saying. It doesn't do any good for someone to tell me to slow down. I can't seem to do that for long.

I don't just talk fast. I move fast. I think fast. I drive fast. If I could find a way to sleep faster, I would, because I'm always afraid I'm missing something. Keep your character's entire personality in mind when giving him a distinctive speech pattern.

THE TURTLE

"Let…me see…if…Richard needs…anything…at…the store."

This is the opposite of the rocket. My best friend happens to be a slow talker, and again, this is because of who she *is*. She moves slowly, thinks slowly, and drives so slowly that it's often painful for me to ride in the car with her, given who I am.

Are there other ways you can indicate a character's slow pattern of speech? Be creative. The exercises at the end of this chapter will give you the opportunity to be creative with each of these speech patterns and consider how you might *show* each one in a page of dialogue.

This character in your story is in no hurry and can't be made to move or talk faster, no matter what. I think it might even be physically impossible for her.

You could indicate her slow pace in narrative that describes her dialogue. *Sue meandered from subject to subject while my soup grew cold. "You're…" yawn…"not…eating…" she looked around the restaurant… "your soup."*

Just for Fun

Using all of the dialogue quirks, write a four-page party scene where each of the guests has at least one of the speech patterns. Some combinations in one character might be fun to try—the turtle combined with the switch-blade, for example: a slow-talking tough guy. What's important here is to creatively practice with all of the speech patterns until you're confident using them.

THE BABY DOLL

This character talks in a high-pitched voice, like a little girl who's never grown up, but who is grown up. I don't know of any males who talk like this—well, besides Michael Jackson. That doesn't mean there aren't any. I just think it's rare.

This character comes from a kind of unsure place inside of herself, perceiving the world through a not-quite-grown-up view. Her voice squeaks, like a vocalist hitting the high notes and her voice cracking. That might be one way you could *show* it. "Let me see"—squeak—"if Richard needs anything at the store"—giggle. Since you can't really *show* a tone because it's a sound, again you have to be creative and think how you might let the reader in on how this character's voice *sounds*.

THE BASS DRUM

This character sounds like Tom Brokaw. Again, because this speech pattern has more to do with sound than it does the *way* the speech is said, you might have to describe the voice rather than *show* it in the actual dialogue. You can simply use narrative, something like: *Whenever he spoke, it sounded like he was inside the chamber of a bass drum, hollow and deep.* Sometimes, you can use famous people to help the reader key into how a character speaks. You might just use the famous newsman to show how a character sounds: *Every time he spoke, I found myself looking toward the television to see if Tom Brokaw was broadcasting the news.*

THE CALCULATOR

This character is constantly weighing his words, talking very carefully and methodically. There is any number of reasons for this. Sometimes this character is concerned about his image, wanting to come off well to others, so he chooses every word. It could be that he wants power over another character and is weighing every word to make sure he's manipulating the situation to his advantage. He could simply be scared and feeling the need to not say anything that would put him in danger or bring on a threat of any kind.

He seemed deep in thought, then finally spoke. "Let me see if...Richard," he paused then continued, "needs anything at the...store."

Put yourself inside of your character's head in order to get to the motivation behind the patterns of speech you give her. Being inside of her head will help you determine what she says and how she says it. Sometimes a speech pattern is a permanent part of a character's speech; other times it's momentary and temporary because of the situation in which she finds herself.

THE ACE

The ace simply doesn't talk much at all and when he does, he gives one-word answers. Or he grunts. He probably wouldn't even complete the sentence about Richard. "Let me see if..." His words may trail off. "Let me see if...Richard...needs..." You can't always understand the ace because he usually doesn't want to be talking to you anyway. A conversation with him might go something like:

> "So, Joe, how's it going?"
> "It's goin'."
> "You have enough work to do?"
> "Yep." (Or a nod.)
> "How's your family? June, the boys?"
> "Fine."
> "You have a vacation planned this year? You taking your family anywhere?"
> "Camping."

Somehow you'll have to characterize this guy, and while the one-word answers help do this, you're going to have to find other ways: his clothes, his mannerisms, and his demeanor. This character just doesn't have a lot to tell you about himself.

THE APOLOGIZER

This character is basically apologizing for being alive. No matter what the subject of conversation, she's saying she's sorry. This dialogue is easy to write, simply being characterized by "I'm sorry" thrown in at regular intervals. Since she's sorry for everything, this is a character who is often full of shame and doesn't like to be seen. She wishes she were invisible, so she talks in low tones and might mumble a lot. You can show this in narrative or you could be creative and use a smaller font for her speech. In dialogue with others, she's easily manipulated and controlled, thinking she's responsible for everything that happens.

THE SHIELD

Have you ever talked to someone who, no matter what you're talking about, is defending himself or whomever you're talking about? His tone of voice shows this. It's like he feels that he's always under attack and has to ward off the next blow, so he's always standing at the ready. To get into this character's mindset, you have to imagine what it would feel like to think that everyone is against you, trying to pin something on you, and working constantly to find the gap in your armor where they can zoom in and get you. This character's face is often pinched as he waits for the next zinger he needs to deflect. He's quick on the draw, as he has a lot of experience deflecting verbal blows and is used to verbal sparring. His answers in conversation are fast and his goal is to keep others away from him.

> "Do you think—"
> "No, of course not," Earl quickly said. "I didn't know anything about it. How could I have been there?" His voice was rising, growing shriller, then, "Let me see if Richard needs anything at the store."

Here Earl is deflecting what he thinks is coming before it can hit him and then quickly changing the subject. He has many strategies to keep others as far away from him as possible.

THE CHANNEL CHANGER

The channel changer speaks in sentence fragments.
"See if Richard needs anything. At the store, you know."

This character is distracted and may not be really thinking about the conversation she's having. Or she may be thinking about another conversation she'd like to be having. Or many other conversations she'd like to be having.

The channel changer talks in circles. He's unfocused, and you have to do mental cartwheels to make any sense of what he's saying. This type of character may suffer from a mental illness that causes him to jump around a lot in his speech. Those with attention deficit disorder often use sentence fragments as do geniuses in social settings. This could be a character on drugs or alcohol, just saying whatever comes into his mind at any moment. Those who find themselves in a state of terror can begin to speak like this.

This character may complete a thought but then make a gigantic leap to the next subject without waiting for a response. This is what marks the non-sensical speaker. He's simply all over the map in conversation. He's disconnected from himself and his own thoughts and isn't often tuned in to those around him, at least not in a rational way. So you want to show his disjointed thoughts by showing his disjointed speech.

"I'll see if Richard, you know, I was thinking that you and I should hook up—I wonder if Richard's even here, I'm going to the store and, hey, he might need something." This character simply changes frequency more often than the other characters may be able to keep up with her. You might want to use this character to keep all of the other characters in the story a little off balance. She comes in handy when the other characters are trying to accomplish something verbally. She may interrupt and take everyone in a completely new direction in which they had no intention of going. Once there, the channel changer is probably either on to a new subject or out of the room altogether.

THE DIALECT

This is one of the most difficult types of speech to do well just because if you use too much of it for any one character, the reader finds it tough going as far as getting through the story. And if it's a novel, it's a lot of pages of dialect. Every once in a while the author gets away with it, of course. Alice Walker's *The Color Purple* is an example of a dialect we all put up with because the story was so compelling. But I wouldn't try that if I were you, unless you have an equally compelling story. And there hasn't been a *The Color Purple* since, well, *The Color Purple*.

The best way to handle dialect is to just sprinkle a few words of the foreign language or slang into the dialogue here and there. For example, if it's hip-hop, you can throw a "yo" into the dialogue once in a while to characterize the speaker and make the dialect sound authentic. But you don't want to write the dialogue exactly like a hip-hopper would talk, as it just becomes too tedious to read.

"Yo, let me see if my man, Richard, needs anything at the store."

Sometimes dialect requires that the writer change the spelling of words here and there to show the character's nationality and/or background. Again, don't go overboard with this in the dialogue, just a subtle change of spelling once in awhile will remind the reader of this character's background.

THE CANNON

In John Irving's novel *A Prayer for Owen Meany*, I would call the protagonist a cannon because of the loudness of his speech.

> "DO YOU THINK I CARE WHAT THEY DO TO ME? "he shouted; he stamped his little foot on the drive-shaft hump. "DO YOU THINK I CARE IF THEY START AN AVALANCHE WITH ME?" he screamed. "WHEN DO I GET TO GO ANYWHERE? IF I DIDN'T GO TO SCHOOL OR TO CHURCH OR TO EIGHTY FRONT STREET, I'D NEVER GET OUT OF MY HOUSE!" he cried. "IF YOUR MOTHER DIDN'T TAKE ME TO THE BEACH, I'D NEVER GET OUT OF TOWN. AND I'VE NEVER BEEN TO THE MOUNTAINS," he said. "I'VE NEVER EVEN BEEN ON A TRAIN! DON'T YOU THINK I MIGHT LIKE GOING ON A TRAIN—TO THE MOUNTAINS?" he yelled. .

And this is the way Irving indicates it—in all caps. It's very effective, and not annoying for the reader, as unlike dialect, the words are all easily pronounced— they're just loud. What a delightful characterization device that immediately signals to the reader when Owen is speaking.

> "LET ME SEE IF RICHARD NEEDS ANYTHING AT THE STORE."

THE SWITCHBLADE

"Let me see if that punk, Richard, needs anything at the store." This character might punch Richard on the shoulder as he asks him this question. He's a tough guy and his voice reflects that. He likes the power he has over others and knows how to use it, physically and in conversation.

Thinking from inside of this character means putting on a tough-guy persona and talking out of that to the other characters. His voice has an edge to it. He needs to be the one in charge at all times, and so much of his speech consists of directives, telling others what to do and how to do it. This is his goal, what he sees as his purpose when relating to others. Sometimes a switchblade's toughness expresses itself more indirectly, and that can be effective, too. In the book *Scene & Structure*, Jack Bickham offers a tip about this that is especially helpful if the switchblade happens to be the antagonist, and he usually is:

> Don't hesitate to use dialogue at cross-purposes once in a while as a scene-building device. Such dialogue can be defined as story conversation in which the conflict is not overt, but where the antagonist either doesn't understand what's really at issue, or is purposely nonresponsive to what the lead character keeps trying to talk about. Dialogue at cross-purposes, or nonresponsive behavior by an antagonist, will be experienced by both the lead character and the reader as conflictual. After all, in such a situation the lead character feels thwarted in some way, and so struggles harder. If the opposing character does not start responding quite directly, the viewpoint character will fight harder.

You can probably think of some ways of speaking that we haven't covered in this chapter. That's okay. Be creative and consider how you might show a particular speech pattern without overwhelming the reader or having it come off corny. Giving your character a particular manner of speech can go a long way in characterizing him and helping your reader recognize him when he appears onstage. It distinguishes him from the other characters, setting him apart. If you have a specific role for a character to play and need to set him apart, then consider giving him a distinct speech pattern.

In the next chapter, we'll be discussing some practical ways to make sure your dialogue continues to do the job it's meant to do—grab the reader and keep her attention.

EXERCISES

The most important thing to remember about dialogue quirks is that they must relate to the story's theme and be connected to the character's is motivation. Using the following story situations, write a one- to two-page scene of dialogue for each quirk, showing how the dialogue relates to the story's theme and motivation.

- The twisted tongue—a male character wanting to succeed at his new telemarketing job
- The rocket—a female character teaching a class at a senior center
- The turtle—a male character on a fast-paced game show
- The baby doll—a female character waiting to be taken seriously as she's buying a new car
- The bass drum—a short, male character at a speed-dating event in a restaurant
- The calculator—a female character being interrupted by her boss after money is missing from the till
- The ace—a male character on his first real date
- The apologizer—a female character being asked the time on a downtown street
- The shield—a male character in the emergency room after slicing his thumb open
- The channel changer—a female character trying to talk her way out of a speeding ticket
- The dialect—an older male beatnik/hippie at his daughter's wedding
- The cannon—a male character who doesn't understand the concept of whispering in his new girlfriend's church for the first time
- The switchblade—a male character stopping to help a woman whose puppy has just been hit by a car

chapter 12

[WHOOPS! DIALOGUE THAT DOESN'T DELIVER—THE MOST COMMON MISTAKES]

"John, I'd like you to meet Steve," Paul said.

"Hi Steve." John expostulated and reached out to shake Steve's hand.

"Hi John. Nice to meet you." Steve shook John's hand.

John wondered where Steve was from. "Where are you from, Steve?" John asked.

"Originally from Alaska, John," Steve orated, "but I now reside in Montana."

"Why Steve, I have an uncle who lives in Alaska!" John exclaimed. "Do you know him?"

There are a number of mistakes here; maybe you can find them. Wink. This reminds me of those pictures of forests we had to study as kids and find the animals hidden there. We thought we were smart if we could find all the animals, but I remember them being in plain sight. The elephant was usually hanging upside down in the tree, and you could recognize him by his trunk, and you could spot the zebra over in the water by his stripes. Anyway, I made the mistakes pretty obvious in the above scene, and you should have no trouble finding them.

We're going to deal with each mistake one by one because I have seen some of the most talented writers make every single one of these mistakes and not even know they're doing it. They're subtle and sneak into our writing style without our even knowing it. Unless we know we're making a mistake, we can't correct it. The purpose of this chapter is to help you learn specifically what weakens your dialogue so you can watch out for these little buggers when they sneak in. I've named each mistake for the sake of convenience and to help you remember.

THE JOHN-MARSHA SYNDROME

There was a silly skit during the sixties about a couple of characters named John and Marsha. I can't even remember who performed it originally, but it went like this:

> "John."
>
> "Marsha."
>
> "John!"
>
> "Marsha!"
>
> "Joooooooohn…"
>
> "Maaaaaarsha…"
>
> "John?"
>
> "Marsha?"

And so on *ad nauseum.* It sounds stupid now, but it was really pretty funny performed by the right comedians.

It's not so funny when it happens in our fiction. And speaking of stupid, guess who sounds stupid when it happens? The author, yes, but especially the characters.

> "Ron, I heard about the party the other night."
>
> "Oh yeah, Karen? What did you hear?"
>
> "Ron, I heard you were drunk."
>
> "Drunk? Karen, you know me better than that."
>
> "Do I? I thought I did, Ron. Now I'm not so sure."
>
> "Karen, I don't even drink—I mean, not much."

Blah, blah, blah. The dialogue, which could easily occur between two people, isn't all that bad without the names. It has some tension and that's good. It has some emotion and it makes you kind of wonder what's going to happen between these two. But the constant direct references ruin it because it just doesn't sound natural.

In real life, when you're talking to your husband, child, sister, or whomever, how often do you really refer to them by their names? Listen to people talk. Written dialogue needs to reflect real conversation. We don't talk like this to each other. I don't even know if they do this in soap operas. Maybe, but do we want our stories to sound like soap operas?

There are exceptions to every rule. One very excellent example of an exception can be found in John Grisham's novel *The Chamber*. Detective Ivy knows or at least suspects that Sam Cayhall is the one who blew up the building with the five-year-old twin boys in it. This is a part of the dialogue between them:

> "Really, really sad, Sam. You see, Mr. Kramer had two little boys, Josh and John, and, as fate would have it, they were in the office with their daddy when the bomb went off."
>
> Sam breathed deeply and looked at Ivy. Tell me the rest of it, his eyes said.
>
> "And these two little boys, twins, five years old, just cute as can be, got blown to bits, Sam. Deader than hell, Sam."
>
> Sam slowly lowered his head until his chin was an inch off his chest. He was beaten. Murder, two counts. Lawyers, trials, judges, juries, prison, everything hit at once, and he closed his eyes.
>
> "Their daddy might get lucky. He's at the hospital now in surgery. The little boys are at the funeral home. A real tragedy, Sam. Don't suppose you know anything about the bomb, do you, Sam?"
>
> "No. I'd like to see a lawyer."
>
> "Of course." Ivy slowly stood and left the room.

The reason this is the exception is because Ivy is using Sam's name for effect. The detective is in a position of power, and he's using that for all it's worth in this scene. He wants Sam to know he's onto him, and using his name like this over and over lets Sam know that his gig is up. But most often, doing this makes a piece of dialogue sound very artificial.

If you're guilty of this dialogue crime, there's no need to go to confession or anything. Simply ask yourself why you're doing it. Sometimes it's because we're trying to make our dialogue between characters very intense. We think that if they keep using each other's names, the reader will know that this is an important conversation and pay attention. The problem is when we keep doing it over and over, it has the opposite effect. Every piece of dialogue in the story is weakened because it sounds so false.

Another possible reason is because we want to identify the characters as they speak, and we think this is the way to do it. There are many ways to tag characters in dialogue, as we'll see in chapter thirteen, but this isn't one of them.

After you've written your first draft, go through your story with a red pen (yes, this calls for a *red* pen) and delete all direct references except maybe a couple—only when they would naturally be used. Your characters will thank you for making them sound just a little bit more intelligent.

THE ADJECTIVE, ADVERB, AND INAPPROPRIATE TAG ADDICTION

Remember how John *expostulated* at the opening of this chapter? Gag.

"Oh Elizabeth," Kenneth harkened as he danced her around the room, "will you marry me?"

Harkened?!

Joseph's face gradually turned the brightest shade of red, matching the lampshade under which shone a 300-watt bulb. He glared at Dolores. "Get out," he said ragingly. Or hotly, or angrily—it doesn't matter. What does matter is that we already know he's standing there turning red under the collar and he's glaring at the other character. Do we really think he's in a good mood? Do we need the author to tell us exactly how the words are spoken—ragingly?

You know the answer. The funny thing about the adverb addiction is that the words chosen are often made up and look ridiculous when written down. Ragingly? But I see them all the time. And laughingly, I edit them out. I see words like disapprovingly, amazingly, and alarmingly. Maniacally, stupidly, surreptitiously. Smilingly—that's one of my favorites. But even more common adverbs, like sweetly, leisurely, and assiduously, are unnecessary if you are working hard on your dialogue so it communicates the emotion and intensity you want it to have.

That's right—it's your job as the writer to make sure your dialogue communicates accurately (whoops). Sometimes you need a couple of assistants—narrative and action. Action does it every time. If a character is a little upset, have him throw a dish or punch a wall, which is better than having him speak ragingly. If he's happy, resist the adverb gleefully and have him grab another character, lift her off the ground, and spin her around.

In the following dialogue from *The Accidental Tourist*, author Anne Tyler throws in a couple of lines of narrative action that show how the character's words are being said:

> "When I was a little girl," Muriel said, "I didn't like dogs at all or any other kinds of animals either. I thought they could read my mind. My folks gave me a puppy for my birthday and he would, like, cock his head, you know how they do? Cock his head and fix me with these bright round eyes and I said, 'Ooh! Get him away from me! You know I can't stand to be stared at.' "
>
> She had a voice that wandered too far in all directions. It screeched

upward; then it dropped to a raspy growl. "They had to take him back. Had to give him to a neighbor boy and buy me a whole different present, a beauty-parlor permanent which is what I'd set my heart on all along."

These two sentences of narrative are enough to show us how Muriel talks. Much better than if she were to say the words *screechingly* or *growlingly*.

I like what the successful horror writer Dean Koontz has to say on this subject in his book *How to Write Best-Selling Fiction.* He says:

> You can find published novels in which authors use one flashy dialogue tag after another. Don't send me a list of those authors, please. I didn't tell you that the frequent use of such tags would prevent you from being published. I only said that they indicate that the author is an amateur or that he lacks the sensitivity to appreciate the musical qualities of language. Books full of inept dialogue tags get published all the time. Of course they do. Not all published writers are good writers.

Readers aren't stupid. If you've offered your reader a clear sense of who the characters are and what they're experiencing, the reader will hear the tone of voice in which they're speaking. Verbs and adverbs can stop the flow of the immediate moment in dialogue if you're always stopping to explain how something is being said.

If you find yourself addicted to adjectives and/or adverbs in your dialogue, what you want to work on is getting inside of your character's skin just as an actor does. Ask yourself, "What is motivating me in this scene? What am I feeling as I speak these lines? What do I want more than anything else right now?" Then write the kind of powerful dialogue that needs no adjective or adverb to give it its oomph. The dialogue should speak for itself.

> "Sarah, did I hear you right?" I cocked the trigger and held it to my left temple. Did it matter—left or right? "Did you say you never wanted to see me again?"

Do I need to tell you how this character is speaking these words?

THE DISCONNECT

A conversation between two or more people has a flow to it. There's give and take—or at least there should be. Of course, so much depends on the characters' personalities and what they want in the scene you've created for them. It's your job, to understand fully what you want to accomplish with the scene, which means being sure of what the viewpoint character wants. So how do you achieve a flow?

The flow of the scene comes from many of the things we've discussed in other chapters: weaving dialogue, narrative, and action, establishing the setting and referring to it throughout the scene, moving your characters steadily forward—externally and internally.

The nuts and bolts part of this is to make sure that each line of one character's dialogue responds to the previous line of the other character's, as well as sets up the one to follow. It really is like playing a game of pool. You hit the balls that were set up for you and when your shot is over, you've set up the balls for the next player.

Real life conversations aren't that smooth, but dialogue captures the essence of real life conversations, so it's okay. We're creating art here. And having fun.

In the following scene, John and Steve are visiting Randy, who owes John some money. John has come to collect on the debt. There's a disconnect between the first and last line.

> "What time do you have to be back at work?" John asked. "Hey, look, I know you don't have any money. I've heard that too many times. I didn't come over here because I thought you had money. I came over here because you happen to owe me. I think we're up to two hundred bucks by now." John lifted a vase from an end table. "Hmmmm, bet you could get at least fifty bucks for this at a pawn shop. Hey, Sue said you took her out to dinner last week, that the bottle of wine alone was forty-five bucks. Not bad for someone—"
>
> "Let's get out of here." Steve looked around nervously. "I don't like—"
>
> "Shut up!" John ordered. "We're here now." He eyed Randy with interest. "And we're going to get what's coming to us."
>
> "Nine o'clock. I'm on the second shift."

Huh? Nine o'clock? What's Randy talking about? Oh yeah, John asked what time he had to be back work—ten sentences ago.

This is definitely a violation of flow. Every speech needs to connect to the one before it, unless there's a very good reason: the character is scattered, trying to change the subject, *or* the writer has lost his place in the dialogue.

Let's hope it's not the latter.

THE AS-YOU-KNOW-BOB TENDENCY

We know that dialogue is often the most effective and interesting way to convey background information, setting details, and description, so we want to use it to do that kind of work whenever possible. But let's not get carried away because, while it's a cardinal sin to bore our readers, there's something else that's equally important—that our characters sound authentic, like our neighbors, family members, or co-workers. Let me give you an example of a time when dialogue is *not* the best way to dispense story background to the reader.

Your viewpoint character George's Aunt Maude is coming to stay with him and his wife, Carol, for a couple of weeks in the summer as she does every summer. You want your readers to understand exactly what Aunt Maude's visit means to George and Carol. You need to give them some background so they'll understand that this is less than pleasant news. George has just gone out to the mailbox and found a letter from Aunt Maude announcing her annual visit. He's reading it as he comes into the house.

> "Well, Carol, my Aunt Maude is coming again in August for her annual visit. You know, that's the aunt from Iowa whose teeth always fall out at the dinner table, the one who was married to my Uncle Willis before he died in 1998, I believe it was. You remember, she chatters on like a runaway train, and even when you're starting to snooze, she doesn't notice. She's the one who wears those plaid housedresses. She has the blue one and the red one—"

It's easy to see why this isn't working. If Aunt Maude comes to visit every summer, Carol already knows all of this. You can't put these words into George's mouth just for the sake of the reader who needs to know it. In this case, this information would be better conveyed in narrative or, if the reader doesn't need to know all of this right away, in action once Aunt Maude arrives.

Make sure each character speaks out of his own need, not that of his listener or the reader. Depending on the purpose of the scene, George might come away from the mailbox with all kinds of thoughts that would lead to a *real* scene of dialogue. Let's say George's goal is to keep Aunt Maude's letter from Carol until he can figure out a way to tell her because she hates it when his aunt comes to visit.

> "Did we get any mail?" Carol asked.
>
> "Nothing exciting." That was the truth. So far so good. He hadn't had to lie. George put the flyers down on the kitchen table, tucking the letter under

them for now. If Carol knew they'd received a letter from Aunt Maude, it wouldn't be a pretty scene and he wanted to avoid the unpleasantness for now. He could take or leave his elderly aunt, but Carol dreaded her visits. He wasn't sure exactly why Carol dreaded his aunt's visits every summer, whether it was the way she kept dropping her false teeth into her food at dinner or because she chattered on like a runaway train most of every day.

"What's that?" she asked, pulling the envelope out from under the flyers.

"Oh, nothing," he said again, grabbing the letter from her hand. Maybe it was Aunt Maude's dresses Carol was tired of. She had the blue plaid one and the red plaid one.

"Not Aunt Maude!" Carol cried.

Much more natural, don't you think? It's not all dialogue, but it's still an effective dialogue scene because these are thoughts George might actually have in light of the fact that he's trying to keep the letter from his wife, and the reader gets all of the necessary information (well, if all of that information is necessary). The amount of information the reader needs is again determined by the plot and where you're taking these characters.

THE SPEECH

In real life, what does it feel like to listen to someone go on and on and on about something—anything—and on and on and on? Even if it's a subject in which you're interested, another person's speech is seldom something we can or even want to listen to for long. Well, unless we're at a lecture or something, and it's *supposed* to be a speech.

Likewise, you don't want to write speeches for your characters. This is something I see quite often in new writers' dialogue. A character has a lot to say on a subject and the writer just lets him run on at the mouth for a page or two or three. Not good. This seldom works in movies, and it definitely doesn't work on the printed page. People who ramble on are often boring their listeners. It just never occurs to these folks that the other people in the room might have something to say or a thought or opinion on the subject.

There are always exceptions—mainly the character who makes speeches because that's who he is. But just know that this character won't be one of your reader's favorites, and his speeches better be few and far between and be there for a purpose that fits in with the story. Otherwise, you're the one who will look bad, not your speech-giving character.

THE HO-HUM MOMENTS

These are passages that do nothing to further the plot, develop the characters, or create tension in the story. The ho-hum moments might appear in the form of introductions.

> "Joe, this is Sally."
>
> Sally stuck out her hand. "Hi Joe."
>
> "Hi Sally," Joe said, shaking her hand.
>
> "Pleased to meet you," Sally said.
>
> "Me too," said Joe.

This is so not interesting. Sometimes this kind of dialogue continues, increasing the pain for the reader.

> "Do you live around here?" asked Sally.
>
> "A couple of miles from here," Joe answered. "Over on Main Street."
>
> Sally smiled. "Oh yes. I have a friend who lives over there."
>
> "What's your friend's name?"

WHO CARES?! This scene needs a mugger, a plane dropping out of the sky, Sally taking off her clothes—anything would help.

With dialogue, we try to capture the essence of a scene, not record every word the characters might say to each other, even if they might engage in this kind of small talk in real life. To be honest, though, even if I happened to get caught in such a conversation, I wouldn't last as long as Sally did.

Other ho-hum moments can easily occur when you're trying to get a character from one place to another. Here's a scene that shows a mother driving her son to soccer practice.

> "Did you do your homework before we left?"
>
> "Uh-huh."
>
> "How about that report for Mr. Colton's class? Get that done?"
>
> "Yup."
>
> "I think I'll stop at the store on my way home. I need some eggs and milk."
>
> "And batteries for my Game Boy."
>
> "Oh, of course. Will you remind me?"
>
> "Uh-huh."
>
> "Is that kid still picking on you at practice?"
>
> "Nope."

Whatever. Which reminds me, I need new batteries for *my* Game Boy. I am so done reading this story.

If you want to get your fiction published, and we know you do, you can't write ho-hum dialogue. You can't create this kind of pain for your readers. Storytelling, by definition, is about conflict and resolution. Nowhere is this truer than in dialogue. Characters that agree with each other are boring. Characters that talk about nothing are boring. Lively dialogue lights up our stories like nothing else. Be sure every line and every scene of every story you write includes lively dialogue—the kind that makes the reader one of your biggest fans.

Following is an example of what could have been a ho-hum, boring scene of characters introducing themselves to one another. It's from a very familiar novel, *One Flew Over the Cuckoo's Nest,* by Ken Kesey. Here we're meeting the main character, R.P. McMurphy, for the first time, a few moments after he's been admitted to a mental institution. The story is actually told by a minor character making some observations. Instead of McMurphy simply entering the room and the other characters saying their names, McMurphy appears on the scene with a flurry of dramatics, and we meet the other characters as they begin reacting to him.

> "My name is McMurphy, buddies, R.P. McMurphy, and I'm a gambling fool." He winks and sings a little piece of a song: " '...and whenever I meet with a deck a cards I lays...my money...down.' ' And laughs again.
>
> He walks to one of the card games, tips an Acute's cards up with a thick, heavy finger, and squints at the hand and shakes his head.
>
> "Yessir, that's what I came to this establishment for, to bring you birds fun

an' entertainment around the gamin' table. Nobody left in that Pendleton Work Farm to make my days interesting any more, so I requested a transfer, ya see. Needed some new blood. Hooee, look at the way this bird holds his cards, showin' to everybody in a block; man! I'll trim you babies like little lambs."

Cheswick gathers his cards together. The redheaded man sticks his hand out for Cheswick to shake.

"Hello, buddy; what's that you're playing'? Pinochle?"

Nothing ho-hum about this scene or this character. And the reader begins to anticipate what McMurphy is going to do next.

THE PERFECT GRAMMAR PROBLEM

"Joseph, I think we should see other people." Janet held her breath as she pushed her carrots around on her plate.

"You think we should see other people? Do you want to break up with me?"

"That is what I am thinking. I believe we have outgrown each other and should date others."

Joseph looked confused. "I do not understand. Just yesterday you spoke about how you thought you might like to spend the rest of your life with me."

"I have changed my mind. Women do that sometimes."

"Oh. You can give me the ring back, then. I think I still have the receipt and can get a refund."

In dialogue, more than in any other element of fiction, you do not have to utilize perfect grammar. If anyone has ever told you that your dialogue sounds "stilted" or "formal," what they're saying is that you're writing too perfectly, not the way people really talk. At least I hope you've never had the above conversation with anyone. The problem is obvious—the characters are speaking to each other in perfect English. To clarify, during some periods in history, people talked like this. But if your story is not set in such a period of history, and you don't want your reader laughing at you, you need to lighten up when it comes to dialogue. Let's try again.

"Joe, I'm thinking maybe we should go out with other people." Janet held her breath as she pushed her carrots around on her plate.

"Huh? What are you talking about? Are you breaking up with me?"

"I guess, I don't know. I mean, I just think maybe we should, you know, go out with others before we settle down, that's all."

Joseph looked confused. "I don't get it. Just yesterday you were saying you wanted to spend the rest of your life with me."

"Okay, I changed my mind. Women do that, you know."

"Oh, sure, that's right. Well, how about taking off the ring, then? I think I kept the receipt and can get my money back."

Fixing Your Own Story

Take a look at your own story and see if you can adjust the weak places according to what you've learned in this chapter.
To summarize:

[1] Take out as many direct references as you can—those places where your characters are constantly using each other's names.

[2] Go through the story and delete all adverbs and adjectives that describe how a passage of dialogue is spoken.

[3] Every passage of dialogue should be connected to the one before and the one after unless, of course, you have a completely disjointed character who has attention deficit disorder or is on drugs and a little distracted.

[4] Find the places where your dialogue is loaded with information that could be more effectively dispensed through narrative. Be brutally honest with yourself as you examine each dialogue passage to make sure that your characters are speaking out of their own needs and not to inform the reader.

[5] The worst sin you can commit with your dialogue is to bore your reader. Go through all of your dialogue and pump up the tension and suspense and increase the conflict or add some if there is none. Would anyone want to eavesdrop on your characters? Or not?

[6] Make sure every passage of dialogue is as loose and natural as it can be for the character speaking it. Unless you have a really anal character, use a lot of contractions and phrases, dashes and ellipses, slang where appropriate, or interruptions by the character speaking and the others around him.

[7] If you find any places at all where you've told your reader something using narrative or shown your reader something using action, resist the urge to repeat it in dialogue.

This is a little better. Not so stilted and formal and perfect.

If you suspect that you write stilted dialogue, try reading it out loud, either to yourself or your writing group. See if it sounds like a conversation real people would have. As always, the better you know your characters, the less likely it is you'll be writing stilted dialogue.

THE REDUNDANCY ISSUE

When our characters say something to each other, we don't have to repeat the information in narrative or action. Once is enough. I see this problem a lot and have caught myself doing it.

> Randy decided he'd go to the store for some milk.
>
> "I'm going to the store for some milk!" he called to Joyce.

Unnecessary. I'm not sure why this problem occurs unless we're simply trying to introduce our dialogue to the reader. Our dialogue needs no introduction. It's better to just jump in. You may not catch yourself doing this, so watch for this problem at the revision stage.

This is all a lot to think about, isn't it? Try not to feel overwhelmed. I learned about the mistakes I was making one by one as I grew as a fiction writer. You can't possibly think about all of this while you're doing the actual writing or you'll drive yourself nuts trying to do it perfectly. This is left brain stuff and thinking about it while creating will paralyze your creativity. When learning a new skill, you can't be constantly thinking about what you might be doing wrong.

A couple of years ago I took a class and learned to ride a motorcycle. The instructor was like a drill sergeant, constantly yelling at us and berating us for life-threatening mistakes we were making: cutting each other off, cutting corners too sharply, looking at the ground instead of around the next corner, etc. I couldn't wait until the class was over and I could ride my bike without someone watching me. I promptly dumped my bike while trying to make it up a hill and turn a sharp corner at the same time. I took off too fast one time and crashed into and through the brush in front of my apartment, but I kept my balance and rode off down the street quite proud of myself.

Someone once told me that if I didn't dump my motorcycle a few times, I wasn't taking any risks.

Just write. Take risks. You'll make mistakes. That's how you learn.

In chapter thirteen, we're going to tie up some of the loose ends about dialogue. There are a lot of little things you can do to tighten your dialogue to deliver more focused punches as well as make your dialogue feel more real.

The John-Marsha syndrome. There are a few too many direct addresses in the following passage. Rewrite it, taking out most of them and making any other adjustments to make it read smoothly.

> "I'm going to the store, Ellen. Need anything?"
>
> "There's a pad and pencil over by the phone, Tom. I'll make a list."
>
> "Ellen, I think we should get some chocolate milk in case Teddy stops by."
>
> "Tom, good idea." She wrote that down. "Oh, and Tom, how about some Oreo cookies to go with the milk?"
>
> "That's too much chocolate, Ellen. Let's get butter cream cookies instead."
>
> "Tom, yes, butter cream cookies." She wrote down butter cream cookies.
>
> "Do you think, Ellen, we should check and see if we're out of sugar? It was pretty low last time I looked."
>
> "You go ahead and check, Tom, I'll just keep making out my list here."

The adjective, adverb, and inappropriate tag addiction. The dialogue that follows has just a few adverbs and adjectives, explaining how the character spoke the dialogue. I've deliberately overdone it so you can have fun rewriting it.

> "We're going to Hawaii!" Curtis said excitedly as he came through the back door and threw down his briefcase. "My boss is sending two guys from the office and—"
>
> "I hate Hawaii," Patty answered tiredly.
>
> "You hate Hawaii?!" Curtis enunciated in shock. "How can anyone hate Hawaii?"
>
> "Easy," Patty reiterated. "It's too hot."
>
> "Too hot?" Curtis repeated hotly. "So what? It's Hawaii, for Pete's sake. It's supposed to be hot."
>
> "I'm just telling you why I don't like it," Patty flusteringly muttered.
>
> "I don't believe this," Curtis shrieked as he sat down hard on one of the kitchen chairs. "We have a free trip to Hawaii and you don't want to go."
>
> "I didn't say I didn't want to go," Patty argued resistantly. "I can sit in the hotel room and eat ice cream bars while you're out snorkeling or whatever."

"Oh, you'll go then?" Curtis asked hesitatingly.

"I suppose," Patty remarked resignedly.

EXERCISE 3

The disconnect. In the dialogue that follows, the characters disconnect a few times. See if you can fix this passage so the characters are responding directly to each other.

"Mom, do you know which direction Dad's going to his meeting? Is he going down Fourth Street?"

"Would you mind emptying the garbage?" Mom said as she passed through the kitchen on her way to the living room.

The phone rang and she answered it. *"No, he's not,"* she said. *"You're welcome."* She put the phone down and thought for a moment. *"I need to go to the store before dinner."*

"Can you get some Fruit Loops? We're out."

"I think he is," she said as she grabbed her purse.

"I'll do it after dinner."

EXERCISE 4

The as-you-know-Bob tendency. Rewrite the following dialogue so the information about Sarah is delivered to the reader in a way that feels natural, not contrived.

Rachel leaned across the table toward Pam. "They're letting Sarah go, you know," she whispered, looking around to make sure no one was listening.

"Oh really?" Pam said through a mouthful of pastrami.

"Yeah, you know how she's always taking those long breaks and on the phone all the time. She talks about her retarded son, but I've never met him. You know how she always says she's calling to check on him. Remember that time we drove her home after work and saw her house—that huge two-storied rundown place on the other side of town? Remember what she said when she got out of the car?"

"Uh-uh."

"That she lived in the house in the back, and remember how we drove around the back down the alley and there weren't no house in the back? Remember that?"

"Kind of." Pam wiped her mouth with her napkin.

"You see how she comes to work every day in that same dress and how her shoes are all worn out and she never wears stockings, you know."

"Yeah."

"I don' t think that's her real hair color, do you? That red color? And she needs to lose some weight. She's bad for the image of this company, having her working at the front desk."

You might want to consider having Sarah show up on the scene, which would be a much more immediate way to describe her to us.

In the following passage, the viewpoint character is making a speech about something she feels strongly about--men. Rewrite this passage from this character's viewpoint, breaking up the speech with other characters
interruptions and the vp's musings and actions.

"Men are like that, you know, always thinking about sex. That's all they think about. I've been dating a few men I've met on the Internet lately, and it comes up every time. Why is that such a big deal with men? Why can't

they just relax and, you know, get to know a woman? I've had it with men. I'm never going out again. It's too stressful, constantly having to play games and hide who you really are in case a guy might be turned off if you,

like, show you have a brain or are actually interested in furthering your career, inter-ested in anything, really, besides the guy. Why do they have to be number one all of the time? I hate to think I might be an old maid or

something. I really want to find a man, but it's so hard. Oh, and another thing, you can't be better than they are at anything because they all have this thing called an ego. It drives me crazy. I' might just be talking about

something I'm good at, but I have to play it down because I wouldn't want the guy to think I might actually be better than the guy at something."

Blah, blah, blah. Even if a character's personality is to talk on and on like this, you can still show this trait, while inserting the viewpoint's thoughts and showing the view-point's actions as well as the actions of the
other characters and letting them interrupt once in a while, or at least try to get a word in.

The ho-hum moments. Rewrite the following passage of dialogue so it has tension, suspense, and/or conflict, so it's interesting to read because there's something at stake. You can use either Lyle's or Alice's viewpoint. Oh, and one other thing—your imagination.

Lyle joined Alice out on the porch, where she was eating popcorn.

"What are you thinking about?" he asked.

She smiled. "Do you really want to know?"

He nodded.

"Everything I have to do tomorrow. The laundry, the grocery shopping, cleaning the house, weeding the flower beds..."

"Hmmmmm." Lyle munched his popcorn thoughtfully. "Did you see that the Grangers got a new car?" he asked, pointing across the street.

"Yeah, it's green, same as the car they traded in."

"Yeah, well, green's a good color."

In case you need a little help, these two could be avoiding talking about Alice's cancer. Or maybe their marriage is dead and there is nothing to talk about. Maybe there's some crazy place you can go with this dialogue that will surprise even you. Let your imagination run wild.

EXERCISE 7

The perfect grammar problem. The following dialogue is way too formal for the two drivers who have just collided in traffic. See what you can to do fix it.

Pat sighed and got out of his car to confront the other driver. "It appears as though we have had a collision. May I see your drivers license and registration?"

"This is my boyfriend's car," the blonde woman told him. "He will kill me. Why were you driving in my lane?"

"I was on my side of the line. You veered over when that motorcycle cut in front of you."

"I did not veer over. I know how to drive. My boyfriend will kill me. I am dead."

"I am sorry to hear that you feel your life is over, but I need to see your proof of insurance."

"You say that like you think I do not have insurance. I will get it. Just a moment. And I would like to see your proof of insurance, as well."

"I do not have insurance."

chapter 13

[PUNCTUATION AND LAST MINUTE CONSIDERATIONS — TYING UP THE LOOSE ENDS]

I received a call one time from an attorney whose client needed "a bit of help" with his novel in the way of grammar, punctuation, and sentence structure.

"It's a fast-moving mystery, but I know of no agent or editor who will look at it in its current form," he told me when he called. He mentioned that he was also Tom Clancy's attorney, so I figured he probably knew what he was talking about. He really believed, otherwise, in the quality of this guy's manuscript.

When I received the manuscript, I saw what he meant. He was absolutely right. It was a great story but had atrocious grammar, punctuation, and sentence structure—mostly in the dialogue scenes.

Even though I've worked on thousands of stories with as many writers over the years, it still surprises me whenever I come across a writer who is an excellent communicator of the written word but stumbles over the mechanics of writing dialogue. I guess I just think that because we've been reading others' stories for so long, we've picked up how to format dialogue so it reads smoothly in our own stories.

But that's not so at all. It's not automatic that because we've been reading dialogue for a long time we'll also know how to write it. If you want to be a fiction writer, one of the most important things you can do for yourself is to learn the mechanics of writing dialogue: where the identifying tags go, how to make dialogue sound most natural, and how to punctuate dialogue. Not knowing these simple little things is sometimes behind the writer's fear of dialogue. If you can get the mechanics down, then you can free your mind to create your story. Oh, and one more minor thing—while knowing

193

the mechanics doesn't guarantee you'll sell your story, it gets you much closer to the editor's desk.

The information that follows will empower you to write the kind of dialogue that will ensure you come across as a professional.

PUNCTUATING TO ACHIEVE RHYTHM

Every story has its own rhythm, and much, maybe most, of that rhythm comes from the way the dialogue scenes are punctuated. A comma put in an awkward place can throw off a sentence and sometimes an entire scene.

I can't think of anything more important when it comes to the practical stuff of writing dialogue than knowing how to punctuate your sentences so your character's voice is authentic and the dialogue is paced for maximum effect: that unique sense of rhythm that makes the story what it is.

Excuse me if I state the basics, but I want to make sure we cover everything so you have no excuse for writing rough and halting dialogue.

- Put quotation marks at the beginning and end of every passage of dialogue.
   Example: "I'm ready to go," Joanie said, standing up.
   Or: Joanie stood up. "I'm ready to go."
   Or: "I think I'm ready," Joanie said as she stood up. "Let's go."
- Use ellipses for words in a character's speech that trail off.
   Example: Unsure of herself, Joanie stood up. "I'm ready to go…"
- Use a dash to show an interruption or a character who breaks off in the middle of a sentence.
   Example: Joanie stood up. "I'm ready to go—"
   "I don't think so." Carl stood in front of her, blocking the doorway.

Study the above sentences and see how every comma, every period, every ellipsis, every dash is inside of the quotation marks. This would also include question marks and exclamation marks. I've seen some published dialogue that used colons and semicolons, but personally, I think this looks rather silly, not like dialogue but a memo. Stay away from any kind of colon in dialogue.

And a word about exclamation marks. Often, new writers rely on them to create the mood of excitement in the scene of dialogue. But using them in this way is to lean on a crutch. They can be quite effective when used once in a while, when a character is over-the-top excited about something. But otherwise, let the spoken words do the work. Write the kind of dialogue for your characters that leaves no doubt in your reader's mind about the level of excitement, anxiety, or anger.

CONSTRUCTING PARAGRAPHS

One of the most difficult things for new writers to learn, it would seem, is how to break a dialogue scene into paragraphs. It's actually quite simple. You only need to give it some conscious thought. There is one basic "rule." Every character gets his own paragraph. This goes for action, narrative, a character's inner musings or dialogue. Everything that pertains to that character goes into one paragraph.

> "And just how do you suppose you're going to break in?" Tom wondered just how much longer he could listen to Dan's stupid ideas.
> Dan smiled. "I'm going to call a locksmith." He pulled out his cell phone.

USING CONTRACTIONS

Which sounds better? "I cannot tell her about Tom," Jill said, her head bowed. "She will think I am the one who started the whole thing." Or, "I can't tell her about Tom," Jill said, her head bowed. "She'll think I'm the one who started the whole thing."

Even without knowing a thing about either Jill or Tom, we have to say the second one because it's the way we talk in real life. And this is usually a "rule" you can trust. If it works in real life, it works in dialogue. Now, of course, there are always exceptions. You might have a very proper character who *will not* use contractions, no matter what. Of course, if the character's personality or upbringing makes it so he talks in very proper English, then let it be. That's another "rule" you can trust—know your characters. But in dialogue, especially, contractions are not only okay, they're usually what sounds the most authentic.

There are other exceptions:

"*I did not have sex with that woman—Ms. Lewinsky.*"

"*I did not, could not, would not kill Nicole.*"

Even if your character normally uses contractions, there comes a time when we need to emphasize something very important, normally a lie. I read once that, under oath, if someone testifying doesn't use a contraction when answering questions, she is lying. Interesting.

USING ITALICS

As a writing coach, I get a lot of questions about italics, when to use them and when not to. There are a couple of "rules" to help guide you.

First, just like with any other tool, you want to use italics sparingly so they don't lose their effectiveness. When you overuse any of the techniques at your disposal, you weaken their ability to communicate whatever it is you want to communicate.

Second, italics have two functions: They add emphasis and indicate a character's thoughts.

When you want to emphasize a word or a phrase in a character's passage of dialogue, use italics, and the reader will be alerted that this is important, something to pay special attention to.

Example: "There's no way he's going with *me* tomorrow, I can tell you that."

Again, don't do this unless you really need to.

When you want to emphasize a character's thoughts, whether in first or third person, use italics. The best reason not to overdo this is because when your protagonist is telling his story, virtually all of his words are actually his thoughts. If you start italicizing everything, the content of his thoughts is weakened simply because you're pointing to all of it and saying it's important. Here is where the *"less is more"* rule is effective. Italicize only those thoughts that are over-the-top emotional or where the character might have some kind of epiphany that you don't want the reader to miss. You can weave the italics right into a passage of dialogue at any point.

"You want it?" the car salesman pressed. "I'll make you a pretty deal."

Of course, Suzanne wanted it. *But I can't afford it,* she thought. *No way.*

USING TAGS

New writers are always asking me how they can get away from using *said* for every line of dialogue. They want to identify their speakers, but they are at a loss how to do it without that one word.

We do need to identify our speakers. Without tags, it's frustrating for readers to have to keep going back ten or so lines to see who the last speaker was and then reading down again, measuring each line in order to keep up with who's saying what. We don't want to make our readers work too hard at reading our story.

Of course, many words come to mind if you're looking for a substitute for *said:* muttered, whispered, exclaimed, explained, reminded, corrected, snarled, sneered, etc. These are all good words. And then there are words like expostulated, reiterated, extrapolated, etc., that we should never use.

The very best way to identify our speakers, though, is with none of the above. What works best is to identify them with action; if it's the viewpoint character, putting his thoughts into his paragraph of dialogue will identify him as well. The following excerpt from Anne Tyler's *A Patchwork Planet* illustrates this. Martine has stopped her car at the curb to pick up the viewpoint character, Barnaby.

> Martine tapped the truck horn. I almost jumped out of my skin.
>
> "Don't do that, okay?" I said, as I opened the passenger door. "A simple 'Hey, you' will suffice."
>
> "What's up?" she asked me. She had already cut the engine. "I thought we were trimming a tree."
>
> "Mrs. Alford died," I said.
>
> "No!"
>
> I hadn't meant to be so blunt about it. I settled in my seat and shut my door. "She had a heart attack," I said.
>
> "Well, damn," Martine said. Then she started the engine again. But she drove very slowly, as if in respect. "She was one of my favorite clients," she said when we reached Falls Road.

In this scene, the action in each paragraph identifies the speaker quite clearly. I'm uncomfortable critiquing published novels, especially when they're written by such a fine writer as Anne Tyler, but the truth is in the above passage, we really don't need any of the *saids*. The action tells us who's speaking in each paragraph. When you use action sentences to identify your speakers, you don't need the *saids* at all.

AVOIDING INAPPROPRIATE TAGS

New writers have their characters nodding, coughing, and laughing sentences in their dialogue, which by the way, doesn't work. A character can only *say* a sentence. Yes, there are variations of *say:* mutter, mumble, whisper, exclaim, snarl, plead, whine, and many more. These work because they're all ways of speaking. But nodding, coughing, and laughing are actions. They can accompany dialogue sentences and should as they add emotion and help your reader visualize what the characters are doing while they're talking. But a character can't nod, cough, or laugh a sentence.

For example, a line of dialogue might read: "I'm out of here," he said, nodding (or coughing or laughing). Not: "I'm out of here," he nodded (or coughed or laughed.) There are many more actions I've seen writers use besides these three: grinned, sniffed, smiled, and more. They usually want to show a character's physical response while speaking the dialogue. This is fine, just do it in a separate sentence or attach it to a sentence tag.

POSITIONING TAGS

There are stronger and weaker places to position our tags in dialogue passages. We need to be aware of this in order to write dialogue with an effective rhythm.

The weakest place for a tag in a dialogue sentence is in the front: *Jane said, "I'd like to try that if you don't mind."*

The next to best place for a tag is in the middle of the sentence: *"I'd like to try that," Jane said, "if you don't mind."* Putting the tag in the middle suggests a pause and changes the rhythm.

The best place for a tag, usually but not always, is at the end of a sentence: *"I'd like to try that if you don't mind," Jane said.*

That said, it's usually a mistake to put the tag at the end of a series of dialogue sentences, and I see this all of the time from new writers who just don't know any better: *"I'd like to try that if you don't mind. I've done it before and I think I could do it again. Let me at least try," Jane said.*

How could this sentence be rewritten and work? If your character's dialogue includes a series of sentences, always place the tag at the end of the first sentence: *"I'd like to try that if you don't mind," Jane said. "I've done it before and I think I could do it again. Let me at least try."*

If you read all of the above sentences out loud, you should be able to tell the difference in rhythm, why they work or don't work. The placement of our tags is important for an overall effect in our dialogue passages.

HANDLING PHONE CONVERSATIONS

The biggest mistake writers make with dialogue in phone conversations is to report only one side of the conversation—the viewpoint character's side. But if we're inside of the viewpoint character's head, that means he's hearing not only his own voice but also the voice of the character on the other end of the phone line. So we need to also write that into the dialogue along with the viewpoint character's response.

Here's an example of what I mean from Anne Tyler's *The Accidental Tourist:*

> "It's Muriel," she said.
> "Muriel," he said.
> "Muriel Pritchett."
> "Ah yes," he said, but he still had no clue who she was.
> "From the vet's?" she asked. "Who got on so good with your dog?"
> "Oh, the vet's!"

Phone conversations in dialogue are a little tricky because, of course, they consist of mostly spoken words—not a lot of action. Cell phones make it easier to incorporate action because a character can be playing racquetball or flying to meet his partner on the opposite trapeze while talking on his cell phone. So there's no excuse for static phone conversations where characters are just sitting in one place talking.

USING HUMOR IN DIALOGUE

Some of us know how to use humor in dialogue and some of us don't. The best way to find out if we're one of the ones who do is to read our work out loud to others or to give it to others and watch them read it—and guess what—if they laugh, we've succeeded in being funny with our dialogue, and if they don't, we'd better stick to writing more serious dialogue for our characters. Ha-ha, laugh-out-loud humor is difficult to write for even the most clever among us. To my surprise, I once heard Dave Barry say that writing humor was *hard work.* Dave Barry! One of the funniest writers around!

Humorous dialogue is best used for comical characters, such as tricksters, mothers-in-laws, crazy next-door neighbors, dumb villains, etc. Humorous dialogue can lighten up a heavy story and allow the reader to breathe again after a tense scene, allow the reader to breathe again.

If you suspect you're not one of the funny ones, try to cultivate the skill of learning to write humorous dialogue so that you can use it at least once in a while, when you need it. Since humor seems to emerge out of the way certain writers view their worlds, if you're not one of them, you'll probably never write comedic fiction, creating the kind of story that is funny all the way through. But to throw in a funny line of dialogue once in a while goes a long way in holding your reader's attention. Humor hooks readers. They know if a character says something funny once, he most likely will again, and so they're watching for that, waiting for you to surprise them and make them laugh again.

Just For Fun

Your female character is walking late at night on a downtown street of a big city. Suddenly she is accosted by three teenage boys who grab her purse. She yells something at them as they run away. What does she yell? Write one line of dialogue for each type of character below. Try to be as original as you can. The goal is to surprise your reader.

- a mom from the suburbs
- a prostitute
- a businesswoman
- an undercover cop
- a grandmother
- a drag queen

UNDERSTANDING THE IMPORTANCE OF RETICENCE

Just a word about the tendency to have our characters spilling their guts to other characters in every scene, thinking we're moving the story along. This isn't normal behavior for most people, so it makes sense that it's not normal for our characters.

Reticence in sharing our souls is something we learn as we grow out of childhood. Sometimes I think it's a kind of loss of innocence that's too bad, but we simply learn whom we can and cannot trust with our heart issues. If we want our characters to be real, we have to let them hold back the same way real human beings would. Of course, there are always the exceptions— those who don't trust anybody and consequently say very little and those who foolishly trust everybody, spilling their guts to everyone they meet.

Just like it's uncomfortable for most of us when someone does this, so is it uncomfortable for the reader when a character does it. So for the most part, rather than jumping into the water fully clothed, your characters should be just putting their toes into the water when it comes to baring their hearts and souls to other characters in your dialogue scene. Not only is this more real, but it also goes a long way in creating suspense. The less your character tells us about himself, while letting on that there's more to know, the more likely we'll be to keep turning the pages to find out the rest.

Just as it takes a lifetime of practice to become skilled as a writer, it takes many years to learn to write dialogue that works on every level and connects with readers. The more of the techniques in this chapter that you can incorporate into your dialogue skills, the more seriously the reader will take your dialogue.

Along these lines, a few dialogue dos and don'ts come to mind. While creating dialogue for our characters is largely intuitive, there are some definite things you can do or avoid doing that will help you write more authentic speech for your characters.

EXERCISE 1

Punctuating to achieve rhythm. All scenes of dialogue have a rhythm to them, and at least part of the rhythm comes from the punctuation. A period, a comma, an exclamation point—they all make a subtle difference and can make a dialogue scene soar or sink. Punctuate the following sentences to achieve the best rhythm.

- I've always loved you she told him and now I'm free to act on it
- He waved a hand in the air yelling Hey Dawn over here
- That's the dumbest thing I ever heard but right then John interrupted him
- Careful he warned you don't want to cut your thumb off
- What do you think I want she asked as she closed the gap between them
- I'll be happy to do that but my voice trailed off and I knew I couldn't finish
- It's over there she pointed a finger behind that car
- You think you know everything she screamed but you have no clue

EXERCISE 2

Constructing paragraphs. Break the following paragraph into three separate paragraphs.

"But I'm not ready to go home yet," Jennifer said as she kept walking straight past her house, picking up her pace as she went. Lisa followed, trying hard to keep up. "Won't your parents be mad if you're not home by nine o'clock?" They'd been through this before and Lisa remembered how Jennifer's dad had yelled. "Who cares if they're mad?" Jennifer slowed down just a bit. "It's my life, and I have to live it my way."

EXERCISE 3

Using contractions. Rewrite the following passages of dialogue and use contractions where there aren't any. See the difference contractions make.

- "He cannot ride the horse as he has never had any riding lessons."
- "I will not run that fast because it is hard on my joints."
- "I have known him for years and he is my best friend."

EXERCISE 4

Using italics. Write a two-page dialogue scene in which your protagonist is trying to make his boss understand that all of the evening overtime he's putting in is hurting his family, that he's not getting to see his kids before they go to bed, and his wife is angry most of the time when he gets home from work. He *wants* his evenings off. Insert into the dialogue italicized words that your protagonist needs to emphasize to his boss. In every scene of dialogue, the words we *don't* say are often the most important ones. In this scene, include at least three lines of internal thoughts that emphasize how he feels, words he knows he can't say out loud.

EXERCISE 5

Using tags. Write a two-page scene of dialogue between three characters without any saids at all. You may use action and your protagonist's thoughts and observations, but no saids.

DIALOGUE

EXERCISE 6

Avoiding inappropriate tags. Study the following sentences and put the word *right* or *wrong* beside each of them. Be sure to cover the answers in the parentheses at the end of this exercise before you start.

[1] He nodded, "Yeah, I think I'll go to the game, after all."

[2] "Hey Brenda," he said with a smirk, "how about meeting after work for a drink?"

[3] "You don't really think I'm going to answer that, do you?" she smiled.

[4] "I can't do that." Brenda laughed. "I might actually look like I know what I'm doing."

[5] "I can't do that," she said, laughing, "I might actually look like I know what I'm doing."

(Answers: 1. Wrong: period after nodded; 2. Right; 3. Wrong: capital S; 4. Right; 5. Right)

EXERCISE 7

Positioning tags. Go through a story you've written, focusing on where you positioned your tags. Change as many of them as you can to action or the protagonist's internal thoughts. If you have to use said, position it at the end of the first line of dialogue in most cases, though sometimes you may want to vary this, especially if you have a lot of lines where you choose to use said instead of an action or a thought.

EXERCISE 8

Handling phone conversations. Write one page of telephone dialogue. Let there be something at stake, something the viewpoint character stands to gain or lose. Make sure we hear both sides of the conversation. Omit all hellos and goodbyes.

EXERCISE 9

Humor. Write a two-page scene of dialogue where two elderly ladies are in conflict about which of them should "go" for the new gentleman, Henry, who just moved into their retirement home. The goal in this exercise is to "try" to write a funny scene. If this idea doesn't appeal to you, try another idea of your own.

EXERCISE 10

Understanding the importance of reticence. Two characters who met on the Internet dating site match.com are meeting for their first date at a coffee shop. They are definitely attracted to each other, but each has a secret in his or her background that could affect the relationship in a negative way. Write two two-page scenes—one from each character's point of view. Concentrate on letting the characters reveal themselves gradually in the dialogue so it feels as natural as possible while being aware of moving the relationship forward.

chapter 14 *

[DIALOGUE DOS AND DON'TS—SOME PRACTICAL TIPS]

"So that's just one of the rules of fiction," I said lightly, ending my instruction for that night.

"Rules?!" one of my students piped up. "What do you mean rules? You're kidding, right?"

"Er, no, well, not exactly."

"Forget that."

"Look, they're not really rules," I backpedaled, feeling horrible for ruining my student's evening. I hated discouraging writing students. That's the last thing I wanted to do. "You know, they're just like, well, stop or yield signs on the road. We have to—"

"No way. Who wants to stop or yield when you're in the middle of a writing frenzy? You know, when you're seriously writing some good stuff?"

He had a point. "Okay, they're not like stop or yield signs, but, well, we need, er, a few guidelines so we look like we know what we're doing."

He finally accepted that.

Look, I don't like "rules" any more than you do, but even more than that, I don't like looking like I don't know what I'm doing. I actually think looking like a dork is worse than having to follow the rules. At least for me, that's true. So I've learned the "rules" of fiction more to save my image than anything else, I suppose. Not that our images are worth a lot, but sometimes we're under the illusion that they are.

This chapter is not about "rules," but it is about providing you with some guidelines so you can be more conscious of the fiction writing process. It's true that knowledge is power. Following are some dos and don'ts that will empower you to write the best fiction that you're capable of writing. I've found that these guidelines also empower me to have a better answer for my students in the future who ask why we need "rules."

When dealing with dos and don'ts, we always start with the dos, but in this case we're starting with the don'ts so we can end with something positive—the dos.

- *Don't try too hard.* I've noticed lately that some stars are falling flat on their faces in their efforts to get their new television shows off the ground. It seems that it's possible to fail no matter how big the star. I have a theory about this, because with each new program I've thought to myself, *Why isn't she just being herself? She's trying too hard and the lines all feel contrived.* I'm never surprised when the show goes down; I know it will from the very first attempt.

  So, guess what happens when we try too hard to write dialogue? It shows. And because it shows, it doesn't work. As I've observed with the failed television programs, when a writer is trying too hard, the dialogue often feels contrived and forced.

  Okay, so we know what not to do. But how do we not do that? How do we not try to write dialogue?

  By simply relaxing into your character to the point that the dialogue is coming out of a place deep inside of you that is the character. And yes, since there are at least two, possibly more, characters in every scene of dialogue, it is a little schizophrenic, but who ever said writers were sane? You created these characters, and because you created them you should be able to speak out of the deepest part of who they are. We only distance ourselves from our characters when we don't like them and don't want to own them, and the result is forced, unnatural dialogue. I know some of this sounds like psychobabble, but that makes it no less true.

  The next time you sit down to work on your story, try some of the exercises at the end of this chapter and see if they help you to write dialogue that is organic with each character.

- *Don't betray your character or reader.* To write bad dialogue is to betray both. How? By putting words in the characters' mouths that they'd never say. It's betraying the character because you're not being true to who he really is, and it's betraying the reader by not writing with integrity.

  We have to let our characters tell their stories. In a sense, yes, these are *our* stories, but we've created characters to play the various parts, so we need to make sure we afford them their dignity and don't exploit them by putting words in their mouths that *we* want them to say.

  To betray and exploit our characters is to:

- have them expressing strong feelings on subjects that might normally put them to sleep
- have them rambling on and on about some issue in which they really have no interest
- put reams of information in their mouths that they would never say out loud just because we need to educate the reader on the story background
- put reams of description in their mouths that they would never say out loud just because we need the reader to see the other characters and/or setting
- give them a voice at any point that isn't who they are
- use them to preach our own personal agenda. Which is our next don't.

- *Don't use your characters to preach your personal agenda.* I feel strongly about the death penalty, child abuse, and chocolate. Prison reform, religious fundamentalists, and weight loss. Road rage. But what kind of a writer would I be if, every chance I got, I was putting words in my characters' mouths about these issues and subjects? I wouldn't be walking in integrity, and I sure wouldn't be creating characters who did.

  Okay, I'd be lying if I said I'm writing stories that don't include my personal pet peeves and issues I feel strongly about. I don't know of a writer who is so detached from his personal agenda that he isn't writing about it at all. We write about subjects that matter to us, that we feel passionately about. We're *supposed* to be doing that. But our characters will only be authentic if we allow them to have their personal issues, too, and to express their thoughts and feelings about those issues in a way that is very much in their own voice.

  For example, I happen to be writing a novel about the death penalty. That's the subject, but the characters all come from different places, and when they make a philosophical statement, I better make sure it's *their* philosophical statement, not mine. One of the main characters has a lot of traits that I don't respect, and sometimes I don't like writing her scenes. She says things that make me so mad, yet I need her because she represents the opposing side of the death penalty (opposing in this case meaning the opposite side of my own) and is the catalyst for many discussions in the story that I want my characters to engage in on this subject that, yes, I feel so strongly about.

- *Don't try to be cute or clever.* This don't is in the same family as *Don't try too hard.* Writers who think every time their characters open their mouths they have to say something entertaining, amusing, or clever are in the same league as actual people who are forever trying to make the rest of us laugh. After a while, these folks are just annoying. You really don't want your characters to annoy your readers. This is not a good thing.

  How do you know if you're trying to be cute or clever? Well, this is the difficult part. I have a sense that real people don't know when they're doing this, so I wonder if writers can know. I'm hoping that just pointing it out will be enough to alert you that it's possible so you'll watch for it and resist the tendency. One sign is if your characters are always laughing at each other. If you find yourself constantly writing, He laughed, She chuckled, He cracked up, They all laughed, They split a gut, you're probably doing a bit of this. It's better to underplay than overplay. Subtlety is always preferable to bowling the reader over with your characters' personalities.

- *Don't let the dialogue drive the scene.* I've read stories by writers (unpublished—an important distinction in this context) that were 80 percent to 90 percent dialogue, and unless you're very good at this or you're writing a specific kind of story in which this could be effective, an all- or mostly-dialogue story just doesn't work.

  Dialogue is a vehicle for moving the plot forward, for characterization, for providing background information to the reader, for description of other characters, for creating suspense and building tension—all purposes we've talked about in this book so far. But dialogue is the means to an end, not the end in and of itself.

  In a plot-driven story, the plot events are what drive the story forward, and in a character-driven story, the protagonist's internal transformation is what moves the story. The dialogue is simply a means of engaging the characters in a scene with each other so they can *move*—externally or internally, preferably both.

  When you allow dialogue to drive a scene, unless you're an expert dialogue writer, your characters end up talking all over the place *about* the story events and the other characters, and so the action and narrative suffers. The characters come off as shallow because they're just *talking*. Not thinking or acting, just flapping their lips. And we know what we think of real people who are all hot air.

You want your story to be three-dimensional, to include action, narrative, *and* dialogue. Of course, there are exceptions—moments when the dialogue will take over a scene—just like there are moments when the action and narrative will take over. This is as it should be. But these are definitely exceptions. For the most part, you want to weave these three elements into each scene you write. In a three-dimensional scene, the dialogue affects the narrative and the narrative affects the action, which affects the dialogue, etc. You can mix all of this up many different ways because most of the time you need all three.

- *Don't worry about perfection.* Dialogue is the one element of fiction where you have to worry the least about getting it "right." By that I mean grammar and sentence structure. You can get by with more in dialogue than you can in any of the other elements of fiction because we want our characters to sound like real people having real live conversations. People talk in sentence fragments, phrases and half phrases, slang, and dialects. Most of us don't care how we sound or come off to one another when we're just hanging out, and our characters don't either. It's only the writer who gets uptight about this stuff.

    There's no such thing as the perfect sentence in dialogue, unless it's "Help!" when a character is drowning or "No!" when a female character doesn't want to have sex. It's that simple. If you could get just this one point from this book, you could relax and never be afraid of dialogue again. Dialogue is just people talking.

    To let go of your need to write perfect dialogue means you'll create dialogue that's more authentic because you'll let your characters be who they are and talk out of that real place inside of them. We're hearing a lot about breathing these days, and sometimes I wonder if we would be less uptight as writers if we could just breathe with our characters when writing their dialogue. It's worth a try.

    When feeling the need to write perfect dialogue, just remember:

    - Your characters are human, definitely not perfect.
    - Your characters aren't thinking nearly as hard about what they're saying as you are.
    - Your characters have something to say and you need to listen instead of think so hard about what *you* want them to say or think they *should* be saying.

- You don't have perfect speech, so why do you think your characters should?
- Who are you trying to impress?

Fixing Your Own Story

Make a list of your own dos and don'ts, those weaknesses you're aware of in your dialogue that affect the pace of your story, the believability of your characters, or the furtherance of the plot.

Now you know everything—almost—that you're not supposed to do when writing dialogue. But what *works?* When writing dialogue, what *can* you do that's effective and engages readers in your characters' conversations with each other?

- *Do write dialogue that's worth eavesdropping on.* It was Gary Provost who originally said it and I thought it was a great thing to remember: "There's no absolute rule about when you use dialogue and when you shouldn't, but here's a good generalization: If a stranger were nearby, would he try to eavesdrop on the conversation? If the answer is no, don't use the dialogue. If the answer is yes, use it."

    That makes perfect sense to me. If we went through every story we wrote with this in mind, I bet we'd get rid of a lot of the ho-hum dialogue we write.

    Every once in a while I take a pad and paper and sit in a restaurant and write. If there are other restaurant patrons nearby, and if they're talking about anything interesting at all, then I'm sunk. I simply can't concentrate. I once heard true crime writer Ann Rule talk about her friendship with horror writer John Saul. When they go out to lunch together, their conversation is often focused on who killed whom and with what kind of weapon. She says they get all kinds of looks from the people around them.

    So the question to remember is: Would anyone want to eavesdrop on your characters' conversation? Why or why not?

- *Do know your characters (especially the minor ones).* I've mentioned it many times in this book, already, but it bears repeating. It's only as you know your characters that you can write dialogue for them that rings true. Otherwise, it sounds like stick people talking, and all of your characters will sound the same—they'll sound like you. I once read in a writing book that if your story could take place anywhere, then you haven't got hold of either your setting or your story because the setting is intricately connected to the story. The same is true of dialogue. If the dialogue you create could be spoken by any of the characters, then you don't know your characters.

Damon Knight gives us some good advice on this subject in his book *Creating Short Fiction:* "Dialogue in fiction should resemble real dialogue with the various hesitations, repetitions, and other glitches edited out of it. Listen to people talk. No two are exactly alike. By the way they talk, their choice of words, the things they talk about, and the attitudes they express, they tell you where they grew up, how they were educated, the kind of work they do, what social class they belong to, and much more. When you know who your character is and where she comes from and what she's like, you should know instinctively what she will say and how she'll say it. If the people in your stories *don't* talk 'in character,' it must be because you don't know them well enough, or because you have not spent enough time listening attentively to people's speech patterns."

We often make special efforts to do character sketches and charts on our protagonists, antagonists, and one or two minor characters, but we need to also know the rest of the cast so the entire story will ring true when all of our characters speak, not just the major players. How are we going to know if a line is false if we don't know the character speaking it?

A couple of years ago, I started writing first-person profiles for all of the characters in my stories. This allows them to tell me who they are in their own voices. This is actually pages and pages of dialogue when you think about it, because I'm letting them talk to me. It has opened my characters up to me like nothing I've ever tried before. All of these years, I've been toiling over those humongous lists of questions in dossiers suggested by writing teachers to get to know your characters. I get so bored answering all of the questions and filling out the dossiers that I have no passion left for the story when it's time to write it. So I've become an advocate of the first-person profile, especially for the antagonist, because writing in first person forces me to get inside of his head.

- *Do pace your dialogue.* Every story has a rhythm, and we need to try to get into our story's rhythm so it moves well. As we learned in chapter eight, we can use dialogue to either speed up a scene or slow it down. When we're conscious of this process, our dialogue works in tandem with the action and narrative to create a flow that's organic to the story we want to tell. For example, if it's an action/adventure story, the dialogue will move as quickly as the action and narrative, unless the action is over the top, and then you can use the kind of nondramatic dialogue that will slow the scenes down a bit. If it's a romance, you may use mostly dialogue to tell your story, and in this case, it will probably move along at a nice clip.

  When you've just come off a fast-paced action scene, you might want to create a scene of interaction between your characters for the purpose of reflecting on what just happened. Whatever your story needs, you want to be conscious enough of how dialogue works in pacing so you can accelerate or brake at will. This will make your dialogue more effective because it will contribute to the story's overall rhythm, making the entire story a smoother ride for your reader.

- *Do write functional dialogue.* Functional dialogue is dialogue that goes somewhere, that has a destination and propels the story forward. It's dialogue with a purpose. As we've read throughout this book, dialogue needs to do a lot of things for the story, sometimes all at once. How can we possibly stay aware of all that dialogue has to do while we're putting words in our characters' mouths?

  The answer to this question is: *Don't think.* About anything. You write dialogue from a place in your gut, not your head. The sooner you learn how to do this, the better you'll become at dialogue.

  "Right," I can hear you saying. "You've told me a hundred things I need to think about while I'm writing dialogue. That's what this book has been all about from the first page. Now you're telling me, 'Don't think'? Are you nuts?"

  Actually, learning the lessons in this book is important so they'll become second nature to you. But while applying them, you don't want to be thinking about them. When learning to ride a motorcycle a couple of years ago, I only thought about the "rules" for the first few months. Now I never think about them because I know what they are. I don't *have* to think about them. They're a part of me. Okay, you can think about the rules in this book because they're new to you, but eventually you have to let go and surrender to the process of writing dialogue. It's as easy as riding a motorcycle; you only need to learn and then let go. There is one way you know if you've learned or not—if the ride is still a bumpy one, you're not quite there. When it's smooth, it's because you've let go. And the result is functional dialogue—authentic dialogue, suspenseful dialogue, purposeful dialogue.

- *Do honor your character's journey.* Your character is going somewhere. You may have had a destination in mind, but now he's happily on his way, not the least bit concerned about your original plan for him. Again, if you want your story to be organic, you need to honor your character and put words in his mouth that are intricately connected to his internal and external journey, which is your story.

  Of course, in order to honor your character's journey, you have to know what it is. Be sure to spend time pondering your character's journey before you begin to write. Then, when he speaks, he will know where he's going and can talk about it with intelligence and integrity. For example, in chapter three we looked at a passage of Atticus Finch's dialogue in *To Kill a Mockingbird.* Here's a man who was very aware of his journey, his stand against racism, from the very beginning of the novel. His words indicate just how aware he was. Let's look at a paragraph of his speech once more:

  > "What was the evidence of her offense? Tom Robinson, a human being. She must put Tom Robinson away from her. Tom Robinson was her daily reminder of what she did. What did she do? She tempted a Negro."

  Harper Lee had a destination for Atticus Finch and in a focused way took him toward that destination in much of the dialogue that he spoke throughout the novel. Not to preach but to speak out what would become his destiny at the end of the story and change an entire town. That's how powerful dialogue can be and how important it is that you commit to honoring your character's journey while writing dialogue.

- *Do search for the essence.* In *How to Write Best-Selling Fiction*, Dean Koontz tells us,

  > Many writers think—erroneously—that fiction should be a mirror of reality. Actually, it should act as a sifter to *refine* reality until only the essence is before the reader. This is nowhere more evident than in fictional dialogue. In real life, conversation is often roundabout, filled with general commentary and

polite rituals. In fiction, the characters must always get right to the point when they talk.

Every scene of dialogue has an essence, and that's what the writer is responsible for re-creating. The goal is to always write authentic dialogue while writing only the dialogue that matters in the current scene as it connects to the overall story problem. There are nuggets in all dialogue, and if we want those nuggets to shine, we have to cut away all of the extraneous words that distract from the essence of the nuggets.

My personal opinion is that most of us write too many words. We would do well to write far less than we do. I don't think I'm exaggerating when I say that probably 75 percent of the writers I work with in a coaching capacity regularly complain about the word limits imposed on them in their writing assignments. They haven't learned to appreciate that word limits are a gift to teach them to write and make every word count for something. When learning to write with word limits, when being open to the process instead of resisting it, certain writers emerge as champions because they embrace the lessons and discover the essence of each scene as they write it.

If you want to get in the habit of searching for the essence in your story dialogue, comb through your characters' words until you find the ones they *have* to say, the ones that without, the story would be lost on the reader. I guarantee you, there are very few of those. Oh, yes, we need the words that characterize and create suspense and tighten the tension, but to find the essence means to tie even these words into the story's theme so every word in every scene connects in some way to the big picture.

I don't believe that you always have to know up front what the dialogue's essence is while writing each scene of your story, but if your intention is to find it and cut away everything around it so it can come forth, then this is what will happen. All it takes is a willingness on your part to find it, to not be satisfied until everything but the essence is cut away.

So these are just a few of the dos and don'ts, guidelines to help you with what's really important in writing dialogue. And back to the writing frenzy my student mentioned in the beginning of this chapter. The creation of the first draft of a story is not the time to be thinking about the guidelines, worrying about whether you're following them, thinking about the rightness or the wrongness of style, voice, form, or anything else. But when you've written the first draft and are into your revisions, using the left side of your brain, these guidelines will come in handy as they will give you something tangible with which to measure the quality of your writing.

Our final chapter addresses our relationship with our readers. This is the most important relationship we have after the one with our characters. If we can understand what dialogue can do for our readers, we'll get more excited about writing the kind of dialogue that delivers substance and connects in ways that sometimes can even change a reader's life.

EXERCISE 1

Don't try too hard. If you want to ease into your character's persona before you write a scene, the following exercises might help:

- Put on a hat that your character would wear when writing his dialogue. (You might want to go out and invest in a few hats for this exercise.)
- Put on music that your character would listen to.
- Rent a movie that includes a character that your character reminds you of and watch it right before your writing time.
- Write up to five e-mails in your character's voice to the other characters in the story to prime the pump before you work on your story.
- Cut a photo out of a magazine that looks like your character and post it nearby while you're writing his dialogue.
- If you can't get into any of the above, you need to do more work on your character's development.

EXERCISE 2

Don't betray your character or reader. Think about what it would mean to write the kind of dialogue that would betray the characters in your story. Pondering this will ultimately indicate how well you know your characters. Write one paragraph for each character. In this paragraph, come up with a subject that would betray that character's basic personality and the goals you have for that character in the story.

Don't use your characters to preach your personal agenda. Take any or all of the following issues and write one paragraph of a character's dialogue that preaches and one that simply shares an opinion. (Of course, there are certain characters who preach because that's who they are, in which case preaching is okay—but they're not usually characters your reader will have a lot of respect for.) If these issues don't light you up, choose different ones.

- abortion
- the environment
- euthanasia
- homelessness
- war
- child abuse

Don't try to be cute or clever. If you're unaware of when you may be writing cute or clever dialogue, this exercise may help you. The goal is for you to become aware of this tendency, so try to answer the following questions as honestly as you can about any of the dialogue you suspect may be too cute or clever.

- Does this line of dialogue ring true for this character?
- Am I trying to lighten things up too much by having my character laughing too hard and too often in this scene?
- Is this line of dialogue necessary or have I just thrown it in, hoping to entertain the reader?
- Do I understand my character's sense of humor and am I being true to it in every scene in my story?
- Is there a way I can show my character's sense of humor more subtly?

Don't let the dialogue drive the scene. Using only dialogue, write one page of a scene that shows one character in conflict with another character over money. Now rewrite the same scene using dialogue, narrative, and action, first from one character's point of view, then from the other character's point of view. The goal of this exercise is to see how action and narrative contribute to a scene what dialogue only can't.

Don't worry about perfection. Write one page of dialogue without thinking about any of the rules of writing dialogue. You can make up a character or use one in a story you've been writing. The goal is to write without thinking, to just go. Let her say anything that comes into her mind, no matter if her dog would turn over in its grave. Don't even punctuate if you don't want to. If you do it often enough, this one exercise may free you up to where you're not afraid of dialogue anymore.

EXERCISE 7

Do write dialogue that's worth eavesdropping on. With your pad and pencil, go sit in a public place like a park or mall and listen to people talk until you hear a conversation that gets your attention. If that never happens (many people talk about nothing), develop one of the nothing conversations into a conversation that would raise the hairs on the heads of anyone nearby.

EXERCISE 8

Do know your characters (especially the minor ones). Write first-person profiles for all of the characters in a story you're working on. If you're not currently working on a story, be spontaneous. Write three first-person profiles of characters you would like to write stories about. It doesn't matter if you like the characters or not. This is organic, so just go for it and see what happens.

EXERCISE 9

Do pace your dialogue. Practice pacing your dialogue. Use the following scenarios for practice and write one-page scenes of dialogue.

Fast-paced
- three friends at a party
- two car thieves on a joyride
- two female friends at a mall

Slow-paced
- two monks in a monastery

- two hikers on a trail
- a woman and her therapist in his office

EXERCISE 10

Do write functional dialogue. Experiment. Write a page of dialogue without thinking about anything at all. You can use characters from a story you're writing or just write dialogue in a vacuum. You're coloring out of the lines, so it doesn't matter.

EXERCISE 11

Do honor your character's journey. Choose five characters from recent short stories or novels you've read and find lines of dialogue that honor each protagonist's journey. Or even the antagonist's journey; antagonists have an agenda and a destiny, too. These lines should indicate who they are and what their goal is in the story. If you want to use a character or characters from your own story in one of these exercises, that's even better. Choose dialogue that clearly indicates who the character is in the story.

EXERCISE 12

Do search for the essence. Choose a character from a movie you've seen recently, a story you've read, or even someone in your real life, and write one page of fictional dialogue about something that's desperately important to this person. When you've completed the page, cut away everything until you have only the essence of the passion and subject left.

chapter 15

[CONNECTING WITH READERS — YOU CAN MAKE A DIFFERENCE]

How many times have we been told, as writers, that we should write for ourselves and no one else? We shouldn't try to please anyone but ourselves. Not family, friends, co-workers, acquaintances, enemies. It's just you and the blank page.

This is partly true. Integrity demands that we write out of the truth that resides in us.

But there's a delicate balance here, because if we are so concerned about being true to ourselves and not pleasing others we become self-serving, and the consequence of that is to exclude our readers. And don't think they can't feel that.

There are too many self-serving writers out there already. This happens to be a personal soapbox of mine, so I'm not going to go on and on about it lest I do the very thing I'm telling you not to do.

In this chapter I want to chat with you about how we can serve our readers through our fictional dialogue to assure their loyalty and commitment to our characters once they've started down the road with them. There is a line in the Bible that has always been a favorite of mine: "...whoever wants to become great among you must be your servant..." (Matt. 20:26) I believe greatness and servanthood are intricately connected. If we can learn to consider our readers with every story we write, we can serve them with our fiction in a way that can empower them and change their lives. For me, this is what writing fiction is all about.

A character's dialogue, delivered with passion and authenticity, can actually change a reader's life. And isn't that what many of us are about when we write—changing lives? Sure, some of us, maybe even most of us, want to make money at this. Some of us would even like a little fame thrown in. We write to entertain our friends, relatives, and strangers out there in readerland. But down deep in the core of our hearts, wouldn't it be wonderful if we knew we had made a difference in someone's life through the way we portrayed a fictional character?

I'm a living example that this can happen. I'm sure, if I thought about it, I could think of many lines of dialogue that have in some way changed my life and made me a better, more loving person. But I can think of one for sure, used earlier in one of the excerpts in this book. It's Emma's words from Larry McMurtry's *Terms of Endearment* to her boys as she lay dying.

> "... you're going to remember that you love me," Emma said. "I imagine you'll wish you could tell me that you've changed your mind, but you won't be able to, so I'm telling you now I already know you love me, just so you won't be in doubt about that later..."

Emma is an unforgettable character to me because of this one moment where she gives her son, Tommy, the gift of knowing in these words. He's being ornery and his heart is closed to her. He's angry with her for dying. She's going past all of that to let him know that her knowing as a mother transcends his behavior and closed heart, that she knows deep down in his heart he loves her and while he's forgotten it right now, he'll remember it later.

I've taken Emma's words and have actually used them with my own grown son at this moment in time when he can't reach out, when his heart is closed to me. "I know that you love me," I've told him over and over again. "I know that you love me." It's my gift to him for this time in our relationship.

I tell you this story to let you know that you can create the kind of dialogue for your characters that your reader will remember, possibly forever. This is what I want to leave with you in this last chapter. To encourage you to, as much as is within you, make an emotional connection with your reader, to serve your reader in such a way that your dialogue will hit its mark in his heart. I've found a few ways to do that.

ENTERTAIN THE READER

As a writer, my mother loved to entertain, especially children. She would write the silliest stories. I remember the one about the man who lived in the crooked house. He would chat with those who came to call from his ceiling or one of the walls. She was skilled at the kind of conversational dialogue

Fixing Your Own Story

Take a hard look at your most recent story. Did you have the reader in mind?
- Does it entertain?
- Does it educate?
- Does it surprise?
- Does it validate?
- Does it evoke emotion?
- Does it challenge?
- Does it empower?

that would make children laugh and laugh. She would capture them with her silly characters and keep them entertained for hours.

Then, in the late sixties and early seventies, something began to happen to, well, all kinds of fiction, but especially children's fiction. First of all, it began to disappear from magazines that had published it for years. But the other thing that happened was that editors began to request that their writers create the kind of fiction that incorporated a "lesson" into the story. The lesson could be about some aspect of children's health or it could be a moral truth, but editors no longer wanted talking animal stories or stories about crooked houses.

Something died inside of my mother that she never quite regained.

I'm personally pleased that the pendulum began to swing in the direction of fiction that actually says something, makes a point of some kind. But I also believe that our fiction can, and should, entertain. I believe that a skilled fiction writer communicates and entertains simultaneously. I'd like to suggest that one of the ways we can serve our readers is to write the kind of dialogue that entertains. This may not seem like such a radical idea, but it is when you consider that editors still want the kind of fiction that, while it entertains, is also "about" something.

When our fiction fails to communicate, our readers are no different after reading our stories. When our fiction fails to entertain, our readers won't stay with our stories long enough for us to communicate with them, and the end result is the same. No change.

At least one of our goals with dialogue should be to hold our reader by entertaining her, putting words in our characters' mouths that will make her laugh, cry, grow, think, smile, remember, feel, gasp, wring her hands, stomp her feet. In short, *move* her in some way. When a reader is entertained, she's relaxed and is open to the truths we want to get across in our characters' interactions with each other.

I like what I heard actor Sean Penn say recently on *Inside the Actors Studio*. He said that if we ever leave a movie theater feeling alone, the movie has failed to communicate its message. That's also true of a reader after putting down a novel.

EDUCATE THE READER

While I don't think it's the primary task of the fiction writer to educate, learning can certainly take place for our readers when engaging with our characters' dialogue. Whether our characters are discussing life in other countries or life in prison, if it's a life our reader hasn't experienced, he learns something.

Ken Kesey's *One Flew Over the Cuckoo's Nest* had a profound effect on me when I read it just because I have no knowledge of what it's like to live in a mental institution. Kesey's novel is full of lively dialogue by quirky characters in a setting completely foreign to most of us. Whether it was Nurse Ratchett or one of the patients speaking, I was turning pages as fast as I could, fascinated with this setting that I knew nothing about. While there was plenty of educational narrative in this story, it was the dialogue that kept me hooked because it was through the dialogue that I really learned what these characters' lives were all about on a daily basis.

The same thing happened when I read Barbara Kingsolver's *The Poisonwood Bible* and Sue Monk Kidd's *The Secret Life of Bees*. Fictional dialogue brings unfamiliar settings to life on the page because dialogue is people.

And dialogue can educate the reader, not only about unfamiliar cultures or settings but also about human interaction because many of the characters in our stories relate to each other very differently than what the reader is used to. The reader learns that there is more than one way to argue, make love, or communicate one's feelings.

Our characters' dialogue can also educate readers about different historical settings. How much more fun to learn about the Civil War through the dialogue of two soldiers than to read a boring narrative history book.

SURPRISE THE READER

Readers love surprises. When your characters keep saying the same things to each other over and over and over again, the reader starts to yawn. I once worked with a writer who must have thought her character had a lot to say, and to a lot of different people. She wrote four restaurant scenes in a row where the protagonist sat down across the table from another character at yet one more restaurant—a different one each time—and poured her heart out. It wasn't just that the setting was the same, but the story this character told was the same.

Now that I think about it, you could actually take this scenario and make it surprise the reader. How? By having her tell a different story to each of the other characters about the same situation. This would surprise the reader because it would show what a liar this character was.

Often the character will say something that surprises even her. Or one of the other characters will say something to surprise all of us and to which your character will have a reaction that could be another surprise. Unpredictability in dialogue—that's what we're after.

Watch out for the tendency to create scenes where characters are simply regurgitating what has just happened in a scene of action. We already know what happened, so unless your character has something new to report, go on to the next scene. Often, after a scene of action, the viewpoint character will need to emotionally and mentally process the event, so you'll need to create a nondramatic scene of dialogue to let him do that. But even here, you'll want to show reactions through his dialogue that we don't expect from him. I don't mean reactions that are out of character, but maybe as he talks about his feelings and shares his thoughts with another character, he'll realize something about himself that he didn't know before or share feelings that he doesn't even understand himself. All of these kinds of elements in scenes of dialogue surprise the reader and keep her engaged.

VALIDATE THE READER

If you validate your reader, he'll love you and read anything you write for the rest of his life. Yes, one of the reasons a reader chooses to read a story in the first place is because he needs validation. This is often on an unconscious level, but if your characters are sharing human emotions and thoughts that aren't always nice about other characters—especially those about a wicked mother or mother-in-law—your reader will embrace your characters and embrace your story.

Readers think they're the only ones with these weird emotions and thoughts, sometimes violent, sometimes loving but toward the wrong people, sometimes inappropriate (to them) sadness. Then, your character is in the car talking to her husband and confesses that she's in love with his best friend. Or whatever. The reader identifies.

Dialogue that validates is dialogue that makes the reader feel okay about himself in a world full of normal people when he feels very abnormal. Validating dialogue in the mouths of your characters is dialogue that emotionally connects your reader to your characters so they truly will be unforgettable in her mind, the lessons learned lasting a very long time, maybe the rest of her life.

Validating dialogue lets the reader know that he's not alone, that he's part of a universal family, which remember, as Sean Penn said above, is what we're after.

CAUSE THE READER TO FEEL

When we create real characters with real feelings about real situations in their lives, the reader is drawn into our story as if it's happening to her. This is how we know we're successful—when the reader so identifies and cares about your characters that she will feel joy, anger, sadness, fear, and all of the other emotions your characters feel as they move through the tragedies and comedies that are their lives.

If we want our readers to remember our characters and their stories, we need to evoke emotion. Think about your own life. The moments in your life that stand out in your mind are those you've experienced with the most emotion. It doesn't matter what the emotion was. Our feelings put us in the present moment, so when we put dialogue in our characters' mouths that plugs into a conversation the reader has had with someone or makes him think about something or someone that means a lot to him, we're creating one more unforgettable moment for him. In a sense, we're recreating his life for him that he's vicariously reliving through our characters.

This is just one more reason to create dialogue with substance. We may talk about nothing in our real lives, but when our characters talk about nothing, our readers aren't engaged with them on an emotional level. It's only when the dialogue is *about* something that really matters that our readers' hearts begin to stir and before they know it, they're *in* the story, reacting to everything that's going on as if they're living it themselves.

This is our goal in writing dialogue that delivers: to engage our readers so they *feel* what our characters feel.

CHALLENGE THE READER

Just as our characters challenge each other in their dialogue with one another, so do we want our readers to be challenged. When one character challenges another character to a duel, our reader feels an adrenaline rush. But that's an external challenge. Internally, we want to challenge our readers to change their lives if they need changing. We want to cause our readers to think about their lives in new ways. We want our readers to transcend old ways of thinking and believing that no longer fit who they are today. When our characters do this kind of work in their dialogue with each other, our reader does, too.

I don't mean sitting a character down in a therapy office. As long as we are committed to writing dialogue for our characters that matters, that has substance, that is *about* something, our readers will be challenged. How can they not be? If one of your characters suggests to another character that she might be addicted or abused or in some kind of illusion about some part of her life, don't you think your reader might wonder the same thing about her own life?

Challenging the reader is the work of literary and mainstream writers more than it is the work of genre writers. But still, even in genre stories, there are obstacles for the viewpoint character to overcome that should challenge the reader to overcome the same kinds of obstacles in her own life.

EMPOWER THE READER

Finally, we want to empower readers to live their best lives, their most authentic lives, lives they can be proud of. Our dialogue can do that because that's what we're creating for our characters—opportunities for them to interact with each other and ultimately come away from these encounters empowered.

Have you ever had a conversation with someone—a friend, relative, or enemy—and came away feeling defeated and exhausted? This is because you gave your power away to that person in that conversation. Likewise, have you ever had a conversation with someone—a friend, relative, or enemy— and came away empowered, knowing that you owned your own truth in the conversation, that you walked in integrity, that you didn't give up who you were? If we write dialogue that's true to who we've created our characters to be, our readers should be able to recognize which are the disempowered characters and which are the empowered ones and in the process learn how to hold on to their own power in conversation with others. Our characters can teach our readers this through their own process of growth in the story situations we create for them.

As you can see, the dialogue in our stories can go a long way in the process of connecting with readers on many levels. And isn't that what writing fiction is all about? We create characters that we come to know and love as we put words into their mouths and breathe life into their souls. When a person unknown to us, on the other side of the country, possibly on the other side of the globe, picks up our story, she gets to know our characters in the same way we do, through the words we've given them. In that way, as writers, we perform an amazing service for the global consciousness on the planet.

Sounds big. It is. That's how important it is to determine to write effective, authentic, and powerful dialogue that makes the kind of connection that will stay with readers, sometimes throughout their entire lives. To inform their lives. To determine their paths. To encourage and inspire them on their life journeys.

You can learn to write this kind of dialogue.

appendix

[CHECKLIST]

[1] Have you found your voice for the story, and does the dialogue resonate for each character and feel authentic?

[2] Have you done everything you know to release your fear and your characters' dialogue is now coming out of the core of who they are?

[3] Have you come to an understanding of the kind of dialogue needed for each type of story so that your dialogue sounds appropriate for the genre, literary, or mainstream story that you're writing?

[4] Does every scene of dialogue in your story move the plot forward?

[5] Does your dialogue also include narrative, action, and character introspection so it feels three-dimensional to the reader?

[6] Does your dialogue capture the essence of each scene and is it focused on what each character wants in the story?

[7] Does your dialogue include at least some details of setting?

[8] Is your dialogue paced so it speeds up and slows down according to what the characters and story events dictate?

[9] Are your dialogue scenes full of tension and suspense?

[10] Does your dialogue clearly show your character's emotion?

[11] Are any dialogue quirks there for a good reason and are they true to who the character is?

[12] Have you learned what the most common mistakes in writing dialogue are so that you can avoid them?

[13] Is your dialogue punctuated and formatted so it achieves a smooth rhythm in each scene?

[14] Have you honored the dos and don'ts of effective dialogue that connects with readers?

[15] Is any one line of dialogue in your story capable of transforming a reader's life?

index